Dorothea Ruggles-Brise

## The Minstrelsy of Scotland

200 Scottish songs, adapted to their traditional airs

Dorothea Ruggles-Brise

**The Minstrelsy of Scotland**
*200 Scottish songs, adapted to their traditional airs*

ISBN/EAN: 9783337240189

Printed in Europe, USA, Canada, Australia, Japan

Cover: Foto ©Thomas Meinert / pixelio.de

More available books at **www.hansebooks.com**

AUGENER'S EDITION,
No. 8930.

THE

# MINSTRELSY OF SCOTLAND

## 200 Scottish Songs,

*ADAPTED TO THEIR TRADITIONAL AIRS;*

ARRANGED FOR VOICE WITH PIANOFORTE ACCOMPANIMENT,

*AND SUPPLEMENTED WITH HISTORICAL NOTES,*

by

## ALFRED MOFFAT.

"What needs there be sae great a fraise
Wi' dringin' dull Italian lays,
I wadna gie our ain strathspeys
   For half a hunder score o' them.
They're dowf and dowie at the best,
   Dowf and dowie, dowf and dowie,
   Dowf and dowie at the best,
   Wi' a' their variorum ;
They're dowf and dowie at the best,
Their *allegros* and a' the rest,
They canna please a Scottish taste
   Compar'd wi' Tullochgorum."

REV. JOHN SKINNER.

Augener & Co., London.
86, NEWGATE STREET, E.C.
1, FOUBERT'S PLACE, AND 81, REGENT STREET, W.

1895.

LONDON :
WILLIAM CLOWES AND SONS, LIMITED, TYPE-MUSIC AND GENERAL PRINTERS,
STAMFORD STREET AND CHARING CROSS.

# PREFACE.

The Editor has great pleasure in here acknowledging the unvarying kindness and courtesy of all to whom he has applied for information in the compiling of this collection of Scottish Folk-Songs. His thanks are due, not only for much valuable information received, historical and otherwise, but also in many instances for use of copyright songs. Among those who have assisted him greatly in his work may be mentioned Mr. Henry Whyte, Glasgow, well known in Gaelic circles as "Fionn," and author of the *Celtic Lyre*; and Mr. Lachlan MacBean, author of *Songs and Hymns of the Scottish Highlands*. From both of these volumes some of the best Highland and Hebridean melodies in the present work have been taken, and the Editor is specially indebted to Mr. Whyte for his kind permission to use many beautiful translations of Gaelic verses, and for much interesting information concerning the airs to which they are set.

The warm thanks of the Editor are also offered to Lady John Scott, the talented composer of "Annie Laurie," and other fine Scottish airs; to Mr. J. MacKay, Editor of the *Celtic Monthly*; Mr. John Glen, author of the *Glen Collection of Scottish Dance Music*; Mr. Frank Kidson, author of *Traditional Tunes*, and *Old English Country Dances*; Mr. Ballentyne Dykes, of Camstraddan, Loch Lomond; Mr. Donald Ross, Edinburgh; Mr. Malcolm MacFarlane, Elderslie, and others.

LUSS, LOCH LOMOND.
*March,* 1894.

# INDEX OF FIRST LINES.

# INDEX OF TITLES.

# A friend o' mine cam here yestreen.

## MY WIFE HAS TA'EN THE GEE.*

*Allegro.*

VOICE.

PIANO. *mf*    *mf*

1. A friend o' mine cam here yestreen, And
2. We sat sae late au' drank sae stout, The
3. And in the morn when I cam doun, The
4. When that she heard, she ran, she flung Her

1. he wad hae me doun    To drink a pot o' ale wi' him In the neist bor-rows toun; But
2. truth I tell to you,    That lang or e'er the mid-night cam', We baith were roar-ing fou. My
3. ne'er a word she spake,    But mo - ny sad and sour looks, And ay her head she'd shake. "My
4. arms a - bout my neck,    And twen - ty kiss - es in a crack, And, puir wee thing, she grat. "If

1. oh! in-deed, it was the waur, An' far the waur for me,    For lang or e'er that I cam' hame My
2. wife sits at the fire - side, The tears aye blind her e'e,    The ne'er a bed will she gae too, But
3. dear," quoth I, "what ail-eth thee, To look sae sour on me?    I'll nev - er do the like a - gain If
4. you'll ne'er do the like a - gain, But bide at hame wi' me,    I'll lay my life I'll be the wife That

1. wife had ta'en the gee!
2. sit and tak' the gee.
3. you'll ne'er tak' the gee!'
4. nev - er tak's the gee!"

*con forza.*

* This song appears in Herd's Collection, 1769. No author's name is given. In Maidment's *North Country Garland*, 1824, there is a song, beginning "My wife shall hae her will," which is often sung to the same tune. The air, which was contributed by Burns to the fifth volume of the *Museum*, is a transformation of an old tune entitled "The Miller."

B

# A Highland lad my love was born.*

Verses by Burns.
*Allegretto.*

Air: "The White Cockade."

VOICE.

PIANO.

*mf*

*mf*

1. A High - land lad my love was born, The Low - land lads he
2. Wi' his phil - a - beg an' tar - tan plaid, And gude clay - more down
3. They ban - ish'd him be - yond the sea; But, e'er the bud was
4. But oh! they catch'd him at the last, And bound him in a

*cres.*

1. held in scorn; But he still was faith - fu' to his clan, My
2. by his side, The lad - ies' hearts he did tre - pan, My
3. on the tree, A - down my cheeks the pearls ran, Em -
4. dun - geon fast; My curse up - on them ev' - ry one, They've

*cres.*

* Burns' verses occur in his Cantata, "The Jolly Beggars." They were written to the tune, "O! an' ye were died, gudman." The old verses, entitled "The White Cockade," first appeared in Herd's Collection, 1776, vol. ii., and in Aird's *Selection of Scotch, etc., Airs,* vol. i., 1782, as "The Ranting Highlandman."

1. gal - lant braw John High - land - man!
2. gal - lant braw John High - land - man!
3. brac - ing my John High - land - man!
4. hang'd my braw John High - land - man!
Sing hey, my braw John
High - land - man! Sing ho, my braw John High - land - man! There's
f
colla voce.
cres.
ff
no' a lad in a' the lan' Was match for my John
High - land - man!
mf

# A wee bird cam' to our ha' door.

## WAE'S ME FOR PRINCE CHARLIE.*

Verses by WILLIAM GLEN.
*Andante espressivo.*

Air: "Johnnie Faa, or the Gipsie Laddie."

VOICE.

PIANO.

*p con molto espress.*

*poco rit.*

*p*

1. A  wee  bird  cam'  to  our  ha'  door,  He  war - bled  sweet  an'
2. Quoth  I,  "My  bird,  my  bon - nie, bon - nie  bird,  Is  that  a  sang  ye
3. "On  hills  that  are,  by  right,  his  ain,  He  roves  a  lane - ly
4. "Dark  night  cam'  on,  the  tem - pest  roar'd  Loud  o'er  the  hills  an'
5. But  now  the  bird  saw  some  red  coats,  An'  he  shook  his  wings  wi'

1. clear - - ly,  An'  aye  the  o'er - come  o'  his  sang,  Was
2. bor - - row,  Are  these  some  words  ye've  learnt  by  heart,  Or  a
3. stran - - ger,  On  ov' - ry - side  he's  press'd  by  want,  On
4. val - - leys,  An'  where  was't  that  your  Prince  lay  down,  Wha's
5. an - - ger, - "Oh!  this  is  no  a  land  for  me;  I'll

* A version of this air appears in the Skene MS. 1615-1620, under the title of "Ladie Cassilles Lilt." William Glen, the author of the lovely verses "Wae's me for Prince Charlie," was a native of Glasgow. He died in that city about 1824 in extreme poverty. The old ballad of "Johnny Faa" is given in *The Tea-table Miscellany*. It treats of the abduction of Lady Cassilis by the gypsies, and according to Ritson, neighbouring tradition strongly vouches for the truth of the story.

The gypsies cam' to our gude Lord's yett
And vow, but they sang sweetly;
They sang sae sweet and sae very compleat,
That down cam' the fair ladye.

Of this ballad, Burns remarks that "it is the only old song which he could ever trace as belonging to the extensive county of Ayr." M'Gibbon inserted the air in his *Scots Tunes*, Bk. II., 1746, as "Johnnie Faa."

*poco cres.*

1. "Wae's me for Prince Char - - - lie!" Oh! when I heard the
2. lilt o' dool and sor - - - row?" "Oh! no, no, no," the
3. ev' - ry side is dan - - - ger. Yes - treen I met him
4. hame should been a pa - - - lace? He row'd him in a
5. tar - ry here nae lan - - - ger!" He hov - er'd on the

1. bou - nie, bon - nie bird, The tears cam' drap - pin' rare - - ly, I
2. wee bird sang, "I've flown sin' morn - in' ear - - ly, But
3. in a glen, My heart maist burst - it fair - - ly, For
4. High - land plaid, That cov - - er'd him but spare - - ly, An'
5. wing a - while 'Ere he de - part - ed fair - - ly, But

*p*    *poco rit.*

1. took my bon - net off my head, For weel I lo'ed Prince
2. sic a day o' wind an' rain— Oh! wae's me for Prince
3. sad - ly chauged in - deed was he— Oh! wae's me for Prince
4. slept be - neath a bush o' broom— Oh! wae's me for Prince
5. weel I mind the fare - weel strain Was, "Wae's me for Prince

*Last time.*

1. Char - - - lie.
2. Char - - - lie!
3. Char - - - lie!
4. Char - - - lie!"
5. Char - - - lie!"

*molto rit.*     *pp*

# A wooer cam' to our town.

### AIKENDRUM.*

Verses by ALLAN CUNNINGHAM.

Allegretto vivo.

VOICE.

PIANO.

1. A woo-er cam' to
2. He bowed fu' laigh at
3. He sighed and praised my
4. There's wit a-neath his

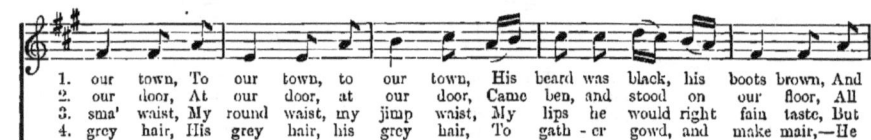

1. our town, To our town, to our town, His beard was black, his boots brown, And
2. our door, At our door, at our door, Came ben, and stood on our floor, All
3. sma' waist, My round waist, my jimp waist, My lips he would right fain taste, But
4. grey hair, His grey hair, his grey hair, To gath-er gowd, and make mair,—He

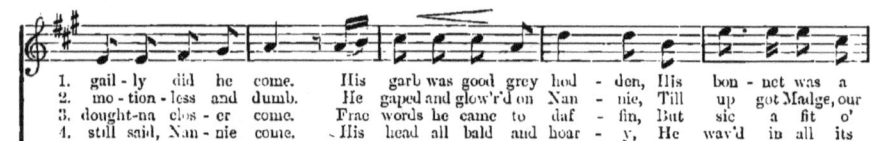

1. gail-ly did he come. His garb was good grey hod-den, His bon-net was a
2. mo-tion-less and dumb. He gaped and glow'rd on Nan-nie, Till up got Madge, our
3. dought-na clos-er come. Frae words he came to daf-fin, But sic a fit o'
4. still said, Nan-nie come. His head all bald and hoar-y, He wav'd in all its

1. broad one; And ay his head gaed nod-din', His name was Ai-ken-drum.
2. Gran-nie, "Lord, carle, are ye no can-nie?" "Mang maids," quo' Ai-ken-drum.
3. cough-in', I could-na keep frae laugh-in' At an-cient Ai-ken-drum.
4. glor-y, Laid lands and bonds a-fore me—'I've wedd-ed Ai-ken-drum!

* Mr. R. Chambers, in *Scottish Songs Prior to Burns*, gives this melody with verses entitled "The Piper of Dundee." The verses here adopted were written for George Thomson's *Select Melodies of Scotland*, vol. v., in 1822. Thomson has marked the air with the letter "A," showing that he considered it to be "of remote antiquity." Gow has a version of it in his fifth Collection as "Aiken Drum." The air is probably a version of the old tune "Johnnie's grey Breeks."

# Adieu, Dundee! *

Verses by CHARLES NEAVES.
*Adagio sostenuto.*

Air: "Adew, Dundee."

1. A - dieu, Dun-dee! from Mar - y part-ed, Here nae
2. But like yon wa - ter saft - ly glid - ing, When the

1. mair my lot may lie; Wha can bear when bro - ken-heart-ed, Scenes that speak o'
2. winds are laid to sleep; Such my life when I con - fid-ing, Gave to her my

1. joys gane bye! A' things ance were sweet and smil-ing, In the light o' Ma - ry's
2. heart to keep! Like on wa - ter wild - ly rush-ing, When the north wind stirs the

1. e'e; Fair - est seem - ings maist be - guil-ing, Love, a - dieu! a - dieu, Dun - dee!
2. sea; Such the change my heart now crush-ing, Love a - dieu! a - dieu, Dun - dee!

* Between 1615 and 1620 a MS. collection of music was compiled by a gentleman of the name of Skene, now generally supposed to have been John Skene of Hallyards, son of Sir John Skene, Clerk Register of Scotland. He appears to have been born about 1575, and to have died in the year 1644. The MS. was left by one of his descendants to the Advocates' Library in Edinburgh, and in 1838 William Dauney translated and published it under the title of *Ancient Scotish Melodies from a Manuscript of the Reign of King James VI.* Dauney's introduction, relative to the history of Scottish music, is particularly valuable. The air "Adew, Dundee," occurs in this MS. The town of Dundee seems to have been a favourite with our Scottish minstrels; there are a great many old songs relating to it.

# Ae fond kiss, and then we sever.*

Verses by Burns.
*Andantino.*

Air : "Rory Dall's Port."

VOICE.

PIANO.

*p con espress.*

*ril.*

*con Ped.*

*p*

1. Ae fond kiss and then we sev - - er; Ae fare - weel and
2. I'll ne'er blame my par - tial fan - - cy, Nae thing could re -
3. Fare thee weel, thou first and fair - - est! Fare thee weel, thou

*sempre ped.*

1. then for ev - - er! Deep in heart - wrung tears I'll pledge thee,
2. sist my Nan - - cy; But to see her was to love her,
3. best and dear - - est! Thine be il - ka joy and trea - - sure,

* Burns wrote these verses in 1790 to the tune of "Rory Dall's Port." This he mentions on his MS. sent to Johnson for *The Scots' Musical Museum*. In Captain Fraser's *Collection of Airs and Melodies Peculiar to the Highlands*, a version of this tune is found under the name of *The Cow-Boy*. The composer of the air was Roderick Morrison, usually called *Dall*, or the blind. He was one of the last native Highland harpers, and died *circa* 1670.

1. War - ring sighs and groans I'll wage thee! Who shall say that
2. Love but her and love for ev - er. Had we nev - er
3. Peace, en - joy - ment, love, and plea - sure! Ae fond kiss and

1. For - tune grieves him, While the star of Hope she leaves him?
2. lov'd sae kind - ly, Had we nev - er lov'd sae blind - ly,
3. then we sev - er; Ae fare - weel, a - las! for ev - er!

1. She nae cheer - fu' twin - kle lights me; Dark des - pair a -
2. Nev - er met, or nev - er part - ed, We had ne'er been
3. Deep in heart - wrung tears I'll pledge thee, War - ring sighs and

1. round be - nights me?
2. bro - ken - heart - ed.
3. groans I'll wage thee!

# Ailie Bain.*
### (Eilidh Bhàn.)

Translated from the Gaelic of Evan MacColl
by Malcolm MacFarlane.

Air: "Buain na rainich."

*Allegretto vivo.*

VOICE.

PIANO.

Ai-lie Bain o' the glen, Bon-nie lassie, winsome lassie;

Ai-lie Bain o' the glen, Wha' could help but lo'e her?

1. Here wi' lips fore-tok'-ning kiss - es,
2. A' the lads are daft a - bout ye,
3. On the cauld nichts tho' my plaid - ie
4. What tho' mo - nied cuifs en - deav - our
5. Would this e'en - ing saw them ris - in'

*cres.*

1. Wait - ing dull and wea - rie;   'Tis nae won - der my heart's wish is—Quick - ly come, my dear - ie.
2. A' the bar - dies praise ye;   Were I ane my - sel', I doubt na   I'd gang rhym - in' cra - zy.
3. Shel - ter'd us but spare - ly,   Yet my part - in' frae be - side ye   Seem'd tae come owre ear - ly.
4. Wi' their gowd tae lure ye,   True tae me yer heart beats ev - er;   Ne'er shall they se - cure ye!
5. Frae our bott - ling, Ai - lie;   Tae Kil - mun tae put the cries in,   I wad trip it gai - ly!

*cres.*

CHORUS. *f*

Ai-lie Bain o' the glen, Bon-nie lassie, winsome lassie; Ai - lie Bain o' the glen, Wha could help but lo'e her?

---

* From the *Celtic Lyre*, by permission. Regarding this song Mr. Whyte sends us the following: " The Gaelic verses are the composition of Mr. Evan MacColl, popularly known as the Lochfyne Bard. The aged Bard was born at Kenmore, Lochfyne, in 1808, but has been resident in Canada for over forty years." The air is associated with a fairy song to which Hogg wrote a paraphrase of the Gaelic words which were published in *Albyn's Anthology*, vol. i., 1816. In this last-named collection the air is entitled "Cnochd a Bheannichd."

# As I was walking by yon river-side.

## HE'S DEAR TO ME THO' HE'S FAR FRAE ME.*

Gaelic air.

*Molto andante con espressione.*

VOICE.

PIANO.

1. As I was walk - ing by
2. I've been in the Lowlands where they
3. If win - ter war' past an' the

*p*

*p*

1. yon riv - er side, My heart it was sair, and O but I was wea - ry, I
2. shear the . . sheep, And up in the High - lands where they pu' the heath - er, I
3. summer come a - gain, When dai - ses an' ro - ses spring sae fresh an' bon - nie, Then

*cres.*  *f*  *dim.*

1. thought up - on the days that are past and gane, For he's
2. ken a bon - ny lad - die that lo'es me weel; But he's
3. I will change my silks for a bonnie plaid - en coat, An' a -

*cres.*  *dim.*

*rit.*

1. dear, dear to me, tho' he's far, far frae me.
2. far, far a - wa' that I lo'e far bet - ter.
3. wa' to the lad that is dear, dear to me.

*rit.*  *poco rit.*

* From Johnson's *Scots' Musical Museum*, vol. vi., 1803. Stenhouse's note to this song is: "This sweet little pastoral made its appearance about the year 1796, as a single-sheet song, written by a gentleman. His name, however, the Editor has not yet learnt. The melody is very pretty, and appears to belong to the ancient class of Scottish airs of one simple strain, such as " Braw, braw lads of Gala Water," to which it bears a strong resemblance."

# And are ye sure the news is true?

## THERE'S NAE LUCK ABOUT THE HOUSE.*

*Allegretto.*

VOICE.

1. And are ye sure the news is true? And are ye sure he's weel? Is
2. Rise up and mak a clean fire-side, Put on the muc-kle pot, Gie
3. There are twa hens in-to the crib Have fed this month and mair, Make
4. Sae sweet his voice, sae smooth his tongue, His breath's like cal-ler air, His

PIANO.

*mf*

1. this a time to think o' wark? Ye gauds fling by your wheel! Is
2. lit-tle Kate her cot-ton gown, And Jock his Sun-day coat, And
3. haste and thraw their necks a-bout, That Col-in weel may fare. Bring
4. ve-ry tread has mu-sic in't As he comes up the stair, And

1. this a time to think o' wark, When Col-in's at the door? Rax
2. make their shoon as black as slaes, Their stock-ings white as snaw, It's
3. down to me my big-on-et, My bish-op-sat-in gown, And
4. will I see his face a-gain And will I hear him speak? I'm

* This air is a slightly modified version of "Up and waur at them a', Willie." Mr. R. Chambers, in *Scottish Song Prior to Burns*, says:— "When William, Duke of Cumberland, came to Edinburgh to put himself at the head of the Government troops for the suppression of the Rebellion (Jan 1745), the music bells of St. Giles' Kirk played "Up and waur at them a', Willie." The authorship of "There's nae luck about the house" has been much disputed. Some attribute it to William Mickle, of Langholm, and others to Mrs. Jean Adams, School-mistress of Crawford, at Crawford's-Dyke, near Greenock, about the middle of last century. The poem first appeared in Herd's *Scots' Songs*, 1776, vol. ii., under the title of "The Mariner's Wife." We have adopted Herd's version.

1. me my cloak, I'll to the quay, And see him come a - shore
2. a' to plea - sure our guid - man, He likes to see them braw.
3. then gae tell the Bai - lie's wife That Col - in's come to town.
4. down - right diz - zy wi' the joy, In 'troth I'm like to greet!

For there's

nae luck a - bout the house, There's nae luck at a'; There's

lit - tle plea - sure in the house, When my gude-man's a - wa'!

1st to 3rd Verses.

Last Verse.

# And we're a' noddin'.*

Moderato.

PIANO.

1. And we're a' nod-din', nid, nid, nod-din', And we're a' nod-din' at
2. And we're a' nod-din', nid, nid, nod-din', And we're a' nod-din' at
3. And we're a' nod-din', nid, nid, nod-din', And we're a' nod-din' at

1. our house at hame. Gude e'en to ye kim-mer, And are ye a-lane? O
2. our house at hame. O sair hae I fought, Ear' an' late did I toil, My
3. our house at hame. When he knockt at the door I kent weel his rap, And

1. come and see how blythe are we, For Ja-mie he's cam' hame; And
2. bair-nies for to feed an' clad; My com-fort was their smile! When I
3. lit-tle Ka-tie cried a-loud, "My Dad-die he's come back!" A

rit.

colla voce.

* The author of these verses is unknown. They are published in Blackie's Book of Scottish Song, 1843. What seems to be an earlier version of this song was published by Johnson in the *Museum*, with amendments by Burns. (See *Scots' Musical Museum*, vol. vi., p. 540). Johnson's version is evidently founded on the original words of "John Anderson, my jo," preserved in the Percy MS. of the 16th century. The air in the *Museum* is different from the one we have adopted, which is apparently modern.

poco rit.

1. O, but he's been lang a - wa', And O, my heart was sair, As I
2. thocht on Ja - mie far a - wa', And o' his love sae fair, A
3. storm gaed thro' my anx - ious heart As thocht - ful - ly I sat; I

1. sob - bed out a lang fare - weel, May - be to meet nae mair.
2. bod - in' thrill cam' thro' my heart, We'd may - be meet a - gain! } Noo we're
3. rase, I gaz'd, fell in his arms And burst - ed out an' grat!

colla voce.

a' nod - din', nid, nid, nod-din', And we're a' nod - din' at our house at hame, Noo we're

f a tempo.

a' nod - din', nid, nid, nod-din', And we're a' nod - din' at our house at hame.

# Argyle is my name.

## BANNOCKS O' BARLEY-MEAL.*

*Spirituoso.*

Old ballad modified by Sir ALEX. BOSWELL.

1. Ar - gyle is my name, and you may think it strange, To
2. Ye ri - ots and re - vels of Lon - don, a - dieu! And
3. And if it chance Mag - gie should bring me a son, He shall

1. live at a court, yet ne - ver to change; To fac - tion or ty - ran - ny
2. Fol - ly, ye fop - lings, I leave her to you! For Scot - land I min - gled in
3. fight for his King as his fa - ther has done; I'll hang up my sword wi' an

* The verses given here are Sir Alex. Boswell's modification of an old ballad attributed to the Duke of Argyle, born 1680, and which is given in Herd's *Collection of Scots' Songs*, 1776, vol. ii. The tune is of Highland origin.

1. e - qual - ly foe; The good of the land's the sole mo - tive I know. The
2. bus - tle and strife— For my - self I seek peace and an in - no - cent life. I'll
3. old sol - dier's pride— Oh, may he be wor - thy to wear't on his side! I

1. foes of my coun - try and King I have faced; In ci - ty or bat - tle I
2. haste to the High - lands and vis - it each scene Wi' Mag - gie, my love, in her
3. pant for the breeze o' my lov'd na - tive place, I long for the smile o' each

1. ne'er was dis - graced; I've done what I could for my
2. rock - lay o' green; On the banks o' Glen - a - ray what
3. wel - com - ing face; I'll aff to the Hie - lands as

1. coun - try's weal; Now I'll feast up - on Ban-nocks o' bar - ley - meal!
2. plea - sure I'll feel, While she shares my Ban-nocks o' bar - ley - meal!
3. fast's I can reel, And feast up - on Ban-nocks o' bar - ley - meal!

# At Polwarth on the Green.*

Verses attributed to ALLAN RAMSAY.

* This song appears in the *Tea-Table Miscellany*, 1724. It is probably an old song corrected by Ramsay. Thomson adapted Ramsay's version to the original air in the *Orpheus Caledonius*, 1725. "Polwarth is the name of a small village in Berwickshire; in the middle of it are two ancient thorn-trees, a few yards distant from each other, around which it was formerly the custom for every newly-married pair, and the company invited to the wedding, to dance in a ring. From this circumstance originated the old song of 'Polwarth on the Green'" (*Museum Illustrations*, p. 177). The air under the title of "Polwarth on the Green" is preserved in the Crockat MS. Book, 1709. Gay chose this melody for song No. 20 in his opera "Polly," 1729, beginning:—

Love now is nought but art,
'Tis who can juggle best,
To all men seem to give your heart,
But keep it in your breast.

1. dance a bout the thorn, A kind - ly wel - come
2. in - ward - ly they blceze; But I will frank - ly

1. you shall meet Frae her wha likes to view A
2. show my mind, And yield my heart to thee, Be

1. lo - ver and a lad com - plete, The lad and lov - er
2. ev - er to the cap - tive kind, That langs na to be

1. you!
2. free!

# Awa', Whigs, awa'!*

*Andante maestoso.*

VOICE.

PIANO.

A - wa', Whigs, a - wa'! A - wa', Whigs, a - wa'! Ye're

but a pack o' trai - tor loons, Ye'll dae nae gude a - va'!

1. Our this - tles flou - rish'd fresh and fair, And bon - nie bloom'd our ros - es; But
2. Our sad de - cay in kirk and state Sur - pass - es my de - scrib - ing; The
3. Grim Ven-geance lang has ta'en a nap, But we may see him wau-ken; But

* These three verses are taken from Hogg's *Jacobite Relics*, Ser. I. p. 76. Hogg gives seven verses in all. Burns also contributed a version of "Awa', Whigs, awa'" to vol. iii. of Johnson's *Museum*. The above tune, which has entirely superseded the one in the *Museum*, was first printed in R. A. Smith's *Scottish Minstrel*, 1822.

1. Whigs cam' like a frost in June, And with-er'd a' our po-sies! A-
2. Whigs cam' o'er us like a curse, And we hae done wi' thriv-ing! A-
3. wae's the day when roy-al heads Are hunt-ed like a mau-kin! A-

1. wa', Whigs, a-wa'! A-wa', Whigs a-wa'! Ye're
2. wa', Whigs, a-wa'! A-wa', Whigs a-wa'! Ye're
3. wa', Whigs, a-wa'! A-wa', Whigs a-wa'! Ye're

1. but a pack o' trai-tor loons, Ye'll dae nae gude a-va'!
2. but a pack o' trai-tor loons, Ye'll dae nae gude a-va'!
3. but a pack o' trai-tor loons, Ye'll dae nae gude a-va'!

# Ay wakin', O! *

1. Ay wa-kin', O! Wa-kin' ay, an' eer-ie, Sleep I can-na get For think-in' on my dear-ie,
2. Ay wa-kin', O! Wa-kin' ay, an' eer-ie, Sleep I can-na get For think-in' on my dear-ie,

1. Ay wa-kin', O! Sure-ly night comes on, A' the lave are sleep-in', I
2. Ay wa-kin', O! Spring's a plea-sant time, Flow'rs o' ev'-ry col-our; The

1. think on my bon-nie lad, An' bleer my een wi' greet-in', Ay wa-kin', O! Wa-kin' ay, an' eer-ie,
2. wa-ter rins owre the heugh, And I long for my lov-er, Ay wa-kin', O! Wa-kin' ay, an' eer-ie;

1. Sleep I can-na get For think-in' on my dear-ie, Ay wa-kin', O!
2. Sleep I can-na get For think-in' on my dear-ie, Ay wa-kin', O!

* The first verse and chorus of this song are traditional. The second verse seems to have been written by Burns. The air is undoubtedly ancient, and, curiously enough, sometimes turns up in common time. Stenhouse, in the *Museum Illustrations*, gives what he considers to be the genuine version. It is in triple time. Ritson is of the opinion that the air "Ay wakin', O," from its intrinsic evidence, is very ancient. *See* the Historical Essay in *Scotish Songs*, p. cix.

# Beneath the pines my dearie, O.*

## (LULLABY.)

*Andante tranquillo.*

VOICE.

PIANO.

*p*

*poco rit.*

Ped.    Ped.    Ped.      *con sempre ped.*

1. Be - neath the pines my dear-ie, O, When
2. Be - neath the pines my dear-ie, O, When

1. a' is still an' ee - rie, O. Be - neath the pines my dear - ie, O, Sleep peace-fu'-ly my
2. a' is still an' ee - rie, O. Be - neath the pines my dear - ie, O, Sleep peace-fu'-ly my

*mf*      *f*

1. dear - ie, O. Oh, ance an' I but lit - tle thocht A lot so hard wad e'er be thine, An'
2. dear - ie, O. Oh, that this with - er'd heart wad beat, Till as a sil-ler birk thou hast grown; That

*rit.*      Last time.

1. see thee flee frae friend an' hame, An' part frae a' that's right-fu' thine.
2. I micht see thy fu - ture fate, Nor leave thee in the warld a - lone.

Ped.    Ped.    Ped.

* A version of this air occurs in R. A. Smith's *Scottish Minstrel*, vol. vi.

# Bannocks o' bear-meal.*

*Allegro energico.*

Air: "The Killogie."

VOICE.

PIANO.

*f*

1. Ban - nocks o' bear - meal, and ban - nocks o' bar - ley;
2. Ban - nocks o' bear - meal, and ban - nocks o' bar - ley;

1. Here's to the High - land - man's ban - nocks o' bar - ley!
2. Here's to the High - land - man's ban - nocks o' bar - ley!

1. Wha' in a brul - zie will first cry a par - ley?
2. Wha' in his days were loy - al to Char - lie?

*sf*

* This Jacobitical fragment was contributed to Johnson's *Scots Musical Museum* by Burns. The tune is old, and was originally known by the first line of the verses which were then sung to it, beginning: "A lad and a lassie lay in a Kilogie." In 1694 the eldest son of the Earl of Lothian wrote new words to the air, which was then called "Cakes of Crowdy"; a copy of this song is published in Hogg's *Jacobite Relics*, Ser. I., p. 26. The tune appears in the *Orpheus Caledonius*, 1725, with verses entitled "I'll never leave thee."

1. Ne - ver the lads wi' the ban - nocks o' bar - ley!
2. Wha' but the lads wi' the ban - nocks o' bar - ley!

1. Ban - nocks o' bear - meal and ban - nocks o' bar - ley;
2. Ban - nocks o' bear - meal and ban - nocks o' bar - ley;

1. Here's to the High - land - man's ban - nocks o' bar - ley!
2. Here's to the High - land - man's ban - nocks o' bar - ley!

# Blink o'er the burn, sweet Betty.*

*Allegretto tenderosa.*

VOICE.

PIANO.

*p*

*rit.*

con Ped.

*p*

1. Blink o'er ... the burn, .. sweet Bet - ty, It is .. a
2. O, Bet - ty shall bake .. my bread, And Bet - ty shall

*p*

1. cauld win - ter nicht; It rains, .. it hails, it
2. brew ... my ale, And Bet - ty shall be my

1. thun - ders, The moon .. she gi'es .. nae - licht; It's
2. love .. When I ... come o'er .. the dale, Blink

* Mr. Robert Chambers points out that songs with the phrase " Blink over the burn, sweet Betty," for their groundwork, have existed as far back as the reign of King Henry VIII. In *King Lear*, Act iii. Sc. 6, we find Edgar saying: " Wantest thou eyes at trial, Madam? Come o'er the bourn, Bessy, to me." The age of the air is unknown, but versions of it are found in the *Orpheus Caledonius*, 1725, and Watts' *Miscellany*, 1730.

1. a' for the .. sake o' sweet Bet - ty That ev - er I
2. 'o'er ... the .. burn, .. sweet Bet - ty, Blink o'er ... the

*mf*

1. tint .... my way; O las - sie, let me sit
2. burn .... to me; An' while I ha'e life, my dear

*poco rit.*

1. by thee, Un - til it be break ... o' day.
2. las - sie, My ain sweet ... Bet - ty thou's be.

*Last time.*

# Blythe, blythe, and merry was she.*

Verses by BURNS.

Air: "Andro and his Cutty Gun."

*Spirituoso.*

VOICE.

PIANO.

Blythe, blythe, and
Blythe, blythe, and
Blythe, blythe, and

mer-ry was she, Blythe was she but and ben, Blythe by the banks o' Earn, And
mer-ry was she, Blythe was she but and ben, Blythe by the banks o' Earn, And
mer-ry was she, Blythe was she but and ben, Blythe by the banks o' Earn, And

FINE.

cres.

blythe in Glen-tur-rit glen. 1. By Auch-ter-tyre there grows the aik, On Yar-row banks the
blythe in Glen-tur-rit glen. 2. Her looks were like a flow'r in May, Her smile was like a
blythe in Glen-tur-rit glen. 3. The Hie-land hills I've wan-der'd wide, And o'er the Low-lands

*poco rit.*

D.S. al FINE.

1. bir-ken-shaw; But Phe-mie was a bon-nier lass, Than braes o' Yar-row ev-er saw.
2. sim-mer morn; She tripp-it by the banks o' Earn, As licht's a bird up-on a thorn.
3. I hae been; But Phe-mie was the blyth-est lass That ev-er trod the dew-y green.

*colla voce.*

* The song, known under the name of "Andro and his Cutty Gun," appears in Ramsay's *Tea-table Miscellany*, 1724. The air is old and seems to have been originally a bagpipe tune. Burns' song, with the melody, appears in Johnson's *Museum*, vol. ii., No. 160. The heroine of the piece was Miss Euphemia Murray, of Lintrose, who was known as "The Flower of Strathmore," on account of her personal beauty.

# Bonnie wee thing.*

Verses by Burns.

Molto andante tenderoso.    p molto espress.

VOICE.

PIANO.

p molto espressione.   ri'ard.   p

Ped.    con Ped.

1. Bon - nie wee thing, can - nie wee thing, Love - ly wee thing,
2. Bon - nie wee thing, can - nie wee thing, Love - ly wee thing,

rit.   p   rit.

1. wert thou mine! I would wear thee in my bo - som, Lest my jew - el I should tine.
2. wert thou mine! I would wear thee in my bo - som, Lest my jew - el I should tine.

rit.   p   rit.

1. Wish - ful - ly I look and lan - guish In that bon - nie face of thine; And my heart it
2. Wit and grace and love and beau - ty, In ae con - stel - la - tion shine! To a - dore thee

rit.

1. stounds wi' an - guish Lest my wee thing be na mine!
2. is my du - ty, God - dess o' this soul o' mine!

rit.   p   rit.

Ped.    Ped.

* These beautiful verses were composed by Burns for the fourth volume of the *Scots' Museum*, issued 1792. The air first appeared in Oswald's *Caledonian Pocket Companion*, vol. viii. A crude version of it, however, is found in the *Straloch Ms. Lute-book*, 1627-29, under the title of " Wo' betyd thy wearie Bodie."

# Bonnie lassie, will ye go?

### THE BIRKS O' ABERFELDY.*

Verses by BURNS.
*Poco Andantino.*

Air: "The Birks o' Aberfeldy."

VOICE.

PIANO.

*p con espress.* — — *poco rit.*

con Ped.

*p*

Bon - nie las - sie, will ye go, Will ye go, will ye go, . .

con sempre Ped.

*poco rit.*

Bon - nie las - sie, will ye go To the birks o' A - ber - fel - dy?

*poco rit.*

* An air styled *The Birks of Abergelde* appears in Playford's Collection, 1700, under the name of "A Scotch Ayre." Abergeldy is in Aberdeen-shire.

1. Now sim - mer blinks on flow - 'ry braes, And o'er the crys - tal stream - let plays; Come,
2. While o'er their heads the ha - zels hing, The lit - tle bur - dies blythe - ly sing, Or
3. The braes as - cend, like lof - ty wa's, The foam - in' stream deep roar - in' fa's, O'er
4. Let For - tune's gifts at ran - dom flee, They ne'er shall draw a wish frae me, Su -

*poco rit.*

1. let us spend the light - some days In the birks o' A - ber - fel - dy.
2. light - ly flit on wan - ton wing In the birks o' A - ber - fel - dy.
3. hung wi' frag - rant spread - ing shaws, The birks o' A - ber - fel - dy.
4. preme - ly bless'd wi' love an' thee, In the birks o' A - ber - fel - dy.

*poco rit.*

*mf*

1. Bon - nie las - sie, will ye go, Will ye go, will ye go; ..
2. Bon - nie las - sie, will ye go, Will ye go, will ye go; ..
3. Bon - nie las - sie, will ye go, Will ye go, will ye go; ..
4. Bon - nie las - sie, will ye go, Will ye go, will ye go; ..

*rit.* D.S.

1. Bon - nie las - sie, will ye go To the birks o' A - ber - fel - dy?
2. Bon - nie las - sie, will ye go To the birks o' A - ber - fel - dy?
3. Bon - nie las - sie, will ye go To the birks o' A - ber - fel - dy?
4. Bon - nie las - sie, will ye go To the birks o' A - ber - fel - dy?

*rit.* *p* *poco rit.*

# Braw, braw lads.
## GALA WATER.*

Verses by R. Burns.

Air: "Galla Water."

*Larghetto con moto.*

PIANO.

*p*

*ritard.*

con Ped.

1. Braw, braw lads on Yar - row braes, Ye wan - der thro' the
2. But there is ane, a se - cret ane, A - boon them a' I
3. Al - though his dad - die was nae laird, An' though I hae nae
4. It ne'er was wealth, it ne'er was wealth, That coft con - tent - ment,

1. bloom - ing heath - er, But Yar - row braes nor Et - trick shaws, Can
2. lo'e him bet - ter; And I'll be his, an' he'll be mine, The
3. mei - kle toch - er; Yet, rich in kind - est, tru - est love, We'll
4. peace, and plea - sure; The bands and bliss o' mut - ual love, O

1. match the lads o' Ga - la Wa - ter!
2. bon - nie lad o' Ga - la Wa - ter!
3. tent our flocks by Ga - la Wa - ter!
4. that's the chief - est warld's . . trea - sure!

*p rit.*

*Burns wrote the verses about the close of 1792. The melody is generally considered very old. In Herd's Collection, 1776, vol. ii., verses appear to this air, commencing:—

Braw, braw lads of Galla-water,
O braw lads of Galla-water,
I'll kilt my coats below my knee,
And follow my love through the water.

Sae fair her hair, sae trent her brow,
Sae bonny blue her een, my dearie;
Sae white her teeth, sae sweet her mou',
I aften kiss her till I'm wearie.

# By yon castle wa'.

## THERE 'LL NEVER BE PEACE TILL JAMIE COMES HAME.*

Verses by BURNS.                    Air : " There are few good fellows when Jamie's awa'. "

Lento.

VOICE.

PIANO.

p        poco rit.        mf

con l'ed.

1. By yon cas-tle
2. My sev-en braw
3. Now life is a

1. wa', at the close of the day, I heard a man sing tho' his
2. sons .. for Jam - ie drew sword, And now I greet round their green
3. bur - - den that bows me down, Sin' I tint my bairns, and

1. head it was grey; And as he was sing - ing, the tears down
2. beds in the yird; It brak the sweet heart o' my faith - fu' auld
3. he tint his crown; But till my last mo - ments my words are the

sf

poco rit.

1. came— There 'll nev - er be peace till Jam - ie comes hame!
2. dame— There 'll nev - er be peace till Jam - ie comes hame!
3. same— There 'll nev - er be peace till Jam - ie comes hame!

p        poco rit.

* Burns wrote these verses for Johnson's *Scot's Musical Museum*. Both Oswald and MacGibbon give versions of the air, but the one we have adopted is from the *Scots' Museum*, No. 315. Hogg also gives this song and air in his *Jacobite Relics*, 1821, Series II. In his note on p. 244, he falls into the curious error of considering Burns' verses "an old song without any alterations."

D

# By yon bonnie banks.*

1. By yon bon-nie banks, and by
2. We'll meet where we part-ed in
3. O brave Char-lie Stuart! dear to
4. The wild bird-ies sing and the

1. yon bon-nie braes, Where the sun shines bright on Loch Lo - - mond, Where
2. yon sha-dy glen, On the steep, steep side o' Ben Lo - - mond, Where
3. the true heart, Wha could re-fuse thee pro-tec - - tion? Like the
4. wild flowers spring, An' in sun-shine the wa-ters are sleep - - in'; But the

* The history of this song is somewhat singular. It has been attributed by many to the talented composer of "Annie Laurie," but through the kindness of Lady John Scott we are enabled to correct this statement. Lady John Scott writes us that she and Sir John picked up both words and air from a poor little boy who was singing on the streets of Edinburgh. She does not think that the song was known before that. That Lady John Scott was credited with this composition at a date prior to its having been printed, we are assured by Mr. J. S. D. Dykes, of Carnstradden, Luss, who was acquainted with the song when it was still being handed about in MS. The first published copy of "By yon bonnie banks," was issued by Messrs. Paterson and Sons, Edinburgh, some fifty years ago. It was arranged by Finlay Dunn (b. 1795, d. 1853), and the verses are marked as being written by a lady.

ten.

1. me and my true love were ev - er wont to gae, On the bon-nie, bon-nie banks o' Loch
2. in pur-ple hue the Hie-land hills we view, And the moon looks out frae the
3. weep - ing birch on the wild hill - side, How grace - fu' he luik'd in de-
4. brok-en heart it kens, nae sec - ond spring, Tho' the wae - fu' may cease frae their

poco rit. ten.

Ped. Ped.

più mosso.

1. Lo - - mond.
2. gloam - - in'.
3. jec - - tion!
4. greet - - in'!

An' ye'll tak' the high - road, an' I'll tak' the low - road, An'

mf

poco rit.

I'll be in Scot - land a - fore ye; But me an' my true love will

poco rit.

Ped. Ped.

ten. cres. rit.

nev - er meet a - gain On the bon - nie, bon - nie banks o' Loch Lo - - mond!

ten. cres. rit.

D 2

# Ca' the yowes to the knowes.*

Ca' the yowes to the knowes, Ca' them where the hea - ther grows,

Ca' them where the burn - ie rows, My bon - nie dear - ie.

1. Hark, the ma - vis' eve - ning sang Sound - ing Clu - den's woods a - mang;
2. We'll gang doun by Clu - den side, Thro' the ha - zels spread - ing wide,
3. Yon - der Clu - den's si - lent tow'rs, Where, at moon - shine mid - night hours,
4. Fair and love - ly as thou art, Thou hast stown my ve - ry heart;

* This air was rescued from oblivion about the year 1787 by Burns. He sent it, with the verses given above, to Johnson for his *Scot's Musical Museum*. The verses are partly traditional. The Cluden is a river in Dumfrieshire.

1. Then a - fauld - ing let us gang, My bon - nie dear - ie.
2. O'er the waves that sweet - ly glide, To the moon sae clear - ly.
3. O'er the dew - y bend - ing flow'rs Fai - ries dance sae cheer - ie.
4. I can die, but can - na part, My bon - nie dear - ie.

1. Ca' the yowes to the knowes, Ca' them where the hea - ther grows,
2. Ca' the yowes to the knowes, Ca' them where the hea - ther grows,
3. Ca' the yowes to the knowes, Ca' them where the hea - ther grows,
4. Ca' the yowes to the knowes, Ca' them where the hea - ther grows,

1. Ca' them where the burn - ie rows, My bon - nie dear - ie.
2. Ca' them where the burn - ie rows, My bon - nie dear - ie.
3. Ca' them where the burn - ie rows, My bon - nie dear - ie.
4. Ca' them where the burn - ie rows, My bon - nie dear - ie.

D.C.

# Cauld blaws the wind frae north to south.

UP IN THE MORNING EARLY.*

Verses by JOHN HAMILTON.

Air: "Cold and Raw."

*Allegro moderato.*

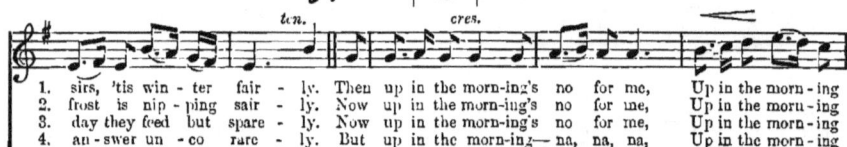

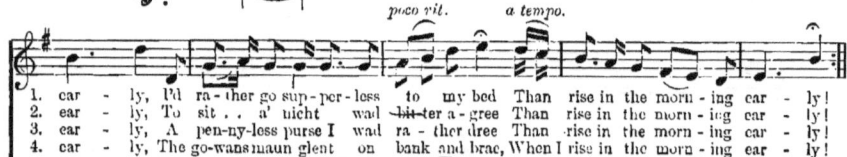

* This air dates back as far as at least the first part of the 17th century. It seems to have been known at an early period in England, and is, in fact, claimed by many as an English melody. Purcell used it as a bass to his song, "May her bright example chace," written in 1692, and published in the *Orpheus Britannicus*, vol. ii. 1702. The anecdote in connection with Purcell's composition is too well known to repeat here. D'Urfey also prints the tune in his *Pills to purge Melancholy*, vol. ii., to verses entitled "The Farmer's Daughter," and in vol. iv. to another song, "The Country Lass." Gay included it in the *Beggar's Opera*.

# Come, all ye jolly shepherds.

## WHEN THE KYE COME HAME.*

Verses by JAMES HOGG.

*Moderato.*

PIANO.

1. Come, all ye jol-ly shep-herds, that whis-tle thro' the glen, I'll tell ye o' a se - cret that
2. There the black-bird biggs his nest for the mate he loves to see, And up up-on the topmost bough, oh,
3. See yon - der paw-ky shep - herd that lin-gers on the hill, His yowes are in the fauld, and his
4. A - wa' wi' fame and for - tune, what com-fort can they gi'e? And a' the arts that prey on man's

1. cour-tiers din - na ken; What is the great-est bliss that the tongue o'-man can name? 'Tis to
2. hap - py bird is he! Then he pours his melt-ing dit - ty, and love, 'tis a' the theme, An' he'll
3. lambs are ly - in' still; Yet he dow - na gang to rest, for his heart is in a flame, To
4. life an' lib - er - tie! Gi'e me the high-est joy that the heart o' man can frame; My

1. woo a bon - nie lass - ie when the kye come hame.
2. woo his bon - nie lass - ie when the kye come hame.
3. meet his bon - nie lass - ie when the kye come hame.
4. bon - nie, bon - nie lass - ie, when the kye come hame.

When the kye come hame,' when the

kye come hame, 'Tween the gloam - in' and the mirk, when the kye come hame.

* This air is a considerably altered version of the one known as, "Shame fa' the gear and the blethrie o't."

## Come, gie's a sang, the lady cried.

### TULLOCHGORUM.*

*Allegro spirituoso.*        *mf*      Verses by Rev. JOHN SKINNER.

1. Come, gie's a sang, the la - dy cried, And
2. O, Tul-loch-go-rum's my de - light, It
3. What needs there be sae great a fraise, Wi'
4. May choic - est bless-ings aye at - tend Each

1. lay your dis - putes a' 'a - side, What sig - ni - fies for folk to chide, For
2. gars us a' in ane un - nite, And on - y sumph that keeps up spite, In
3. driug - ing dull I - ta - lian lays, I wad - na gie our ain strath-speys For
4. hon - est o - pen-heart - ed friend, And calm and qui - et be his end, And

1. what was done be - fore them. Let Whig and To - ry a' a - gree,
2. con - science I ab - hor him. For blythe and mer - ry we'll a' be,
3. half a hun - dert o' them. They're dowf and dow - ie at the best,
4. a' that's gude watch o'er him. May peace and plen - ty be his lot,

* These verses owe their creation to the following episode: One evening when Skinner was visiting his friend, Montgomery of Ellon, Aberdeenshire, a violent political dispute arose between two gentlemen of opposite views. To restore good humour, Mrs. Montgomery called for a sang, providing Skinner at the same time with the idea which he has so admirably versified to the tune of "Tullochgorum." The poem was a great favourite of Burns, who called it " this first of songs," and " a masterpiece." Mr. R. Chambers says that, " Though belonging to a clerical body generally reputed as Jacobites, and though he himself suffered imprisonment during the *Forty-five* on suspicion, it does not appear that Skinner had any strong partisan feelings, except in favour of mirth and social harmony in general." (*Songs Prior to Burns*.)
"The tune of 'Tullochgorum' is very old, and is mentioned on Habbie Simson's Epitaph :—

"Sae weill's he keepit his decorum,
And all the stottis of Quhipp Meg Morum.

Stottis means notes; Quhipp Meg Morum is the old name of the air, and the sense is, therefore, Notes of Whig Meg Morum" (Mitchison's *Garland of Scotia*, 1841).

1. Whig and To - ry, Whig and To - ry, Whig and To - ry a' a - gree To
2. Blythe and mer - ry, blythe and mer - ry, Blythe and mer - ry we'll a' be, And
3. Dowf and dow - ie, dowf and dow - ie, Dowf and dow - ie at the best, Wi'
4. Peace and plen - ty, peace and plen - ty, Peace and plen - ty be his lot, And

1. drop their Whig - meg - mo - rum; Let Whig an' To - ry a' a - gree To
2. make a hap - py quo - rum; For blythe and mer - ry we'll a' be As
3. a' their va - ri - o - rum; They're dowf and dow - ie at the best, Their
4. dain - ties, a store o' them; May peace and plen - ty be his lot, Uu -

1. spend this night in mirth an' glee, An' cheer - fu' sing a - lang wi' me The
2. lang as we hae breath to draw, And dance till we be like to fa', The
3. al - le - gros and a' the rest, They can - na please a High - land taste, Com -
4. stain'd by an - y vi - cious spot, And may he nev - er want a groat, That's

*Last time.*

1. reel o' Tul - loch - go - rum!
2. reel o' Tul - loch - go - rum!
3. par'd wi' Tul - loch - go - rum!
4. fond o' Tul - loch - go - rum!

f

42

# Come o'er the stream, Charlie.*

Verses by JAMES HOGG.

Air: "MacLean's Welcome."

*Allegro con brio.*

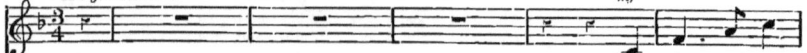

1. Come o'er the stream,
2. Come o'er the stream,
3. Come o'er the stream,

1. Char - lie, dear Char - lie, brave Char - lie, Come o'er the stream,
2. Char - lie, dear Char - lie, brave Char - lie, Come o'er the stream,
3. Char - lie, dear Char - lie, brave Char - lie, Come o'er the stream,

1. Char - lie, and dine wi' Mac - Lean; And though you be
2. Char - lie, and dine wi' Mac - Lean; And though you be
3. Char - lie, and dine wi' Mac - Lean; And though you be

1. wea - ry, we'll make your heart chee - ry, And wel - come our
2. wea - ry, we'll make your heart chee - ry, And wel - come our
3. wea - ry, we'll make your heart chee - ry, And wel - come our

* Hogg has included this song in his *Jacobite Relics*, Ser. II., p. 90. The verses are a free translation from the Gaelic. The air is of Highland origin.

1. Char - lie and his roy - al train. We'll bring down the red deer, we'll
2. Char - lie and his roy - al train. And you shall drink free - ly the
3. Char - lie and his roy - al train. If aught will in - vite you, or

1. bring down the black steer, The lamb from the brack - an, and
2. dews o' Glen Sheer - ly, That stream in the star - light where
3. more will de - light you, 'Tis rea - dy— a troop of our

1. doe from the Glen; The salt sea we'll har - ry, and bring to our
2. kings din - na ken; And deep be your meed o' the wine that is
3. bold High - land - men Shall range on the hea - ther, wi' bon - net and

1. Char - lie, The cream from the bo - thy, and curd from the pan.
2. red, ... To drink to your sire and his friend the Mac - Lean.
3. fea - ther, Strong arms and broad clay - mores, three hun - dred and ten.

# Cope sent a letter frae Dunbar.

### JOHNNIE COPE.*

Air: "Fy to the hills in the morning."

Con spirito.

VOICE.

PIANO.

*mf*

1. Cope sent a let - ter frae Dun - bar: O,
2. When Char - lie look'd the let - ter up - on, He
3. Now, John - nie, be as gude's your word, Come,
4. When John - nie Cope he heard of this, He
5. Fye, John - nie, now get up and rin, The
6. When John - nie Cope to Ber - wick cam', They

*mf*

*cres.* *f*

1. Char - lie, meet me an ye daur, And I'll learn ye the art o' war, Gin ye'll
2. drew his sword the scab - bard from: Come, fol - low me, my mer - ry men, And
3. let us try baith fire and sword; And din - na rin like a fright - ed bird, That's
4. thocht it wad - na be a - miss To hae a horse in rea - di - ness To
5. High - land bag - pipes mak' a din; It's best to sleep in a hale skin, For 'twill
6. speer'd at him, "Where's a' your men?" "The deil con - found me, gin I ken, For I

* Two versions of this clever ballad are given by Joseph Ritson in his *Scotish Songs*, p. 82, etc. They differ considerably from the version in Johnson's *Scot's Musical Museum*, No. 234. Stenhouse declares them to be "merely variations of the original satirical song which was written by Mr. Skirven, author of the song called 'Tranent Muir'" (*Museum Illustrations*, p. 220). For full historical information regarding Sir John Cope, see Hogg's *Jacobite Relics*, 1821, Ser. II., p. 308. A version of the tune appears in Oswald's *Caledonian Pocket Companion*, Bk. ix, under the title of "Johny Cope."

1. meet me in the morn - ing.
2. we'll meet Cope i' the morn - ing.
3. chased frae its nest i' the morn - ing.
4. flee a - wa' i' the morn - ing.
5. be a blui - dy morn - ing.
6. left them a' i' the morn - ing."

Hey, John-nie Cope, are ye wauk-in' yet? Or

are your drums a - beat - in' yet? If ye were wau - kin', I wad wait To

go to the couls i' the morn - ing.

# Come under my plaidie.*

Verses by HECTOR MACNEILL.

Air: "Johnnie M'Gill."

*Con anima.*

1. Come un-der my plaid-ie, the night's gaun to fa', Come in frae the cauld blast, the
2. Gae wa' wi' your plaid-ie, auld Don-ald, gae 'wa, I fear na the cauld blast, the
3. Dear Ma-rian, let that flea stick fast to the wa', Your Jock's but a gouk and has
4. My fa-ther aye tell'd me, my mi-ther and a', Ye'd mak a gude hus-band and
5. She crap in a-yont him be-side the stane wa', Whar John-nie was list'-ning and

1. drift an' the snaw; Come un-der my plaid-ie an' sit down be-side me, There's
2. drift, nor the snaw! Gae 'wa wi' your plaid-ie! I'll no sit be-side ye! Ye
3. nae-thing a-va; The haill o' his pack he has now on his back, He's
4. keep me ay braw, It's true I lo'e John-nie, he's gude and he's bon-nie, But
5. heard her tell a', The day was ap-point-ed, his proud heart it dunt-ed, Aud

* Of this song Mr. Patrick Buchan writes: "This is the best song Macneill ever wrote, and early gained that popularity to which it is justly entitled. It is somewhat strange that in most of Macneill's songs we find the lovers unequally matched, either by a young lassie and an old man, or vice versâ. The air, 'Johnny MacGill,' is by a Dumfries fiddler of the same name, and is truly a spirited and lively production" (*Garland of Scotia*, 1841). John MacGill, of Girvan, Dumfries, flourished about the beginning of last century. The air was first published in Joshua Campbell's *A Collection of the Newest and best Reels*. Glasgow, 1778.

1. room in't, dear las - sie, be - lieve me, for twa. Come un - der my plaid - ie, an'
2. might be my gut - cher, auld Don - ald, gae 'wa! I'm gaun to meet John - nie, he's
3. thret - ty, and I am but three-score and twa. Be frank now and kind - ly, I'll
4. wae's me! ye ken he has nae - thing a - va! I hae lit - tle to - cher you've
5. struck 'gainst his side as if burst - in' in twa. He wan-der'd hame wea - ry, the
1. sit down be - side me, I'll hap ye frae ev' - ry cauld blast that can blaw; Come
2. young and he's bon - nie, He's been at Meg's bri - dal fu' trig an' fu' braw; Nane
3. busk ye aye fine - ly, To kirk or to mar - ket there'll few gang sae braw; A
4. made a gude of - fer, I'm now mair than twen - ty, my time is but sma', Sae
5. night it was drea - ry, And thow - less he tint his gate deep in the snaw; The
cres.
poco rit.
a tempo.
1. un - der my plaid - ie, an' sit down be - side me, There's room in't, dear las - sie, be -
2. dan - ces sae licht - ly, sae grace - fu' or ticht - ly, His cheeks like the new rose, his
3. bien house to bide in, a chaise for to ride in, And flun - kies to tend ye as
4. gi'e me your plaid - ie, I'll creep in be - side ye, I thocht ye'd been auld - er than
5. how - let was scream - in', while John - nie cried, "Wo - men Wad mar - ry auld Nick if he'd
cres.
poco rit.
a tempo.
1. lieve me, for twa.
2. brow's like the snaw!
3. aft as ye ca'.
4. three-score and twa!
5. keep them aye braw!"
p
poco rit. a tempo.

# Dear, dear are the Highlands.*

### (Is toigh leam a' Ghaidhealtachd.)

Translated from the Gaelic of
JOHN CAMPBELL by FINDLAY MACRAE.

*Moderato con spirito.*

Gaelic air.

PIANO. *mf*

*Con Ped.*

1. Dear, dear are the High-lands, be - lov - ed the glens, Each cas - cade and dell in the
2. And dear are the maid - ens, so hand-some and fair, In their smiles oft I sought to soothe
3. And dear is the Gae - lic—its mu - sic and song Oft cheered our sad hearts, wrung by
4. O'er our coun - try be - loved now the red deer bound free, While use - less o'er o - cean wide

1. land of the Bens; And dear are the gal - lants in gay tar - tau there, With
2. sor - row and care; With a bride by my side from my own High-land home, Light -
3. grief or by wrong; The ac - cents we lisped, as in child - hood we strayed, Shall
4. scat - tered are we; But should bat - tle threat-en, who then shall stand true? O,

*ten.*

1. fea-thered glen-gar - ries and thick curl-ing hair.
2. heart - ed and free o'er the world I would roam.
3. ne'er be for - got till in dust we are laid.
4. then for the boys in the bon - nets of blue!

* From the *Celtic Lyre*, by kind permission of the Editor, Mr. Henry Whyte. This is a patriotic song by the poet postmaster of Ledaig, Argyllshire, which has attained a large amount of popularity. The air is associated with an older song known as "*Cogadh no sith*"—War or Peace. Mr. John Campbell was born at Oban in 1823. For an interesting sketch of his life, see *Good Words*, July and August, 1869. A volume of poems by this bard was published in 1884.

# Duncan Gray.*

Con spirito.

mf     Verses by BURNS.

VOICE.

PIANO.

1. Dun-can Gray cam' here to woo—
2. Dun-can fleech'd, and Dun-can pray'd—
3. Time and chance are but a tide—
4. How it comes let doc-tors tell—
5. Dun-can was a lad o' grace—

1. Ha, ha, the woo-ing o't! On blyth yule night, when we were fu'— Ha, ha, the woo-ing o't!
2. Ha, ha, the woo-ing o't! Meg was deaf as Ail-sa Craig—Ha, ha, the woo-ing o't!
3. Ha, ha, the woo-ing o't! Slight-ed love is sair to bide—Ha, ha, the woo-ing o't!
4. Ha, ha, the woo-ing o't! Meg grew sick, as he grew well—Ha, ha, the woo-ing o't!
5. Ha, ha, the woo-ing o't! Mag-gie's was a pi-teous case—Ha, ha, the woo-ing o't!

1. Meg-gie coost her head fu' high, Look'd a-sklent and un-co skeigh, Gart poor Dun-can
2. Dun-can sigh'd baith out and in, Grat his een baith bleer'd and blin'; Spak' o' low-pin'
3. "Shall I, like a fool," quoth he, "For a haugh-ty hiz-zie dee? She may gae to-
4. Something in her bo som wrings, For re-lief a sigh she brings; And her e'en, they
5. Dun-can could na be her death, Swell-ing pi-ty smoor'd his wrath; Now they're crouse and

1. stand a-beigh; Ha, ha, the woo-ing o't!
2. o'er a linn; Ha, ha, the woo-ing o't!
3. France for me!" Ha, ha, the woo-ing o't!
4. spak' sic things! Ha, ha, the woo-ing o't!
5. can-ty baith, Ha, ha, the woo-ing o't!

* This air appears in MacGibbon's and Oswald's Collections, and, according to Dr. Blacklock, was composed about 1700 by a carter in Glasgow. Burns wrote these verses in the winter of 1792.

E

# Fal il o ro, fal il o.

## SONG TO THE CHIEF.*

Translated from the Gaelic by LACHLAN MacBEAN.

*Moderato.*

PIANO. *mf* *p*

*mf*

Fal il o ro, fal il o, Day a - round me spring - ing, Hee

*mf*

ri - hil u - hil i - hil o, No heart have I for sing - ing.

1. At dawn I rise with weep - ing eyes, No heart have I for sing - ing; A -
2. A - round me shrill the breez - es chill Of east - ern winds are sting - ing; Oh,
3. Oh, that it brought the bon - nie boat, Light o'er the bil - lows swing - ing, And
4. Oh, would that he right gal - lant - ly His way to Sleat were wing - ing, Where
5. Where songs a - rise and har - mo - nies, With harps and pi - brochs ring - ing; But

* From *Songs and Hymns of the Scottish Highlands*, by kind permission. This song is generally understood to belong to the Isle of Skye, and the reference to Sleat goes a long way to confirm this belief. It belongs to last century, but the author's name is unknown. The air is very ancient.

1. round me shrill the breez - es thrill Of east - ern winds are sting - ing.
2. I would hail the west - ern gale With bless - ings round it fling - ing.
3. safe may float the bon - nie boat, Our gal - lant chief - tain bring - ing.
4. songs a - rise and har - mo - nies With harp and pi - broch ring - ing.
5. now I rise with weep - ing eyes, No heart have I for sing - ing.

Chorus. f

Fal il o ro, fal il o, Day a - round me spring - ing, Hee

ri - hil u - hil i - hil o, No heart have I for sing - ing.

D.S.

E 2

# Fareweel, O, fareweel! *

Gaelic air.

**VOICE.** / **PIANO.**

*Andante.*

*p con molto espressione.*

*con Ped.*

*poco rit.*

1. Fare - weel, O, fare -
2. His staff's at the

1. weel! My heart it is sair; Fare - weel, O, fare - weel! I'll ...
2. wa', Toom, toom is his chair, The ban - net an a'! An' ...

1. see him nae more. Lang, lang was he mine, Lang, lang, but nae
2. I maun be here. But O! he's at rest, Where hearts ne'er were

*poco rit.* / *rit.*

1. mair I maun - na re - pine, But my heart is sair.
2. sair, O to meet him a - gain, To ... part nev - er mair!

*poco rit.* / *rit.*

---

\* These verses are from R. A. Smith's *Scottish Minstrel*, 1822, vol. iv. They are by Lady Nairne. Smith gives a version of the tune in eight bars. He has marked it "very old."

# Farewell, thou fair day.

## ORAN AN AOIG, OR, THE SONG OF DEATH.*

Verses by BURNS.

. Isle of Skye Song.

*Lento, con molto maestoso.*

VOICE.

PIANO.

*mf*

1. Fare-well, thou fair day, thou green
2. Thou strik'st the dull peasant, he

*cres.*

1. earth, and ye skies, Now gay with the broad setting sun: Farewell, loves and friendships, ye dear tender ties! Our
2. sinks in the dark, Nor saves e'en the wreck of a name; Thou strik'st the young he-ro, a glo-ri-ous mark! He

*cres.*

*p* *dim.*

1. race of existence is run! Thou grim King of terrors, thou life's gloomy foe, Go frighten the coward and
2. falls in the blaze of his fame. In the field of proud honour, our swords in our hands, Our King and our country to

*p* *dim.*

*cres.*

1. slave! Go teach them to trem-ble, fell ty-rant, but know, No terrors ex - ist for the brave! . .
2. save; Where vic - to - ry shines on life's last ebb-ing sands, Oh, who would not die with the brave! . .

*cres.*

* Burns wrote these verses in the winter of 1791. He obtained the melody from Macdonald's *Collection of Highland Airs.* † In some editions C♯.

## Far over yon hills.

### FLORA MACDONALD'S LAMENT.*

*Andante tranquillo e con molto espressione.*

Verses by. JAMES HOGG.

1. Far o - ver yon hills of the
2. The moor - cock that crows on the
3. The tar - get is torn from the

1. hea - ther sae green, And down by the cor - rie that sings by the sea, The
2. brows o' Ben Con - nal, He kens o' his bed in a sweet mos - sy hame; The
3. arm of the just, . The hel - met is cleft on the brow of the brave, The

1. bon - nie young Flo - ra sat sigh - ing her lane, The dew on her plaid, an' the
2. ea - gle that soars on the cliffs o' Clan Ron - ald, Un - aw'd and un - hunt - ed his
3. clay - more for ev - er in dark - ness must rust, But red is the sword of the

* This favourite air is by Niel Gow, Junr., and the verses by James Hogg, who published them in his *Jacobite Relics.*

*poco cres.*

1. tear in her e'e. She look'd at a boat wi' the breez - es that swung, A -
2. ey - rie can claim. The so - lan can sleep on the shelf of the shores; The
3. stran-ger and slave. The hoof of the horse and the foot of the proud, Have

*poco cres.*

1. way on the waves like a bird on the main; An' ay as it les - sen'd she
2. cor - mo - rant roost on his rock of the sea; But ah! there is one whose hard
3. trode o'er the plumes on the bon - net of blue; Why slept the red bolt in the

*f*

1. sigh'd as she sung, "Fare - weel to the lad I shall ne'er see a - gain! Fare -
2. fate I de - plore, Nor house, ha', nor hame in his coun - try has he, The
3. breast of the cloud When ty - ran - ny re - vell'd in blood of the true? Fare -

*poco energia.*  *dim.*  *rit.*

1. weel to my he - ro, the gal-lant and young, Fare-weel to the lad I shall ne'er see a - gain!"
2. con-flict is past and our name is no more, There's nought left but sor - row for Scot-land and me!
3. weel, my young he - ro, the gal-lant and good! The crown of thy fa-thers is torn from thy brow!

*poco energia.*  *dim.*  *rit.*

# Flow gently, sweet Afton.

## AFTON WATER.*

Verses by BURNS.

*Andante tranquillo.*

VOICE.

PIANO.

*p molto legato.*

*con Ped.*

1. Flow  gent - ly,  sweet  Af - ton,  a -
2. Thou  stock - dove,  whose  e - cho  re -
3. How  lof - ty,  sweet  Af - ton,  thy
4. Flow  gent - ly,  sweet  Af - ton,  a -

*sempre con Ped.*

1. mong  thy  green  braes,  Flow  gent - ly,  I'll  sing  thee  a
2. sounds  thro'  the  glen,  Ye  wild  whist - ling  black - birds  in
3. neigh - bour - ing  hills,  Far - mark'd  with  the  cours - es  of
4. mong  thy  green  braes,  Flow  gent - ly,  sweet  ri - ver,  the

* Burns wrote this poem in 1786. He presented it to Mrs. Stewart of Afton Lodge, as a tribute of gratitude for the kindness she had shown to the poet. He afterwards sent it, with the air, to Johnson for *The Scot's Museum*. There is some doubt regarding the heroine of this song, but Miss Dunlop and Gilbert Burns affirmed that they remembered hearing Burns say that it was written upon his dearly loved "Highland Mary." The author of the air is unknown. The Afton is a small river in Ayrshire, a tributary stream of the Nith.

1. song in thy praise; My Ma - ry's a - sleep by thy
2. yon flow' - ry den; Thou green - crest - ed lap - wing, thy
3. sweet wind - ing rills! There dai - ly I wan - der as
4. theme of my lays; My Ma - ry's a - sleep by thy

1. mur - mur - ing stream, Flow gent - ly, sweet Af - ton, dis -
2. scream - ing for - bear, I charge you dis - turb not my
3. morn ri - ses high, My flocks and my Ma - ry's sweet
4. mur - mur - ing stream, Flow gent - ly, sweet Af - ton, dis -

*colla voce.*

1. turb not her dream.
2. slum - ber - ing fair.
3. cot in my eye.
4. turb not her dream.

*p*

*dim.*

# Gin a body meet a body.*

**Molto moderato.**

VOICE.

PIANO.

1. Gin a bo-dy meet a bo-dy Comin' thro' the rye,
2. Gin a bo-dy meet a bo-dy Comin' frae the well,
3. Gin a bo-dy meet a bo-dy Comin' frae the toun,
4. In the train there is a swain I dear-ly lo'e mysel'; But

*cres.* *ten.* p

1. Gin a bo-dy kiss a bo-dy, Need a bo-dy cry? Il-ka lassie has her lad-die, Nane they say ha'e I; Yet
2. Gin a bo-dy kiss a bo-dy, Need a bo-dy tell? Il-ka lassie has her lad-die, Ne'er a ane ha'e I; But
3. Gin a bo-dy greet a bo-dy, Need a bo-dy gloom? Il-ka lassie has her lad-die, Nane they say ha'e I; But
4. whaur his hame or what his name I din-na care to tell. Il-ka lassie has her lad-die, Nane they say ha'e I; Yet

*ten.*

*poco rit.*

1. a' the lads they smile to me, When comin' thro' the rye.
2. a' the lads they smile on me, When comin' thro' the rye.
3. a' the lads they lo'e me weel, And what the waur am I?
4. a' the lads they lo'e me weel, And what the waur am I?

*poco rit.* *mf poco rit.*

* The first three verses of this song with its air appeared in Johnson's *Scot's Musical Museum* (No. 418). The fourth verse seems to have been added by some public singer. Mr. John Dunlop, Collector of Customs, Port Glasgow, and Lord Provost of Glasgow in 1794, wrote verses beginning: "Oh, dinna ask me gin I lo'e thee," which enjoyed much popularity during the first half of the century. The following is the first verse from the song in the *Museum* (No. 417). Although the verses are marked there as being "written for this work by Robert Burns," we are inclined to believe that this verse is a fragment of some old traditional song :—

Comin' thro' the rye, poor body,
Comin' thro' the rye,
She draigl't a' her petticotie
Comin' thro' the rye.
*Chorus.*—Oh, Jenny's a' weet, poor bodie,
Jenny's seldom dry ;
She draigl't a' her petticotie
Comin' thro' the rye.

In *The Musical Repository*, published in Glasgow in 1799—two years after vol. v. of the *Museum*—the same song appears with a *fourth* verse, which also smacks of an earlier period. Burns' name is not mentioned in connection with the song in the *Repository*, which is headed : "Original words to the foregoing tune." The theory that by the "rye," some stream or ford is indicated, is quite erroneous. In every version of the song which we have seen, the word has been written *rye*—not with a capital R. The state of a rye-field in damp weather would be quite sufficient to reduce the "petticotie" of a careless young lady to a "draigl't" condition. A version of the tune is given in Gow's Collection (Bk. I., p. 19), 1754, under the title of "The Miller's Daughter."

# Good-night, and joy be wi' ye a'.*

Verses by SIR ALEXANDER BOSWELL.

*Moderato.*

VOICE.

PIANO.

*mf*        *mf*

1. Good-night, and joy be
2. When on yon muir our
3. The auld will speak, the

1. wi' ye a', Your harm-less mirth has cheer'd my heart; May life's fell blasts out-o'er ye blaw! In
2. gal-lant clan Frae boast-ing foes their ban-ners tore, Who show'd him-sel' a bet-ter man, Or
3. young maun hear, Be can-ty, and be good and leal; Your ain ills aye hae heart to bear, An-

1. sor-row may ye nev-er part. My spi-rit lives, but strength is gone, The moun-tain fires now
2. fierc-er wav'd the red claymore? But when in peace—then mark me there, When thro' the glen the
3. i-ther aye hae heart to feel. So, e'er I set, I'll see you shine, I'll see you tri-umph

1. blaze in vain; Re-mem-ber, sons, the deeds I've done, And in your deeds I'll live a-gain.
2. wan-d'rer came, I gave him of our har-dy fare, I gave him here a wel-come hame.
3. e'er I fa'; My pant-ing breath shall boast you mine, Good-night, and joy be wi' you a'.

* Hogg also wrote verses to this air, beginning: "The year is wearin' to the wane." Each stanza closes with, "Guid nicht an' joy be wi' you a'." A tune occurs in the Skene MS. named "Good-night, and joy be wi' you." This title is supposed to be the origin of the songs written by so many poets on the same theme. In his *Border Min-trelsy,* Sir Walter Scott prints two stanzas which tradition has preserved as the farewell of one of the Armstrongs on the eve of his execution for the murder of Sir John Carmichael of Edrom, an event which took place in 1600. These verses close with, "I hope ye're a' my friends as yet, good-night, and joy be wi' ye all!" The air is very old, and was first published by Playford in his *Scotch Tunes,* 1700.

# Gin I had a wee house.

### BYDE YE YET.*

**VOICE.**

*Allegretto.*

**PIANO.**

*p*

1. Gin I had a wee house an' a can - ty wee fire, A
2. When I gang ... a - field and come hame ... at e'en, I'll
3. And if there should hap - pen then ev - er to be A

1. bon - nie wee wi - fie to praise an' ad - mire, A bon - nie wee yar - die a -
2. get my wee wi - fie fou neat and fou clean, A bon - nie wee bair - nie up -
3. diff' - rence a - tween my wee wi - fie an' me, In hear - ty good hu - mour, al -

1. side a wee burn; Fare - weel to the bod - ies that yam - mer and mourn.
2. on ... her knee, That cries out dear pa - pa, or dad - dy to me.  } Sac
3. though she be teazed, I'll kiss her and clap her un - til she be pleased.

---

* This song was first printed in Herd's *Antient and Modern Scottish Songs*, vol. ii., 1776. Its author is unknown. A clever parody on
" Byde ye yet " was written by Miss Jenny Graham of Dumfries (b. 1724), beginning, " Alas! my son, you little know the sorrows that from
wedlock flow." It was published by Herd under the title of " The Wayward Wife." The air is of Highland origin.

byde ye yet, an' byde ye yet, Ye lit - tle ken what may be -

tide me yet; Some bon - nie wee bod - ie may fa' to my lot, An' I'll

aye be can - ty wi' think - in' o't, wi' think - in' o't, wi'

think - in' o't, I'll aye be can - ty wi' think - in' o't.

# Hame, hame, hame!*

*Adagio appassionata.*

VOICE.

1. Hame, hame, hame, O hame fain wad I be, . .
2. Hame, hame, hame, O hame fain wad I be, . .
3. Hame, hame, hame, O hame fain wad I be, . .

PIANO.

*p*    *rit.*    *p*

con Ped.

1. Hame, hame, hame to my ain coun-trie! There's an eye that ev-er weeps, and a fair face will be fain, As I
2. Hame, hame, hame to my ain coun-trie! The green leaf o' loy-al-tie is be-gin-ning for to fa', And the
3. Hame, hame, hame to my ain coun-trie! The great now are gane, a' who ventur'd for to save, And the

1. pass thro' An-nan-wa-ter wi' my bon-nie bands a-gain; When the flow'r is in the bud and the
2. bon-nie white rose it is with-er-ing and a'; But I'll wa-ter't wi' the bluid o' u-
3. new grass is grow-ing a-bove their blui-dy grave, But the sun in the mirk blinks

*p*

1. leaf up-on the tree, The lark shall sing me hame in my ain coun-trie.
2. surp-ing ty-ran-nie, And green it will grow in my ain coun-trie.
3. blythe in my e'e, I'll shine on ye yet in my ain coun-trie.

*rit.*

last time.

*rit.*    *p*    *rit.*

* This air is evidently a modification of "The Bridegroom Grat," the tune to which Lady Anne Lindsay wrote her celebrated ballad "Auld Robin Gray." Another version of the song is given by Hogg in his *Jacobite Relics*, Ser. I., Song lxxx.

# Heavy the beat of the weary waves.

### ISLE OF MULL DIRGE.*

Air: "An cronan Muillach."

1. Hea - vy the beat of the wea - ry waves, Fall - ing, fall - ing o'er and o'er Up - on the rock - y shore, Where he comes no more, a - las! no more. Och-one! Ev - - er-more, och - one! . . . . .

2. Tears of des - pair from the weep - ing sky, Fall - ing to the earth be-neath, And o'er the gloo - my heath Hangs a mis - ty pall of death, of death! Och-one! Ev - - er-more, och - one! . . . . .

* A somewhat different version of this melody is included in Captain Fraser's *Airs Peculiar to the Scottish Highlands*, 1816.

# Hear me, ye nymphs, and every swain.

## THE BUSH ABOON TRAQUAIR.*

Verses by ROBERT CRAWFORD.

*Andantino.*

VOICE.

PIANO.

*poco rit.*

1. Hear me, ye nymphs, and
2. That day she smil'd and
3. Yet now she scorn - ful
4. Ye ru - ral pow'rs, who

1. ev' — ry swain, I'll tell how Peg — gy grieves me; Tho'
2. made .... me glad, No maid seem'd ev — er kind — er; I
3. flies .... the plain, The fields we then — fre - quent - ed; If
4. hear .... my strains, Why thus should Peg — gy grieve me? Oh!

* This air first appears in the *Orpheus Caledonius*, 1725, p. 3, adapted to Crawfurd's verses. It is one of the seven tunes ascribed by the editor of that work to "David Rizzio." In Watt's *Musical Miscellany*, vol. ii., p. 97, 1729, we find a slightly different version of the melody under the title of "The Bonnie Bush o' boon Traquhair." Crawfurd was drowned in 1732. These verses have been often wrongly ascribed to William Crawfurd (of Auchinames). The song beginning :

"The crow or daw thro' all the year
No fowler seeks to ruin,"

in Gay's opera *Polly*, 1729, is marked to be sung to the air, "The Bush a-boon Traquair." Traquair is a parish in Peeblesshire; it is watered by the stream Quair.

1. thus I lan - guish and . . . . com-plain, A - las! she ne'er be -
2. thought my - self the luck - iest lad, So sweet - ly there to
3. e'er we meet she shows . . . dis - dain, And looks as ne'er ac -
4. make her part - ner of . . . . my pains, Then let her smiles re -

1. lieves me. My vows . . . and sighs, like si - lent air, Un -
2. find her. I tried . . to soothe my am' - rous flame, Its
3. quaint - ed. The bon - nie bush bloom'd fair in May, Its
4. lieve me. If not, . . . my love will turn des - pair, My

1. heed - ed . . nev - er move . . . . her; The bon - nie bush . . a -
2. words that I thought ten - - - - der; If more there pass'd . I'm
3. sweets I'll e'er re - mem - - - ber; But now her frowns . make
4. pas - sion . no more ten - - - der; I'll leave the bush . . a -

*cres.*

Ped.     Ped.     Ped.

1. boon . . . Tra - quair, Was where I first . . . did meet her.
2. not . . . to blame, I meant not to . . . . of - fend her.
3. it . . . de - cay, It fades as in . . . . De - cem - - ber.
4. boon . . . Tra - quair, To lone - ly wilds . . . I'll wan - - der.

*colla voce.*     *f*     *dim.*

F

# Here awa', there awa'!*

Verses by BURNS.

*Andante affettuoso.*

VOICE.

PIANO.

1. Here a - wa',
2. Win - ter winds blew
3. Rest, ye wild
4. But, oh, if he's

1. there a - wa', wan - der - ing Wil - lie! Here a - wa', there a - wa'
2. loud and cauld at . . . . . our part - in'; Fears . . . for my Wil - lie brought
3. storms, in the caves of your slum - bers! How . . . . your dread howl - ing a
4. faith - less, and minds na his Nan - nie, Flow . . . still be - tween us, thou

1. haud a - wa', hame! Come to my bo - som, my ain . . . on - ly
2. tears to my e'e; Wel - come now, sum - mer, and wel - come, my
3. lov - er a - larms! Wau - ken, ye breez - es, row gent - ly, ye
4. wide roar - in' main! May I ne'er see . . . . it, may . . . I ne'er

*cres.*

1. dear - ie, Tell me thou bring'st me my Wil - lie the same.
2. Wil - lie; The sum - mer to Na - ture, my Wil - lie to me.
3. bil - lows! And waft my dear lad - die ance mair to my arms.
4. trow it, But, dy - ing, be - lieve that my Wil - lie's my ain!

*rit.*

* Oswald has preserved this beautiful air in his *Caledonian Pocket Companion*, Bk. vii. Burns' verses are based upon an old song published in Herd's Collection of 1776, vol. ii., the first verse of which is:—

Here awa', there awa', here awa', Willie,
Here awa', there awa', here awa' hame;
Lang have I sought thee, dear have I bought thee,
Now I have gotten my Willie again.

† In some editions C ♯.

# Here's a health to them that's awa'.*

**PIANO.**

*Allegretto.*

1. Here's a health to them that's a - wa', Here's a health to them that's a - wa'; And, wha
2. Here's a health to them that's a - wa', Here's a health to them that's a - wa'; Here's a

1. win - na wish gude luck to the cause, May ne - ver gude luck be their fa, Hin-ny! It's
2. health to Char - lie, the chief of the Clans, Al - though that his hand be but sma', Hin-ny! Here's

1. gude to be mer - ry and wise; . . It's gude to be hon - est and true; . . . It's
2. free - dom to him that would read; . . . There's free - dom to him that would write; . . . There's

1. gude to be aff wi' the auld . . . . love Be - fore we be on wi' the new, Hin-ny!
2. nane ev - er fear'd that the truth should be hear'd But they whom the truth would in - dite, Hin-ny!

* Hogg, in his *Jacobite Relics*, Series I., introduces this air to words beginning, "Here's a health to them that's awa'!" In his note to the song, p. 217, he remarks: "This has always been a popular air, and one of those songs that Allan Ramsay altered into a love song for the sake of preserving the old chorus, which he has done in many instances, and for which he can scarcely be blamed; because to have published any of the Jacobite songs at that day was risking as much as his neck was worth." Burns wrote the above verses in 1792. They are supposed to be in honour of the Liberal leaders of the House of Commons. By "Charlie, the Chief of the Clans" is meant the Right Hon. Charles Fox.

# Hie upon Hielands and laigh upon Tay.

## BONNIE GEORGE CAMPBELL.*

VOICE.

PIANO.

1. Hie up-on Hie-lands and
2. Doun cam' his mith-er dear,
3. Sad-dled and boot-ed and

1. laigh up-on Tay, Bon-nie George Camp-bell rade out on a day; He
2. greet-in' fu' sair; And out cam' his bon-nie wife ri-vin' her hair; "My
3. bri-dled rade he, A plume in his hel-met, a sword at his knee; But

1. sad-dled, he bri-dled, and gal-lant rade he, And hame cam' his
2. mea-dows lie green, and my corn is un-shorn, My barn is to
3. toom cam' the sad-dle a' blui-dy to see, Oh, hame cam' his

1. guid horse, but nev-er cam' he!
2. bigg, and I'm left a' for-lorn!"
3. guid horse, but nev-er cam' he!

*Last time.*

* This ballad is supposed to be a Lament for one of the adherents of the house of Argyle, who was killed in the battle of Glenlivat, 3rd October, 1594. The air is included in Smith's *Scottish Minstrel*, 1822.

# How blythe ilk morn was I to see.

## THE BRUME O' THE COWDENKNOWES.*

*Andante con molto espressione.*

VOICE.

1. How blythe ilk morn was
2. I want-ed nei-ther
3. He tun'd his pipe and
4. Hard fate, that I should
5. A-dieu, ye Cow-den-

PIANO.

1. I to see My swain come o'er the hill! He skipt the burn and
2. yowe nor lamb While his flock near me lay; He ga-ther'd in my
3. play'd sae sweet, The birds sat list'-ning bye; E'en the dull cat-tle
4. ban-ish'd be, Gang hea-vi-ly and mourn, Be-cause I lov'd the
5. knowes, a-dieu! Fare-weel a' plea-sures there; Ye gods, re-store me

1. flew to me; I met him with good-will.
2. flock at night, And cheer'd me a' the day.
3. stood and gaz'd, Charm'd with the mel-o-dye.
4. kind-est swain That ev-er yet was born.
5. to my swain, Is a' I crave or care!

Oh, the brume, the bonnie, bonnie brume! The

brume o' the Cow-den-knowes! †I wish I were with my dear swain, With his pipe and my yowes.

---

* This ballad appears in Ramsay's *Tea-Table Miscellany*, 1724; it is there signed with the initials S.R. The air belongs to a much earlier period. Stenhouse (*Johnson's Scots' Museum Illustrations*) considers it to be one of the Scottish tunes introduced into England not long after the union of the crowns, 1603. We have adopted the older version of the air as given by Thomson, Oswald, and McGibbon. The more modern version is found in Watt's *Musical Miscellany*, vol. vi., 1729, and in the last number of the first act of *The Beggar's Opera*, 1727, the duet between Polly and Macheath, beginning: "The miser thus a shilling sees."

† Thomson's version differs here—"I wish I were at hame again To milk my daddy's ews" (see *Orpheus Caledonius*, 1725, p. 10).

# Hush-a-by, darling.*

(LULLABY.)

Ancient Lochaber "Cronan" or Lullaby.
Translated from the Gaelic by LACHLAN MACBEAN.

VOICE.

Andantino.

*p*

1. Hush - a - by, dar - ling, and
2. Lul - la - by, lit - tle one,
3. Soft - ly and si - lent - ly
4. Pla - cid - ly, peace - ful - ly,

PIANO.

*p*    *dim.*    *p*

con Ped.

1. hush - a - by, dear O, Hush - a - by, darl - ing will yet be a he - ro,
2. bon - nie wee ba - by, He'll be a he - ro, and fight for us may - be;
3. eye - lids are clos - ing, Dear - est wee jew - el, so gent - ly he's doz - ing;
4. slum - ber has bound him, An - gels are lov - ing - ly watch - ing a - round him;

*pp*    poco a poco crescendo.    ten.____ *f*

1. None will be big - ger or brav - er or strong - er, Lul - la - by, lit - tle one,
2. Cat - tle and hor - ses and sheep will his prey be, None will be bold - er or
3. Soft - ly he's rest - ing by slum - ber o'er - tak - en, Sound - ly he's sleep - ing and
4. Beau - ti - ful spi - rits, his sor - row be - guil - ing, Sweet - ly they whis - per and

*pp*    poco a poco crescendo.    colla voce. *f*

poco rit.

1. cry - ing no lon - ger.
2. brav - er than La - by.
3. sweet - ly he'll wak - en.
4. ba - by is smil - ing.

poco rit.    *p*    rit.

* From *Songs and Hymns of the Scottish Highlands*, 1888, by the kind permission of the editor, Mr. Lachlan MacBean. The melody is very old and was published for the first time by Mr. MacBean.

# Hush ye, my bairnie.*

### (Cagavan Gavlach.)

Old Lochaber Lullaby.
Translated from the Gaelic by Malcolm MacFarlane.

1. Hush ye, my bairn-ie, my bon-nie wee lad-die, When ye're a man, ye shall
2. Hush ye, my bairn-ie, my bon-nie wee lam-mie, Routh o' guid things ye shall
3. Hush ye, my bairn-ie, my bon-nie wee dear-ie, Sleep! come and close the e'en

1. fol - low ye're dad - die; Lift me a coo and a goat and a we - ther,
2. bring to your mam - mie; Hare frae the mea - dow, and deer frae the moun - tain,
3. hea - vy and wear - ie; Closed are the wear - ie e'en, rest ye are tak - in'—

1. Bring - ing them hame to yer Min - nie thi - ge - ther.
2. Grouse frae the muir - land, and trout frae the foun - tain.
3. Soun' be your sleep - in', and bright be your wak - in'.

* This is another ancient Lochaber lullaby. It speaks of a time when "cattle lifting" was considered an honourable occupation, and engaged in by every chief who could venture to do so. The Clan MacKay were known as *Clan Aoidh nan creach*, MacKay of the Raids; while the gathering tune of the Clan MacFarlane is *Thogail nam bo*, To lift the cattle.

# I dream'd I lay where flow'rs were springing.

## THE DREAM.*

Verses by Burns.

1. I dream'd I lay where flow'rs were springing, Gai-ly in the sun-ny beam, And list'ning to the wild birds sing-ing, By a fall-ing cry-stal stream; Straight the sky grew black and dar-ing, Thro' the woods the whirlwinds rave; Trees with aged arms were war-ring, O'er the swell-ing drum-lie wave.

2. Such was my life's de-ceit-ful morn-ing, Such the pleasures I en-joy'd; But lang or noon, loud tempests storm-ing, A' my flow'-ry bliss de-stroy'd; Tho' fickle for-tune has de-ceiv'd me, She promis'd fair, and perform'd but ill; Of mony a joy and hope be-reav'd me, I bear a heart, shall support me still.

*\* Burns composed these two stanzas when he was seventeen years of age. The air first appears in Johnson's Scots' Musical Museum, Song No. 146, and seems to have an Irish ring about it.*

# I'll bid my heart be still.*

Verses by THOMAS PRINGLE, died 1834.

*Andante.*

Ancient Border Melody.

PIANO.

*p espress, con poco ritardando.* *sf*

*p*

1. I'll bid my heart be still, And check each strug - gling
2. They bid me cease to weep, For glo - ry gilds his
3. My cheek has lost its hue, My eye grows faint and

*rit.*

1. sigh; And there's none e'er shall know My soul's cher-ish'd woe, When the
2. name; Ah! 'tis there - fore I mourn, He can nev - er re - turn To en -
3. dim; But 'tis sweet - er to fade In grief's gloo - my shade, Than

*rit.*

1. first tears of sor - row are dry.
2. joy the bright noon of his fame.
3. bloom for a - no - ther than him.

*p* *sf*

* This song was first published in *Albyn's Anthology*, 1816. On p. 41 of that work, Alexander Campbell, the Editor, has the following note: " This sweetly rural and plaintive air, like many others of the more ancient Border melodies, has but one part, or rather or e measure. It was taken down by the Editor from the singing of Mr. Hogg and his friend Mr. Pringle, author of the pathetic verses to which it is united." Campbell gives three of the original verses beginning, "O once my thyme was young."

# I climb the mountains.

## THE BOATMAN.*
### (Fear a Bhàta.)

Translation from the Gaelic by Lachlan MacBean.

1. I climb the moun-tains, and scan the o-cean For thee, my
2. From pass-ing boat-men I'd fain dis-cov-er If they have
3. My lov-er pro-mised to bring his la-dy A silk-en
4. My heart is wea-ry with cease-less wail-ing, Like wound-ed

1. boat-man, with fond de-vo-tion, When shall I see thee? to-day? to-
2. heard of, or seen my lov-er; They nev-er tell me—I'm on-ly
3. gown and a tar-tan plai-die, A ring of gold which would show his
4. swan when her strength is fail-ing, Her notes of an-guish the lake a-

* From *Songs and Hymns of the Scottish Highlands*, by the kind permission of the Editor, Mr. Lachlan MacBean. This melody is one of the many ancient Gaelic airs, about which it is almost impossible to obtain any historical information. It is evidently very old, and is one of the most beautiful and popular melodies of the Scottish Highlands.

1. mor - row? O do not leave me in lone - ly sor - row!
2. chid - ed, And told my heart has been sore mis - guid - ed.
3. sem - blance, But, ah! I fear me for his re - mem - brance.
4. wa - ken, By all her com - rades at last for - sak - en.

O, my boat - man, na - ho - ro ei - le, O, my
Fhir a bhà - ta, na ho - ro ei - le, Fhir a

boat - man, na - ho - ro, ei - le, O, my boat - man, na - ho - ro
bhà - ta, na ho - ro, ei - le, Fhir a bhà - ta, na ho - ro

ci - le, Hap - py be thou, when - e'er thou sail - est!
ri - le, Gu ma slan duit's gach ait' an teid thu!

## I hae laid a herrin' in saut.*

Allegretto.

Verses by James Tytler.

VOICE.

PIANO.

1. I hae laid a her-rin' in saut, Lass, gin ye lo'e me,
2. I hae a house on yon - der muir, Lass, gin ye lo'e me,
3. I hae a hen wi' a hap-pi-ty leg, Lass, gin ye lo'e me,

1. tell me noo! I hae brew'd a for-pet o' maut, An' I
2. tell me noo! Three spar - rows may - be dance on the floor, An' I
3. tell me noo! And il - ka day it lays me an egg, An' I

* The construction of this air proves it to be of considerab'e antiquity. Tytler's poem is merely a slightly altered version of a fragment published in Herd's Collection, 1776, vol. ii, p. 22, beginning, "I hae layen three herring in sa't." An old English song on a similar subject can be traced back as far as Henry VIII.'s time. A version of it occurs in D'Urfey's *Pills to Purge Melancholy*, vol. iii., p. 114, and each verse closes with "I cannot, cannot come every day to wooe." The air is in Aird's *Selection of Scotch, etc., Airs*, vol. ii., 1782.

cres.
1. can - na come il - ka day to woo! I hae a cauf 'twill
2. can - na come il - ka day to woo! I hae a but, and
3. can - na come il - ka day to woo! I hae a keb - bock up -
cres.
poco rit.
1. sune be a coo, Lass, gin ye lo'e me, tell me noo!
2. I hae a ben, Lass, gin ye lo'e me, tell me noo!
3. on . . my shelf, Lass, gin ye lo'e me, tell me noo!
poco rit.
mf a tempo.
1. I hae a stook 'twill sune be a mowe, An' I can - na come il - ka
2. I hae three chick - ens and a fat hen, An' I can - na come il - ka
3. I dow - na eat it a' my - self, An' I can - na come il - ka
f
mf a tempo.
f
Last time.
1. day to woo!
2. day to woo!
3. day to woo!
p

## I lo'e na a laddie but ane.*

1st Verse by JOHN CLUNIE of Borthwick,
the three following Verses by HECTOR MACNEILL.

1. I lo'e na a lad - die but ane, .... He
2. Let ith - ers brag weel o' their gear, .... Their
3. "O Me - nie! the heart that is true .... Has
4. He ends wi' a kiss and a smile— .... Wae's

1. lo'es na a las - sie but me; .... He's will - ing to make me his
2. land and their lord - ly de - gree; .... I care - na for ought but my
3. some - thing mair cost - ly than gear; .... Ilk e'en it has nae - thing to
4. me, can I tak' it a - miss! .... My lad - die's un - prac - tis'd in

1. ain; .... And his ain I am will - ing to be. .... He
2. dear, .... For he's il - ka thing lord - ly to me. .... His
3. sue, .... And ilk morn it has nae - thing to fear. .... Ye
4. guile, .... He's free aye to daut and to kiss! .... Ye

* This air belongs to the 17th century; it is the composition of Matthew Locke, and is therefore English. The old title is "My lodging it is on the cold ground." The Rev. John Clunie was born 1757, and died 1819.

1. coft me a roke-lay o' blue, .... And a pair o' mit-tens o'
2. words are sae su-gar'd, sae sweet! ... And his sense drives ilk fear a-
3. world-lings, gae hoard up your store, .... And trem-ble for fear ought ye
4. las-ses, who lo'e to tor-ment .... Your woo-ers wi' fause scorn and

*mf*

*cres.*

1. green; .... He vow'd that he'd ev-er be true; .... And I
2. wa'! .... I lis-ten, poor fool, and I greet, .... Yet how
3. tyne, .... Guard your trea-sures wi' lock, bar, and door, .... True
4. strife, .... Play your pranks—I hae gi'en my con-sent, .... And

*cres.*

1. plight-ed my troth yes-treen. ..
2. sweet are the tears as they fa'! ..
3. love is the guar-dian o' mine!" ..
4. noo I am Ja-mie's for life! ...

*f*

# I met ayont the cairnie.*

Air: "Jenny Nettles."

VOICE.

Poco allegro.

PIANO.

1. I met a-yont the cair-nie
2. I met a-yont the cair-nie
3. I met a-yont the cair-nie

1. Jen-ny Net-tles, trig an' braw, A-mang the shaws o' Bar-nie, Skip-ping light-ly bare-foot. The
2. Jen-ny Net-tles, trig an' braw, A-mang the shaws o' Bar-nie, Skip-ping light-ly bare-foot. My
3. Jen-ny Net-tles, trig an' braw, A-mang the shaws o' Bar-nie, Skip-ping light-ly bare-foot. My

1. spread-ing ro-ses, wet wi' dew, Are no sae sweet as Jen-ny's mou', Her
2. had-din' stands on yon-der glen, I hae a but, I hae a ben; Gin
3. bon-nie las-sie' trig an' neat, Nay fair-er trips on Lon-don street, Her

1. dim-pled cheek, and e'en sae blue, A-mang the hea-ther bare-foot. I
2. ye'll be la-dy o' my ain, Ye'll gang nae lang-er bare-foot. A
3. glanc-ing e'en sub-dues my heart A-mang the hea-ther bare-foot. The

* The author of these verses is unknown. An older and coarser version is found in Ramsay's *Tea-Table Miscellany*. A tune occurs in the Skene Ms., entitled, "I love my love for love again," which is considered to be an early version of the air "Jenny Nettles." For an interesting account of the strange being known as Jenny Nettles, see Mr. R. Chambers' note to the song in *Songs of Scotland prior to Burns*. The tune is inserted in Bremner's *Scots Reels*, 1757.

1. took her hand, I press'd it,— I ask'd if she could fan - cy me; My
2. silk - en gown then ye shall hae, A clead - in' new frae tap to tae, A
3. sprend - ing ro - ses, wet wi' dew, Are no sae sweet as Jen - ny's mou', Her

1. heart ye hae dis - tress'd it, A - com - ing frae the mar - ket.
2. pair o' shoon an' stock - in's tae, To keep you frae gaun bare - foot.
3. dim - pled cheeks and e'en sae blue, A - mang the hea - ther bare - foot.

I met a - yont the cair - nie Jen - ny Net - tles, trig an' braw, A - mang the shaws o' Bar - nie,

Skip - ping light - ly bare - foot.

# I met four chaps yon birks amang.

### JENNY'S DAWBEE.*

Verses by Sir Alex. Boswell.

1. I
2. The
3. A
4. A
5. Drest
6. She
7. Then

1. met  four chaps yon birks a - mang  Wi'  hing - ing  lugs  an' fa - ces lang; I
2. first,  a  cap - tain  to  his trade,  Wi'  skull  ill  lin'd,  but back weel clead, March'd
3. law - yer neist wi' blath - rin' gab,  Wha  speech - es  wove  like on - y  wab,  In
4. Nor - land laird niest trot - ted  up  Wi'  baw - sand naig,  and sil - er  whip,  Cried
5. up  just like  a  knave o' clubs,  A  Thing cam' niest (but life has rubs); Foul
6. bade  the laird gae kame his wig,  The  sod - ger  no  to strut sae  big,  The
7. John - nie cam',  a  lad  o' sense,  Al - though he  had  na mon - y  pence,  And

* A fragment of the old song is given in Herd's *Scots' Songs*, 1776, vol. ii., p. 204. Boswell's verses were published anonymously in 1803. He shortly afterwards presented them to George Thomson for his collection of Scottish melodies. Sir Alexander Boswell was a son of the biographer of Dr. Johnson. He was born in 1775, and died in 1822. The air is derived from an old Scottish dance tune.

1. spier'd at nee-bour Bal - dy Strang, Wha's they I see? Quo'
2. round the barn and by the shed And pap-pit on his knee. Quo'
3. ilk ane's corn aye took a dab, And a' for a fee. Ac -
4. "There's my beast, lad, haud the grup Or tie't to a tree. What's
5. were the roads, and fu' o' dubs, And jaup-it a' was he. He
6. law - yer no to be a prig; The fool, he cried, "Te - hee! I
7. took young Jen - ny to the spence, Wi' her to crack a wee. Now

Ped. ✻

1. he, "Ilk cream-fac'd, paw - ky chiel, Thoch he was cun - ning as the de'il, An'
2. he, "My god - dess, nymph, and queen, Your beau - ty's daz - zled baith my e'en!" But
3. counts he owed through-out the toun, And trades-men's tongues nae mair could dr[o]un; But
4. gowd to me? I've walth o' lan'! Be - stow on ane o' worth your han'!" He
5. danc'd up squint - in' thro' a glass, And grinn'd "I' faith, a bon - nie lass!" He
6. kenn'd that I could ne - ver fail!" But she preen'd the dish - clout to his tail, And
7. John - nie was a cle - ver chiel, And here his suit he press'd so weel, That

1. here they cam' a - wa' to steal Jen - ny's baw - bee."
2. de'il a beau - ty he had seen But Jen - ny's baw - bee.
3. now he thocht to clout his gown Wi' Jen - ny's baw - bee.
4. thocht to pay what he was awn Wi' Jen - ny's baw - bee.
5. thocht to win, wi front o' brass, Jen - ny's baw - bee.
6. soused him wi' the wa - ter pail, And kept her baw - bee.
7. Jen - ny's heart grew saft as jeel; She birl'd her baw - bee.

sf    p

G 2

# I mourn for the Highlands.*

(FUADACH NAN GÀIDHEAL.)

Gaelic words and translation by
HENRY WHYTE (Fionn).

Air : "Lord Lovat's Lament."

*Andante, con espressione.*

1. I mourn for the Highlands, now drear and for-sa-ken, The lands of my fa-thers, the gal-lant and brave, To make
2. O where are the par-ents and bairns yonder rov-ing? The scene of their gladness is far o'er the main; No

1. room for the sportsman their lands were all ta - ken, And they had to seek out new homes o'er the wave. O
2. blithe-hearted milkmaid now cheers us at gloaming, The herd-boy no long-er is seen on the plain. The

1. shame on the ty-rants who brought de - so - la - tion, Who ban-ish'd the brave and put sheep in their place, Where
2. lark still is soar - ing, and sings in her glo - ry, With no one to list - en her sweet morning lay; The

1. once smil'd the gar - dens, rank weeds have their sta - tion, And deer are pre-ferred to a leal-hearted race.
2. clans-men are gone,—but their deeds live in sto - ry,—Like chaff in the wind, they were borne far a-way.

* From the *Celtic Lyre*, by kind permission. Mr. Henry Whyte wrote these verses to suit a pipe-tune called "Lord Lovat's Lament," which has since become very popular as a vocal air.

# I'm wearin' awa', John.

## THE LAND O' THE LEAL.*

Verses by Lady NAIRNE.

*Adagio, con espressione.*

1. I'm wear-in' a-
2. Ye aye were leal and
3. Then dry that tear-fu'

1. wa', John, Like snaw-wreaths in thaw, John, I'm wear-in' a-wa' To the
2. true, John, Ye're task is end-ed noo, John, And I'll wel-come you To the
3. eye, John, My soul laugs to be free, John, And an-gels wait on me— To the

1. Land o' the Leal. There's nae sor-row there, John, There's nei-ther cauld nor
2. Land o' the Leal. The bon-nie bairn's there, John, She was baith good and
3. Land o' the Leal. Now fare ye weel, my ain John, This warld's care is

1. care, John, The day is aye fair In the Land o' the Leal.
2. fair, John, And we grudg'd her sair To the Land o' the Leal.
3. vain, John, We'll meet and aye be fein In the Land o' the Leal.

* This beautiful lyric was written by Lady Nairne as a token of sympathy to a friend whose child died. It was long considered to be the composition of Robert Burns. The melody is another version of "Hey, tuttie tattie," see p. 195.

# I'm ower young to marry yet.*

**VOICE.**

**PIANO.**

*Con spirito.*

*mf*

*mf*

1. I'm ower young, I'm ower young, I'm
2. I'm ower young, I'm ower young, I'm
3. I'm ower young, I'm ower young, I'm

1. ower young to mar - ry yet, I'm ower young, 'twad be a sin To
2. ower young to mar - ry yet, I'm ower young, 'twad be a sin To
3. ower young to mar - ry yet, I'm ower young, 'twad be a sin To

1. tak' me frae my mam - mie yet. I am my mam-mie's ae bairn, Nor
2. tak' me frae my mam - mie yet. For I hae had my ain way, Nane
3. tak' me frae my mam - mie yet. Fu' loud and shrill the frost - y wind Blaws

* The chorus of this song is old; the rest was written by Burns for Johnson's *Scots' Musical Museum*. Burns' verses have, however, gradually undergone a considerable change to suit modern taste. The original melody to which the song was set, was the old tune, "Loch Erroch Side," now better known as "The Lass o' Gowrie"; but since the beginning of the present century it has been entirely displaced by the modern sprightly strathspey tune given above.

1. of my hame am wea - ry yet; And I wad hae ye learn, lad, That
2. dares to con - tra - dict me yet; Sae soon to say I wad o - bey, In
3. through the leaf - less tim - mer, sir, But if you come this gate a - gain, I'll

*cres.*

1. ye for me maun tar - ry yet. For I'm ower young, I'm ower young, I'm
2. truth I daur - na ven - ture yet. For I'm ower young, I'm ower young, I'm
3. auld - er be gin sim - mer, sir. For I'm ower young, I'm ower young, I'm

*f*

1. ower young to mar - ry yet, I'm ower young, 'twad be a shame To
2. ower young to mar - ry yet, I'm ower young, 'twad be a shame To
3. ower young to mar - ry yet, I'm ower young, 'twad be a shame To

1. tak' me frae my mam - mie yet.
2. tak' me frae my mam - mie yet.
3. tak' me frae my mam - mie yet.

*mf*

# I've seen the smiling.

## THE FLOWERS O' THE FOREST.*

Verses by Miss RUTHERFORD (Mrs. COCKBURN).

*Adagio, con molto espressione.*

VOICE.

PIANO.

*p*

*poco rit.*

con Ped.

*p*

*p*

sempre con Ped.

1. I've seen the smil - ing of for - tune be - guil - ing, I've
2. I've seen the morn - ing wi' gold the hills a - dorn - ing, The

*poco rit.*

1. felt .. all its fa - vours, and found its de - cay. Sweet was its bless - ing,
2. dread tem - pest roar - ing be - fore part - ing day. I've seen Tweed's sil - ver streams

*p*

*poco rit.*

*p*

*poco cres.*

1. Kind ... its car - ess - ing, But now 'tis .... fled, .... 'tis
2. Glitt'ring in the sun - ny beams, Grow drum - lie and dark as they

*poco cres.*

* A version of this melody appears in the Skene MS., circa 1615–'620, as "the Flowers of the Forreste." Miss Rutherford, the authoress of the verses, was born in 1712. She married Mr. Patrick Cockburn of Ormiston in 1731, and died at Edinburgh in her 85th year. By *The Forest* in this song is meant the whole of Selkirkshire and a part of Peeblesshire. In olden times this district of Scotland was called *The Forest*, and was the favourite hunting ground of the Scottish kings and nobles. Miss Rutherford's poem was first published in *The Lark*, Edinburgh, 1765, p. 37.

1. fled far a - way. I've .. seen the for - est a -
2. roll'd on their way. O . . . fic - kle For - tune! ..

1. dorn - ed the fore - most, Wi' flow - ers o' the fair - est, most
2. why this cru - el sport - ing? O why .. thus per - plex .. us, poor

1. plea - sant and gay; Sae bon - nie was their bloom - ing, Their
2. sons . . . of a day? Thy frowns can - not fear me, Thy

1. scent the air per - fum - ing But now they are wi - ther'd, and a' wede a-way!
2. smiles can - not cheer me, For the Flowers of the For - est are a' wede a-way!

# I winna marry ony man.

### HE'S AYE A KISSING ME.*

1. I win - na mar - ry on - y man but San - dy owre the lea: I
2. I win - na hae the min - is - ter, for a' his god - ly looks, Nor
3. I win - na hae the sod - ger lad, for he gangs to the war; I

1. win - na mar - ry on - y man but San - dy owre the lea; I
2. yet will I the law - yer hae, for a' his wi - ly crooks; I
3. win - na hae the sai - lor lad, be - cause he smells o' tar; I

1. win - na hae the Do - min - ie, for guid he can - na be, But
2. win - na hae the plough - man lad, nor yet will I the mil - ler, But
3. win - na hae nor lord, nor laird, for a' their muc - kle gear, But

* In Gow's *Second Collection of Reel's*, 1788, a tune occurs, entitled "Sandy o'er the lee, or Mr. Baird's favourite Reel," and again in his *Complete Repository*, pt. ii., another, entitled "He's aye kissing me." But both these airs are entirely different from the one above, which is taken, with the verses, from the *Scots' Musical Museum*, vol. ii. (1790), No. 274. In his note to the song, Stenhouse writes, "'I winna marry ony man' is an Anglo-Scottish production. In 1776, Mr. James Hook adapted the words to a new air composed by himself, which was published in 1777, in a collection of songs, sung at Vauxhall by Mr. Vernon," etc.—*Museum Illustrations*, p. 257. A good version of the tune occurs in Aird's *Selection of Scotch, etc., Airs*, vol. ii., 1782, as "Sandy o'er the Lee."

1. I will hae my San - dy lad, my San - dy owre the lea.
2. I will hae my San - dy lad, with - oot a pen - ny sil - ler.  } For he's
3. I will hae my San - dy lad, my San - dy ev - er dear.

aye . . . . a - kiss - ing, kiss - ing, aye a - kiss - ing me;  For he's

aye . . . . a - kiss - ing, kiss - ing, aye a - kiss - ing me.

Last time.

# I wish I war where Eelin lies!*

*Andante, con espressione.*

Air: "Fair Helen of Kirkconnel."

PIANO.

*p*

*poco rit.*

con Ped.

*p*

*sempre Ped.*

1. I wish I war where Ee - lin lies, For
2. Curse on the hand that shot the shot, Like
3. O think na ye my heart was sair To
4. O Ee - lin fair, with - out com - pare, I'll

*poco a poco cres.*

1. nicht and day . . . On me scho cries, O! that I war where
2. wise the gun . . . That ga'e the crack, Fair Ee - lin in my
3. see her lie . . . And speak na mair! There scho did swoon, wi'
4. mak' a gar - land o' thy hair, And wear the same for

*poco a poco cres.*

*poco rit.*  *molto rit.*

1. Ee - lin lies, On fair Kirk - con - nel lee!
2. arms scho lap, And diet for love o' me.
3. mic - kle care, On fair Kirk - con - nel lee.
4. ev - er - mair, Un - til the day I dee.

*poco rit.*  *molto rit.*

* We give Charles Kirkpatrick Sharpe's version of the melody. He considered it to be the genuine old Annandale tune. The tragedy of "Fair Helen" is too well known to repeat here; an interesting account of it is given in the *Museum Additional Illustrations,* p. 208*.

# I wish I were now in that Isle of the Sea.

### (Eilean an Fhraoich.)

Translated from the Gaelic of M. MacLeod
by "Fionn" (Henry Whyte).

**Allegretto.**

VOICE.

1. I wish I were now in that Isle of the sea, The
2. This dear-est of Isles is so fer-tile and fair, That
3. At dawn-ing of day when there's mist on the hill, The
4. The notes of the cuc-koo are welcomed in May, And the
5. There ne'er was a pic-ture more love-ly to see, Than the

PIANO.

*p*  *mf*

1. Isle of the Hea-ther, and hap-py I'd be; With deer in its moun-tains, and
2. no o-ther is-land may with it com-pare; Here Gae-lic was spo-ken in
3. milk-maids go skip-ping by foun-tain and rill, When milk-ing their cat-tle they
4. black-bird sings blithe 'mong the sil-ve-ry spray; The lark and the ma-vis pour
5. sun as he sinks in the blue west-ern sea, When home-ward the cat-tle are

1. fish in its rills, Where he-roes have liv'd 'mong its heath-cov-er'd hills.
2. a-ges gone by, And here it will live till the o-cean runs dry.
3. raise a sweet song, And soft-ly the e-choes the cho-rus pro-long.
4. forth their sweet lay, While the lambs in the mea-dows are spright-ly at play.
5. wend-ing their way, 'And all things are still at the close of the day.

*f*  *mf*

* From the *Celtic Lyre*, by kind permission of the Editor, Mr. Henry Whyte, Glasgow. This is a song in praise of the Island of Lewis. The air is of native growth, and the Gaelic verses were written by Mr. M. MacLeod, a native bard. The song has attained considerable popularity in Celtic circles.

# In a Simmer gloamin'.*

Verses by WILLIAM MOTHERWELL.

Gaelic Air: "Gu ma slan a chi mi."

*Andante teneramente.*

1. In a Sim-mer
2. We heard, and we
3. Farewell, and for

1. gloam - in', In yon dow-ie dell, 'Twas there we twa first met By...
2. saw nought A - bove, or a - round, We felt that our love liv'd And
3. ev - er! My first love, and last, May thy joys be to come— Mine

1. Wea - rie's cauld well. We sat on the brume bank And luik-it in the
2. loath'd i - dle sound. I gaz'd on thy sweet face Till tears fill'd my
3. live in the past! In sor - row and in sad - ness, This hour fa's on

1. burn, But side - lang we look'd on Ilk... ith - er in turn.
2. e'e, And they drapp't on your wee loof A warld's wealth to me.
3. me; But light as thy love, May it fleet o - ver thee!

* Alexander Campbell, in his *Albyn's Anthology,* vol. i., 1816, has included this air with new verses by himself beginning, "Blythesome may I see thee." We have, however, given the preference to Motherwell's beautiful poem. A Gaelic song, entitled "Mo chailin dileas donn," by Hector MacKenzie, Ullapool, and set to the same tune, has in latter years become very popular in the Highlands. Translations of MacKenzie's verses are given in *The Celtic Lyre,* and in *Songs and Hymns of the Scottish Highlands.*

# Is there, for honest poverty.

## FOR A' THAT, AN' A' THAT.*

*Spirituoso.*      *mf*      Verses by Burns.

VOICE.

1. Is there, for hon-est pov-er-ty, That
2. What though on hame-ly fare we dine, Wear
3. Ye see yon bir-kie, ca'd a lord, Wha
4. A king can mak' a belt-ed knight, A
5. Then let us pray that come it may, As

PIANO.

*mf*      *mf*

1. hangs his head, an' a' that? The cow-ard slave, we pass him by, We
2. hod-den-grey, an' a' that? Gi'e fools their silks, and knaves their wine, A
3. struts, an' stares, an' a' that; Tho' hun-dreds wor-ship at his word, He's
4. mar-quis, duke, an' a' that; An hon-est man's a-bune his might—Gude
5. come it will for a' that, That sense an' worth, o'er a' the earth, May

1. dare be puir for a' that! For a' that, an' a' that, Our toils obscure, an' a' that; The
2. man's a man for a' that; For a' that, an' a' that, Their tin-sel show, an' a' that; The
3. but a cuif for a' that! For a' that, an' a' that, His rib-bon, star, an' a' that; The
4. faith he maun-na fa' that! For a' that, an' a' that, Their dig-ni-ties, an' a' that; The
5. bear the gree, an' a' that! For a' that, an' a' that, It's com-in' yet, for a' that, That

*Last time.*

1. rank is but the gui-nea-stamp, The man's the gowd for a' that.
2. hon-est man, tho' e'er sae puir, Is king o' men for a' that.
3. man of in-de-pen-dent mind, He looks an' laughs at a' that.
4. pith o' sense, the pride o' worth Are high-er ranks than a' that.
5. man to man, the warld o'er, Shall bro-thers be for a' that.

*f*

* The authorship of this melody is unknown. Burns wrote the verses in 1794. "They were handed about in manuscript a considerable time before they appeared in print. They unfortunately came out at a period when political disputes ran very high, and his enemies did not fail to interpret every sentence of them to his prejudice" (Stenhouse). Burns also wrote his song, beginning "Tho' women's minds, like winter winds," to the same air. It appears in vol. iii. of the *Scots' Musical Museum.* In Gow's *Collection of Reels,* pt. i., 1784, the tune occurs as "Sir John Whiteford's Strathspey, by Nath. Gow"; and again, in the *Repository,* pt. iii., as "There's nae luck about the house; or, for a' that and a' that." In pt. ii. of the same Collection the Editor gives a somewhat different version of the melody as "Lady Mackintosh's Reel." In Aird's *Selection of Scotch, etc., Airs,* vol. i., issued in 1782, and therefore twelve years prior to Burns' composition, there is a tune which has but little in common with the one above, entitled "Far a' that and a' that."

# In winter, when the rain rain'd cauld.

## TAK' YOUR AULD CLOAK ABOUT YE.*

Moderato.

VOICE.

PIANO.

*mf*

*p*

1. In win - ter, when the rain rain'd cauld, An'
2. My Crum - mie is a use - fu' coo, An'
3. My cloak was ance a gude grey cloak, When
4. In days when gude King Ro - bert rang, His
5. Now il - ka land has its ain lauch, Ilk
6. Guid - man, I wat, it's thret - ty year Sin'
7. Now, Bell, my wife, she lo'es na strife, But

*p*

1. frost an' snaw on il - ka hill, An' Bo - reas, wi' his blasts sae cauld, Was
2. she is come of a gude kine; Aft has she wet the bairns mou', And
3. it was fit - ting for my wear; But now its scant - ly worth a groat, For
4. trews they cost but half - a - crown; He said they were a groat owre dear, And
5. kind o' corn has its ain hool; I think the warld has a' gane wrang, When
6. we did ane an - ith - er ken; An' we hae had a - tween us twa Of
7. she wad guide me if she can; And to main - tain an ea - sy life I

* This humorous ballad with its air may be assigned to the 16th century. It appears in Ramsay's *Tea-Table Miscellany*, 1724. A slightly altered stanza from the song is sung by Iago in *Othello*. It occurs in act ii., sc. 3, " King Stephen was a worthy peer," etc. The accidentals found in some versions of the air in bars 8 and 11 are spurious and not in accordance with the age of the melody

1. threat-'nin' a' our kye to kill. Then Bell, my wife, who lo'es na strife, She
2. I am laith that she should tyne. Get up, guidman, it is fu' time, The
3. I have worn't this thret-ty year. Let's spend the gear that we hae won, We
4. ca'd the tai-lor thief and loon. He was the King that wore the croun, And
5. il-ka wife her man wad rule. Do ye na see Rob, Jock, and Hab, As
6. lads and bon-nie las-ses ten. Now they are wo-men grown au' men, I
7. aft maun yield, tho' I'm gude-man. Nocht's to be gain'd at wo-man's haud, Un-

1. said to me richt hast-i-lie, "Get up, guid-man, save Crummie's life, And
2. sun shines i' the lift sae hie; Sloth ne-ver made a gra-cious end, Gae,
3. lit-tle ken the day we dee; Then I'll be proud sin' I hae sworn To
4. thou's the man o' laigh de-gree; It's pride puts a' the coun-try doun, So
5. they are gird-ed gal-lant-lie; While I sit hurk-liu' i' the asse?—I'll
6. wish and pray weel may they be; If you would prove a gude hus-band, E'en
7. less ye gi'e her a' the plea; Then I'll leave aff where I be-gan And

1. tak' your auld cloak a - bout ye."
2. tak' your auld cloak a - bout ye.
3. hae a new cloak a - bout me.
4. tak' thy auld cloak a - bout ye.
5. hae a new cloak a - bout me.
6. tak' your auld cloak a - bout ye.
7. tak' my auld cloak a - bout me.

# It fell about the Mart'mas time.

## GET UP AND BAR THE DOOR*

**Allegretto vivo.**

VOICE.

1. It fell a-bout the Mart'-mas time, And a
2. "My hand is in my hus - sy'f-skap, Gude-
3. Then by there came twa gen - tle-men, At
4. Then said the one un - to his friend, "Here,
5. O, up then start-ed our guid-man, And an

PIANO.

1. gay time it was then, O! When our guid-wife had puddin's to make, And boil them in the
2. man, as ye may see, O! Should't nae be barr'd this hun-dred year, It's no be barr'd for
3. twelve o' clock at night, O! They could-na see ne'er house nor ha', Nor coal nor can-dle
4. man, tak' ye my knife, O! Do ye tak' aff the auld man's beard, And I will kiss the
5. an-gry man was he, O! "Ye'd kiss my wife be - fore my e'en, And scald me wi' pud-din'

1. pan, O! The wind blew cauld, frae east to west, And blew in-to the floor, O! Quoth
2. me, O!" They made a pac-tion 'tween them twa', They made it firm and sure, O! Wha
3. light, O! So first they eat the pud-din's white, And then they eat the black, O! Though
4. wife, O?" "But there's nae wa-ter in the house, And what shall we do then, O?" "What
5. bree, O?" Then up an' start-ed our guid-wife, Gied three skips on the floor, O! "Guid-

1. our guid-man to our guid-wife, "Get up an' bar the door, O!"
2. ev - er spak' the fore-most word, Should rise an' bar the door, O!
3. muc-kle thought the guid-wife then, Yet ne'er a word she spak', O!
4. ails ye at the pud-din' bree, Thats boil - in' in the pan, O!
5. man, ye've spoke the fore-most word, Get up and bar the door, O!"

* From Herd's Collection, vol. ii., p. 159, printed in 1776, under the title of "The Barring of the Door," the tune is included in Aird's *Selection*, vol. ii., 1782.

# It fell on a day.

### THE BONNIE HOUSE O' AIRLIE.*

Moderato.

Old Ballad.

PIANO.

1. It fell on a day, a bon-nie simmer day, When the corn grew green and yel - low, That
2. The la - dy look'd o'er her win-dow sae hie, An' oh! but she look't wear' - ly, And
3. He's ta'en her by the left shoul - der (An' oh! but she grat sair - ly), And

1. there fell out a great dis - pute Be - tween Ar - gyle and Air - lie. The
2. there she spied the great Ar - gyle Come to plun-der the bonnie house o' Air - lie. "Come
3. led her down to yon green bank, Till he plunder'd the bonnie house o' Air - lie. "O

1. Duke o' Montrose has writ-ten to Ar-gyle, To come in the morn - in' ear - ly, An'
2. down, come down, my la - dy," he says, "Come down and kiss me fair - ly, Or
3. gin my ain lord so brave had been at hame, As this nicht he's wi' Char - lie, There

1. lead in his men, by the back o' Dunkeld, To plun-der the bonnie house o' Air - lie.
2. o'er the morn - in' clear day-light, I'll no leave a standin' stane in Air - lie."
3. durst na a Campbell in a' the west Hae plunder'd the bonnie house o' Air - lie."

rit. sf p

* In the year 1640, the Earl of Airlie having joined the Duke of Montrose in the Royal cause, Argyle in his absence attacked the unpro-
tected estates of Airlie. The "Bonnie House o' Airly" was completely plundered and burnt to the ground.

# It was upon a Lammas night.*

Verses by R. BURNS.

Air: "Corn Riggs."

*Allegretto.*

PIANO.

*p*

*poco rit.*

*p*

1. It was up-on a Lam - mas night, When corn rigs are
2. The sky was blue, the wind was still, The moon was shin - ing
3. I lock'd her in my fond em - brace; Her heart was beat - ing
4. I hae been blythe wi' com - rades dear, I hae been mer - ry

*p*

*sf*

1. bon - nie, O! Be - neath the moon's un - cloud - ed light I held a - wa to
2. clear - ly, O! I set her down, wi' right good will, A - mang the rigs o'
3. rare - ly, O! My bless - ings on that hap - py place A - mang the rigs o'
4. drink - in', O! I hae been joy - fu' gath' - rin' gear; I hae been hap - py

1. An - nie, O! The time flew by wi' tent - less heed, Till 'tween the late and
2. bar - ley, O! I ken't her heart was a' my ain; I loved her most sin -
3. bar - ley, O! But by the moon and stars so bright, That shone that hour so
4. think - in', O! But a' the plea - sures e'er I saw, Though three times dou - bled

* These verses were written by Burns in his younger years. The tune "Corn Riggs" is very old. D'Urfey has preserved a good version of it in the first volume of his *Pills to Purge Melancholy*, 1719, p. 317, to verses beginning, "Sawney was tall and of noble race." It also appears in Gay's Opera *Polly*, 1729, in Craig's Collection, 1730, and in *Universal Harmony; or, the Gentleman and Lady's Social Companion*, London, 1743. Allan Ramsay wrote the closing song in his *Gentle Shepherd*, "My Patie was a lover gay," to this tune. There is, however, a much older song connected with the air, dating probably from the earlier part of the 17th century, the chorus of which begins, "O corn rigs, and rye rigs, And corn rigs are bonnie."

1. ear - ly, O! Wi' sma' per - sua - sion she a - greed To see me through the
2. cere - ly, O! I kiss'd her owre and owre a - gain A - mang the rigs o'
3. clear - ly, O! She aye shall bless that hap - py night A - mang the rigs o'
4. fair - ly, O! That hap - py night was worth them a' A - mang the rigs o'

1. bar - ley, O!
2. bar - ley, O!
3. bar - ley, O!
4. bar - ley, O!

Corn rigs, an' bar - ley rigs, Corn . . rigs are

mf

bon - nie, O! I'll ne'er for - get that hap - py night, . . A

mang the rigs wi' An - nie, O!

p

# It's here awa', there awa', how they did rin.

## LOONS, YE MAUN GAE HAME.*

Jacobite Song.

VOICE.

*Vivace.*     mf

1. It's here a - wa', there a - wa',
2. They got to their feet just as
3. Whigs, fare ye a' - weel, ye may
4. Our lang Scot - tish miles they will

PIANO.

mf

*cres.*

1. how they did rin, When they saw the clans march, an' in earn-est be - gin; It's
2. sure as a gun, 'Twas when-e'er they heard Char - lie to Scot-land was come; "Haste,
3. scam - per a - wa', For it's haith, here nae lang - er ye'll whip an' ye'll ca'; Nor
4. tire ye right sair, An' it's ai - blins in moss - es, an' bogs ye will lair; But

*cres.*

1. here a - wa', there a - wa', how they did flee, When they heard that Prince Char-lie was
2. haste ye a - wa'," cried the auld wives wi' glee; "And its joy, for now Char - lie has
3. mair look on Scot - land wi' light - li - fu' e'e, For our Char - lie at last has come
4. rest an' be thank - ful gin hame ye may see, For I rede ye that Char - lie has

1. come owre the sea. It's loons ye maun gae hame!...
2. come owre the sea." An' loons ye maun gae hame!...
3. owre the sea. An' loons ye maun gae hame!...
4. come owre the sea. An' loons ye maun gae hame!...

* Smith has included this song in his *Scottish Minstrel*, vol. ii., p. 85. The author of the verses is unknown.

# John Anderson, my jo.*

Verses by R. Burns.

*Andante con molto espressione.*

PIANO.

1. John An-der-son, my jo, John, When we were first a-queut, Your locks were like the
2. John An-der-son, my jo, John, We clamb the hill the-gi-ther, . . And mony a can-ty

1. ra — ven, Your bon-nie brow was brent; But now your brow is
2. day, John, We've had wi' ane au-ither, . . . Now we maun tot-ter

1. beld, John, Your locks are like the snaw; But bless-ings on your fros-ty pow, John
2. down, John, But hand in hand we'll go; And we'll sleep the-gith-er at the foot, John

1. An-der-son, my jo.
2. An-der-son, my jo.

* A version of this air occurs in the Skene MS., *circa* 1615-1620, but it is very probable that it belongs to a much older date. Burns wrote the verses in 1789 for Johnstone's *Scots' Musical Museum*, where it appears in the third volume, song No. 260. In Percy's *Reliques of Ancient English Poetry*, vol. i., some stanzas of the old song are given. Tradition says that John Anderson was town-piper of Kelso.

# John Grumlie.*

*Allegretto.*

PIANO.

1. John Grum - lie swore by the light o' the moon And the green leaves on    the tree, . . . That
2. O,  he  did dress   his chil - dren fair, And he  put   them in  their gear; . .  But
3. The haw - ket crum - mie loot  nae milk,  He kirn'd,   nor but - ter gat, . .  And
4. John Grum - lie's wife  cam' hame  at e'en, And laugh'd  as she'd  been mad; . .  The
5. "The De'il wi' that,"   quo' sur - ly John, "I'll   do   as 'twas  be - fore;" . .  Wi'

1. he  could do  more work in  a day Than his wife could  do  in  three. . .  His
2. he  for - got  to  turn  the malt,  And  so  he  spoiled the  beer. . .  And he
3. a'  gaed wrang, and nought gaed right,  He  danced wi'  rage and  grat. . .  Then
4. house  it was  in  sic-can a plight,  And  John  sae  glum and  sad. . .  Quoth
5. that  his wife took up  a  rung,  And  John  made  off to the  door. . .  "Stop,

1. wife  rose up in the  morn - ing,  Wi'  cares  an' trou-bles e - nou; — .  "John
2. sang  a - loud as he  reel'd  the tweel  That his wife  span yes - ter - day; . .  But
3. up  he ran to the  head o' the knowe,  Wi'  mon - y  a  wave  and shout — . .  She
4. he,  "I gie up my  house - wife-skep,  I'll  be  nae mair  gude - wife." . .  "In
5. stop, gude-wide, I'll  haud  my tongue, I  ken  I'm sair  to blame; . .  But

* These verses seem to have been based on the old ballad entitled, "The Wife of Auchtermuchty," which has come down to us in an uncorrupted state, owing to its preservation in the Bannatyne Manuscript. Regarding this ballad Mr. William Gunnyon says: "In the whole range of our ballad literature, there is nothing more thoroughly humorous than 'The Wife of Auchtermuchty,' which is preserved in the Bannatyne Manuscript, and is supposed to be the production of a Sir John Moffat, a 'Pope's Knight,' and was therefore probably composed about 1520. It has suffered no alteration or corruption."—*Illustrations of Scottish History*, 1877.

1. Grum - lie bide at hame, John, and I'll go haud the plow." Sing - ing
2. he for - got to mind the hens, And the hens a' laid a - way. Sing - ing
3. heard him as she heard him not, And steer'd the stots a - bout. Sing - ing
4. deed," quo' she, "I'm weel con - tent, Ye may keep it the rest o' your life." Sing - ing
5. hence - forth I maun mind the plow, And ye maun bide at hame." Sing - ing

1. fal de lal lal de ral lal, Fal lal lal lal lal la! . . . . "John
2. fal de lal lal de ral lal, Fal lal lal lal lal la! . . . . But
3. fal de lal lal de ral lal, Fal lal lal lal lal la! . . . . She
4. fal de lal lal de ral lal, Fal lal lal lal lal la! . . . . "In -
5. fal de lal lal de ral lal, Fal lal lal lal lal la! . . . . "But

1. Grum - lie bide at hame, John, And I'll go haud the plow." . .
2. he for - got to mind the hens, And the hens a' laid a - way. . . .
3. heard him as she heard him not, And steer'd the stots a - bout. . . . .
4. deed," quo' she, "I'm weel con - tent, Ye may keep it the rest o' your life." . . .
5. hence - forth I maun mind the plow, And ye maun bide at hame." . .

# Last May a braw wooer.*

Verses by BURNS.

*Allegretto vivo.*

Air: "The Lothian Lassie."

VOICE.

PIANO.

*mf*

1. Last
3. A
5. But
7. I

*mf*

1. May a braw woo - er cam' doun the lang glen, And sair wi' his love he did deave me; I
3. weel stock-it mail - in', him - sel' o't the laird, And marriage aff-hand, was his prof - fer; I
5. a' the next week, as I fret-ted wi' care, I gaed to the tryst o' Dal - gar - knock, And
7. spier'd for my cou - sin, fu' cou-thie and sweet, Gin she had re - cov - er'd her hear - in', And

*cres.*

1. said there was nae-thing I hat - ed like men,—The deuce gae wi' him to be -
3. ne - ver loot on that I kennt it, or cared, But thocht I micht hae a waur
5. wha but my braw fic - kle woo - er was there!—Wha glow - er'd as he'd seen a
7. how my auld shoon fit - ted her shauch-l'd feet,—Gude sauf us! how he fell a -

*cres.*

1. lieve me, be - lieve me, The deuce gae wi' him to be - lieve me!
3. of - fer, waur of - fer, But thocht I micht hae a waur of - fer.
5. war - lock, a war - lock, Wha glow - er'd as he'd seen a war - lock.
7. swear - in', a - swear - in', Gude sauf us! how he fell a - swear - in'!

* "This humorous song was written by Burns in 1787, for the second volume of the *Museum*; but Johnson, the publisher who was a religious and well-meaning man, appeared fastidious about its insertion, as one or two expressions in it seemed somewhat irreverent. Burns afterwards made several alterations upon the song and sent it to Mr. George Thomson for his collection, who readily admitted it into his second volume, and the song soon became very popular. Johnson, however, did not consider it at all improved by the later alterations of our bard. . . . . He therefore published the song as originally written by Burns for his work."—(*Museum Illustrations*, p. 460.) The song and air appear in the sixth volume of the *Museum*, p. 538. Stenhouse gives the original name of this tune as "The Queen of the Loathians." A copy of the old verses is given after Burns' song in the *Museum*. We have adopted the version of "Last May a braw wooer," sent by Burns to George Thomson.

2. He spak o' the darts o' my
4. But what do ye think? in a
6. Out ower my left shoul - ther I
8. He begg'd, for Gude-sake, I wad

*mf* *mf*

2. bon - nie black e'en, And vow'd for my love he was dee - in'; I
4. fort - nicht or less,— The de'il's in his taste to gang near her! He
6. gied him a blink, Lest nee - bours micht say I was sau - cy; My
8. be his wife, Or else I wad kill him wi' sor - row; Sae,

*cres.*

2. said he micht dee when he lik - ed for Jean,—Now Gude for - gie me for
4. up to the Gateslack to my cou - sin Bess,—Guess ye how, the jaud! I could
6. woo - er he ca - per'd as he'd been in drink, And vow'd that I was his dear
8. e'en to pre-serve the puir bo - dy in life, I think I maun wed him to -

*cres.*

2. lee - in', for lee - in', Now Gude for - gie me for lee - in'!
4. bear her, could bear her, Guess ye how, the jaud! I could bear her!
6. las - sie, dear las - sie, And vow'd that I was his dear las - sie!
8. mor-row, to - mor-row, I think I maun wed him to - mor - row!

*mf*

108

# Let us haste to Kelvin Grove.

## KELVIN GROVE.*

Verses by THOMAS LYLE.

Air: "O the shearin's no for you."

*Poco allegretto.*

VOICE.

PIANO.

*p*     *poco rit.*     *p*

1. Let us haste to Kel - vin Grove, bon - nie
2. Let us wan - der by the mill, bon - nie
3. O Kel - vin banks are fair, bon - nie
4. Then fare - well to Kel - vin Grove, bon - nie

1. las - sie, O! Thro' its maz - es let us rove, bon - nie las - sie, O! Where the
2. las - sie, O! To the cove be - side the rill, bon - nie las - sie, O! Where the
3. las - sie, O! When in sum - mer we are there, bon - nie las - sie, O! There the
4. las - sie, O! And a - dieu to all I love, bon - nie las - sie, O! To the

*cres.*

1. rose in all her pride Paints the hol - low din - gle side, Where the
2. glens re - bound the call Of the roar - ing wa - ters' fall, Thro' the
3. May - pink's crim - son plume Throws a soft but sweet per - fume Round the
4. riv - er wind - ing clear, To the fra - grant scent - ed brier, E'en to

*cres.*

1. mid - night fai - ries glide, bon - nie las - sie, O!
2. moun-tains rock - y hall, bon - nie las - sie, O!
3. yel - low banks of broom, bon - nie las - sie, O!
4. thee, of all most dear, bon - nie las - sie, O!

*Last time.*

*rit.*

* This air appears in R. A. Smith's *Scottish Minstrel*, vol. ii., 1824, under the title of "Kelvin Water." It seems to have been long known as "O the shearin's no for you," which is the first line of the old verses to which the tune was sung. Kelvin Grove is on the river Kelvin, near to where it joins the Clyde at Glasgow.

# Maxwellton braes are bonnie.

### ANNIE LAURIE.*

1. Max-well-ton braes are bon-nie Where ear-ly fa's the dew, .. An' it's there that An-nie Lau-rie Gi'ed me her pro-mise true; Gi'ed me her pro-mise true, Which ne'er for-got will be, And for bon-nie An-nie Lau-rie, I'd lay me doun and dee.

2. Her brow is like the snaw-drift, Her neck is like the swan, .. Her face it is the fair-est That e'er the sun shone on; That e'er the sun shone on, And dark blue is her e'e; And for bon-nie An-nie Lau-rie, I'd lay me doun and dee.

3. Like dew on the gow-an ly-ing Is the fa' o' her fair-y feet; .. And like winds in summer sigh-ing Her voice is low and sweet; Her voice is low and sweet, She's a' the world to me, And for bon-nie An-nie Lau-rie, I'd lay me doun and dee.

* The older version of this song has been attributed to a Mr. Douglas, of Fingland, who seems to have lived about the end of the 17th century. The heroine of the song was Annie, daughter of Sir Robert Laurie, first baronet of Maxwellton—so created in 1685. Allan Cunningham is said to have found the verses in the little *Ballad Book* collected by Charles Kirkpatrick Sharp, of Hoddam; see note upon "Annie Laurie" in Cunningham's *Songs of Scotland*, Edinburgh, 1825, vol. iii. Regarding the verses and charming melody which we give, Lady John Scott has kindly informed us that the tune of "Annie Laurie" is her composition, and that she altered the second verse and entirely composed the third verse of the song. Lady John Scott also states that Allan Cunningham wrote the original verses.

# Mirk an' rainy is the nicht.

## O! ARE YE SLEEPIN', MAGGIE?

Verses by TANNAHILL.

*Andante.*

VOICE.

PIANO.

1. Mirk an' rain - y is the nicht; There's
2. Fear - fu' soughs the bour-tree bank, The
3. 'Boon my breath I daur - na speak For
4. By the door she let him in, He

1. no a star in a' the car - ry; Ligh'-nings gleam a - thwart the lift, The
2. rift - ed wood roars wild and drear - ie; Loud the i - ron yett does clank; And
3. fear I rouse your wauk - rife dad - dy; Cauld's the blast up - on my cheek; Oh,
4. cuist a - side his dreep - in' plaid - ie; "Blaw your warst, ye rain and win', Since,

1. dri-vin' win' has win-ter's fu-ry. O! are ye sleep-in', Mag-gie? O! are ye sleep-in', Mag-gie?
2. cry o' how-lets make me eer-ie. O! are ye sleep-in', Mag-gie? O! are ye sleep-in', Mag-gie?
3. rise, oh, rise, my bon-nie led-dy! O! are ye sleep-in', Mag-gie? O! are ye sleep-in', Mag-gie?
4. Mag-gie, noo I'm in a - side ye. Noo, since ye're wauk-in', Mag-gie, Noo, since ye're wauk-in', Mag-gie,

1. Let me in, for loud the linn Is roar-in' owre the war - lock craig-ie.
2. Let me in, for loud the linn Is roar-in' owre the war - lock craig-ie.
3. Let me in, for loud the linn Is roar-in' owre the war - lock craig-ie.
4. What care I for how-lets' cry, For bour-tree bank, or war - lock craig-ie?"

---

\* The following is Buchan's note to this song in *The Garland of Scotia*, 1841: "This song, by Robert Tannahill, was written to the tune of a very old song of the same name. There are few, who have ever lifted a foot on a barn floor, that have not danced to 'Sleepy Maggie.' It is a favourite all the country over. The present air is modern, and more *vocal* in its nature."

# Mòrag.

Translated from the Gaelic by LACHLAN MACBEAN.

1. †Mòr - ag with the tress - es flow-ing, I will praise thee with de - vo - tion.
2. Far too soon has been thy go-ing, Soon come back a - cross the o - cean.
3. Bring a band of maids for spread-ing And for dress - ing cloth of scar - let.
4. Thou shalt not go to the stead-ing, Leave vile work for loon and var - let.
5. Oh, my Mòr - ag is the sweet-est, With her love - ly locks in clus - ter.
6. Coiled and curled in folds the sweet-est, Gleam - ing bright with gold - en lus - tre.
7. Ma - ny lov - ers has my la - dy, In the main - land and the Is - lands.
8. Ma - ny men with sword and plai - die She could sum - mon from the High-lands.
9. Cer - tes but our maids are clev - er When they get their wea - pons rea - dy.
10. Ma - ny webs they've sort - ed ev - er, Firm - ly han - dled close and stea - dy.
11. Thick an' close and firm in press-ing, Bloo - dy-red and dye un - fad - ing.
12. Come, then, with thy maids for dress-ing, We are rea - dy here for aid - ing.

CHORUS.

ff Then ho - ro, Mòr - ag, ho - ro the love - ly la - dy,

Then ho - ro, Mòr - ag!

Last time.

* By kind permission from Songs and Hymns of the Scottish Highlands. Regarding this song, Mr. Henry Whyte writes us: "These verses were composed by the Jacobite Bard, Alex. MacDougald—commonly called Mac Mhaighstir Alasdair, who was born at the beginning of the 18th century. His father was Episcopal Clergyman at Ardnamurchan. The Bard attended Glasgow University, and was teacher and catechist in Ardnamurchan in 1729. When Prince Charlie landed in 1745, MacDougald joined his standard, and composed soul-stirring songs to animate his fellow-Highlanders. The song 'Mòrag' has always been popular. It is set to the tune of a waulking-song—i.e. an action song, used by those engaged in waulking the home-made cloth, to ensure unanimity of motion. Prince Charlie is represented under the similitude of Mòrag, a young girl with flowing locks of yellow hair. She had gone over the seas, and the Bard invokes her to return with a party of maidens (i.e. soldiers) to dress the red cloth, in other words, to beat the English red-coats." † Pronounced Vorack.

# My heart's in the Highlands.*

Verses by BURNS.
*Andantino.*

Air: "Crodh Chailean."

VOICE.

PIANO.

*mf*     *f*     *mf*

1. My heart's in the
2. Fare-well to the
3. Fare-well to the
4. My heart's in the

1. High-lands, my heart is not here; My heart's in the High-lands, a - chas-ing the
2. High-lands, fare-well to the North! The birth-place of va - lour, the coun-try of
3. moun-tains, high co - ver'd with snow! Fare-well to the straths and green val-leys be-
4. High-lands, my heart is not here; My heart's in the High-lands, a - cha-sing the

1. deer; A - chas-ing the wild deer, and fol-low-ing the roe— My heart's in the
2. worth; Wher - ev - er I wan - der, wher - ev - er I rove, The hills of the
3. low! Fare - well to the for - ests and wild - hang-ing woods! Fare - well to the
4. deer; A - cha - sing the wild deer, and fol-low-ing the roe— My heart's in the

*f*

*poco rit.*

1. High - lands wher - ev - er I go.
2. High - lands for - ev - er I love.
3. tor - rents and loud - pour-ing floods!
4. High - lan is wher - ev - er I go.

*poco rit.*     *f*     *poco rit.*

* This is an ancient Gaelic air. It is included in Captain Fraser's *Airs peculiar to the Scottish Highlands*, 1816, under the title of "Crodh Chailean," and in R. A. Smith's *Scottish Minstrel*, 1822, as "Crochallan." Burns adapted his verses to an old Highland tune entitled, "Failte na moirg," and it is in conjunction with this air that the poem appears in Johnson's *Scots' Musical Museum*, vol. iii., No. 259.

# My heart is sair, I daurna tell.

## MY HEART IS SAIR FOR SOMEBODY.*

Verses by BURNS.

VOICE.

*Moderato.*

PIANO.

1. My heart is sair, I daur - na tell, My
2. Ye Pow'rs that smile on vir-tuous love, O,

1. heart is sair for some - bo - dy! I could wake a win-ter-night For the sake of some - bo - dy.
2. sweet-ly smile on some - bo - dy! And frae dan - ger keep him free, And send me safe my some - bo - dy.

*cres.* *rit.*

1. Och - hone, for some - bo - dy! Och - hey, for some - bo - dy! I could range the world a - round,
2. Och - bone, for some - bo - dy! Och - hey, for some - bo - dy! I would do—what would I not?—

1. For the sake o' some - bo - dy!
2. For the sake o' some - bo - dy!

* Ramsay has a song in the *Tea-table Miscellany*, the first verse of which is :—

For the sake of somebody,     I cou'd wake a winter-night
For the sake of somebody,     For the sake of somebody.

Burns wrote his song, "My heart is sair," to an old tune published by Oswald in the *Caledonian Pocket Companion*, and to this work, in a note annexed to his manuscript verses, the poet refers Johnson for the music. Johnson's air, however, has been entirely superseded by the one which we adopt. Regarding it Mr. Peter Buchan writes: "The air is well known and beautiful. We have found it in a Collection which we have every reason to believe is very old."—*Garland of Scotia*, 1841. It occurs in Gow's *Fifth Collection of Reels and Strathspeys*, 1809, and is there entitled "Some Body, Old."

I

# My love built me a bonnie bouir.

*Molto andante.*

PIANO.

*poco rit.*

1. My love built me a bon - nie bouir, And clad it a' wi'
2. There cam' a man at mid - day hour, He heard my song and
3. He slew my knicht, to me sae dear, And burnt my bouir, and
4. The man lives not I'll love a - gain, Since that my come - ly

1. li - ly flow'r; A braw - er bouir ye ne'er did see, Than
2. saw my bouir; And he brocht arm - ed men that nicht, And
3. drave my gear; My ser - vants a' for life did flee, And
4. knicht is slain; Wi' ae lock of his yel - low hair I'll

*rit.*

1. my true lov - er built for me.
2. brake my bouir, and slew my knicht.
3. left me in ex - trem - i - tie.
4. bind my heart for ev - er - mair.

*rit.* *rit.*

* Sir Walter Scott published this song as a "fragment obtained from recitation in the Forest of Ettrick." He considered it as probably relating to the death of Cockburn, of Henderland, a noted robber, who was executed in 1529 by command of James V.

# My Luve's in Germanie.

Verses by HECTOR MACNEILL.

Poco lento.

VOICE.

PIANO.

*p*

*rit.*

*p*

con Ped.

con sempre Ped.

1. My Luve's in Ger-man-ie, Send him
2. He's brave as brave can be, Send him
3. Our foes are ten to three, Send him
4. He'll ne'er come owre the sea, Wil-lie's

1. hame, send him hame; My Luve's in Ger-man-ie, Send him hame. My
2. hame, send him hame; He's brave as brave can be, Send him hame. He's
3. hame, send him hame; Our foes are ten to three, Send him hame. Our
4. slain, Wil-lie's slain; He'll ne'er come owre the sea, Wil-lie's gane! He'll

1. Luve's in Ger-man-ie, Fight - ing for roy-al-tie; He may ne'er his Jean-ie see; Send him
2. brave as brave can be, He wad ra-ther fa' than flee; But his life is dear to me; Send him
3. foes are ten to three, He maun ci-ther fa' or flee, In the cause o' loy-al-tie; Send him
4. ne'er come owre the sea To his love and ain coun-trie; This world's nae mair for me, Wil-lie's

cres.

1. hame, send him hame; He may ne'er his Jean-ie see, Send him hame.
2. hame, send him hame; Oh, his life is dear to me, Send him hame.
3. hame, send him hame; In the cause o' loy-al-tie, Send him hame.
4. gane, Wil-lie's gane; This warld's nae mair for me, Wil-lie's gane!

---

\* In Hogg's *Jacobite Relics*, Ser. II., p. 22, this melody is given with verses beginning, "Ken ye how to fight a Whig, Aikendrum, Aikendrum?" Its first appearance in print seems to be in Johnson's *Museum*, vol. iv. (1792), No. 371, where it is adapted to Jacobitical verses by Burns beginning, "Ye Jacobites by name." A ballad on the celebrated pirate Paul Jones, who flourished about the middle of last century, was sung to the same tune. Both Stenhouse and G. F. Graham consider it to be an old Lowland melody.

## My Love, she's but a lassie yet.*

Verses by James Hogg.

*Con spirito.*

Voice.

Piano.

1. My Love she's but a las - sie yet, A light-some love - ly las - sie yet; It
2. She's nei - ther proud nor sau - cy yet, She's nei - ther plump nor gau - cy yet; But
3. I'm jea - lous o' what bless - es her, The ve - ry 'breeze that kiss - es her; The

---

* The old name for this tune, according to Charles K. Sharp, was " Put up your dagger, Jamie." Burns also wrote verses to it, but we have given the preference to Hogg's song. Robert Bremner has a version of the air in his *Scots Tunes*, 1757, as " Miss Farquharson."

1. scarce wad do To sit an' woo, Down by the stream sae glass - y yet. But
2. just a jin - kin', Bon - nie blink - in', Hil - ty - skil - ty las - sie yet. But
3. flow - 'ry beds On which she treads, Tho' wae for ane that miss - es her. Then

*cres.*

1. there's a braw time com - in' yet, Where ye may gang a - roa - min' yet, An'
2. O! her art - less smile's mair sweet Than hin - ny or than mar - ma - lete; An'
3. O! to meet my las - sie yet, Up in that glen so gras - sy yet; For

*cres.*

1. hint wi' glee O' joys to be, When fa's the mod - est gloam - in' yet.
2. right or wrang, E'er it be lang, I'll bring her to a par - ley yet.
3. all I see Are nought to me, Save her that's but a las - sie yet!

*f*

## My Misty Dell.*

Translated from the Gaelic by LACHLAN MACBEAN.

1. My mis - ty Cor - rie, by deer fre - quent - ed, My love - ly
2. The wa - ter - cress - es sur - round each foun - tain With gloom - y
3. How sweet when dawn is a - round me gleam - ing, Be - neath the

1. val - ley, my ver - dant dell, Soft, rich, and grass - y, and sweet - ly
2. eye - brows of dark - est green; And groves of sor - rel as - cend the
3. rock to re - cline, and hear The joy - ous moor - hen so hoarse - ly

* By kind permission from *Songs and Hymns of the Scottish Highlands*. With regard to these verses Mr. Henry Whyte writes: This pastoral song is the composition of Duncan Ban MacIntyre, the Glenorchy Bard, who was born in 1721. In this song, as in his famous poem in praise of Ben Dorain, the poet dwells with loving minuteness on all the varied features and the everchanging aspects of nature as these are displayed in the Misty Dell. The poem, which contains eighteen verses, has been translated by Robert Buchanan, and will be found in his work entitled *The Laird of Lorne*. MacIntyre died in Edinburgh in 1812, and was buried in Greyfriars Churchyard. The Bard and his poetry was the subject of one of the lectures delivered by the late Principal Shairp, of St. Andrews, from the Chair of Poetry at Oxford, 1877; this lecture is published in the work entitled *Aspects of Poetry*, published by the Clarendon Press, 1881.

1. scent - ed With ev' - ry flow'r that I love so well; All thick - ly
2. moun - tain, Where loose white sand lies all soft and clean; Thence bub - bles
3. scream - ing, And gal - lant moor - cock soft crood - ling near! The wren is

1. grow - ing, and bright - ly blow - ing, Up - on its shag - gy and dark green
2. boil - ing, yet cold - ly coil - ing, The new - born stream from the dark-some
3. bust - ling and brisk - ly whist - ling, With mol - low mu - sic, a cease - less

1. lawn, Moss, can - ach, dai - sies a - dorn its maz - es, Thro' which skips
2. deep; Clear, blue, and curl - ing, and swift - ly swirl - ing, It bends and
3. strain; The thrush is sing - ing, the red - breast ring - ing Its cheer - y

1. light - ly the grace - ful fawn.
2. bounds in its head - long leap.
3. notes in the glad re - frain.

# My Mither's ay glowran owre me.*

Verses by ALLAN RAMSAY.

Air: "A Health to Betty."

**Allegretto.**

VOICE.

PIANO.

*mf*

*poco rit.*

*mf*

1. My Mi - ther's ay glow - ran owre me, Though she did the same be - ty
2. For though my fa - ther has plen - ty Of sil - ler an' plen-ish-ing

*mf*

*p*

*cres.*

1. fore me; I can - na get leave to look at my loove, Or
2. dain - ty, Yet he's un - co sweer to twine wi' his gear, An'

*p*

*cres.*

---

\* These verses were written by Allan Ramsay for his *Tea-table Miscellany*, 1724. They are entitled "Katy's Answer," and refer to the preceding song, "The Young Laird and Edinburgh Katy." Stenhouse considers that the tune is one of those which were introduced into England about the union of the crowns. It appears in John Playford's *Dancing Master*, 1657, and in Durfey's *Pills to Purge Melancholy*, vol. ii., 1719, in connection with a coarse song, headed "The Female Quarrel; or, a lampoon upon Phillida and Chloris. The words made to the tune of a country dance, call'd A Health to Betty." The original verses, entitled "A Health to Betty," are given by Thomson in his *Orpheus Caledonius*, 1725, p. 25. The second strain of the air, commencing at the ninth bar, is a modern addition.

1. else she'll be like to de - vour me! Right
2. sae we had need to be ten - ty. But

1. fain wad I tak' your of - fer, Sweet sir, but I'll tine my
2. tu - tor my parents wi' cau - tion; Be wy - lie in il - ka

1. toch - er; Then San - dy ye'll fret, an' wyte your poor Kate, When-
2. mo - tion; Brag weel o' your land, an' there's my leal hand, Win

1. e'er you keek in your toom cof - fer.
2. them, I'll be at your de - vo - tion!

# My name it is Jack.

## THE PLOUGHMAN.*

Verses by J. Hamilton.

*Con spirito.*

VOICE.

PIANO.

*p*

1. My name it is Jack, an' a ploughman my trade, Nae kirk or State mat-ters o'er
2. Wha's out or wha's in a-mong Tor-ies or Whigs Is nae-thing to me, I will
3. What tho' when I hap-pen to gae to the toun, The lass-es there ca' me a

1. trou-ble my head; A call-ing mair hon-est I'll e-ver pur-sue, The
2. turn up my riggs; Nae par-ty or pen-sion shall e'er make me bow, For
3. coun-try cloun; But sait-ens and silks they would hae un-co few, With-

* This song appears in *A Collection of Twenty-four Scots Songs*, by John Hamilton, 1797.

1. sweet-est em - ploy - ment is haud - in' the plough. I rise in the morn, as the
2. I'm in - de - pen - dent by haud - in' the plough. Am - bi - tion I ban - ish an'
3. out the ef - fects of my haud - in' the plough. My Peg - gy at hame is far

1. lark I am gay, Be - hind my twa hors - es I whis - tle a - way; Health,
2. poor - tith de - fy; There's nane on the earth sae hap - py as I; The
3. bet - ter than they, She's ten times mair frank an' is e - qual - ly gay, Baith

1. bloom, an' con - tent - ment is wreath'd round my brow, An' a' my de - light is in
2. plea - sures of Na - ture a' sea - sons I view, So blest is the man that at -
3. card - in' an' spin - nin' fow weel she can do, And lo'es the young lad - die that

1. haud - in' the plough.
2. tend - eth the plough!
3. fol - lows the plough!

# My Pretty Mary.

**PRETTY MARY.\***
(MÀIRI BHÒIDHEACH.)

Verses translated from the Gaelic by C. M. P.

1. My pret-ty Ma-ry, my love-ly Ma-ry, O, who can mea-sure the love I
2. Could I but so - - journ with thee on - ly In some green glen, .. se-cure and
3. Who ev - er saw thee, but felt thy pow - er? Of Beau-ty's hand-maids thou art the

1. bear thee? My charm-ing Ma-ry, I great-ly fear me, A-way from
2. lone - ly, Then nei - ther glo - ry, fame, nor trea - sure Could ev - er
3. flow - er; And sense and worth, all else ex - cell - ing, With-in thy

\* From the *Celtic Lyre*, by kind permission of Mr. Henry Whyte, Glasgow, who sends us the following note: "'Pretty Mary' is an ancient Hebridean air. The verses are old, and the author's name is unknown. He is said to have been a schoolmaster in the island of North Uist, Invernessshire. The song was published as early as 1819."

1. thee there is nought can cheer me. In storm or sun - shine, wher - e'er I
2. bring me half such plea - sure. Thy ab - sence has . . . of joy be -
3. vir - tu - ous mind are dwell - ing. O ne'er may e - - - vil chance come

1. wan - der, My wont is on . . . thy charms to pon - der; Thy im - age
2. reft me, And nought but sor - - - row now is left me; From day to
3. near thee, With grief or gloom - - y doubts to fear thee; But plea - sant

1. ri - - ses up be - fore me, And throws love's witch - - ing gla-mour
2. day . . . 'tis sigh - ing, pin - ing, For thy sweet face like a sun-beam
3. hopes . . and mus - ings thine be, To cheer the days . . un - til thou

1. o'er me.
2. shin - ing.
3. mine be.

# My Sandy gi'ed to me a ring.

### I LOVE MY LOVE IN SECRET.*

1. My San — dy gi'ed to me a ring, 'Twas a' be - set wi'
2. My San — dy brak' a piece o' gowd, While doun his cheeks the

1. dia - monds fine; But I gi'ed him a bet - ter thing, I
2. saut tears row'd; He took a hauf an' gi'ed it me, And I'll

* This air appears in Mrs. Crockat's *MS. Music Book*, 1709, and later in MacGibbon's and Oswald's Collections. The verses were slightly altered by Burns for the third volume of Johnson's *Scots' Musical Museum*, issued February, 1790.

1. gi'ed my love this heart o' mine! My San - dy, O! my
2. keep it till the hour I dee! My San - dy, O! my

1. San - dy, O! My bon - nie, bon - nie San - dy, O! My
2. San - dy, O! My bon - nie, bon - nie San - dy, O! My

1. love for thee I daur - na show, Yet I love my love in
2. love for thee I daur - na show, Yet I love my love in

1. se - cret, O!
2. se - cret, O!

# Nae mair we'll meet again.*

**Lento.**

VOICE.

1. Nae
2. Yet
3. Now

PIANO.

*p*

*rit.*

con Ped.

1. mair we'll meet a-gain, my love, by yon burn-side, Nae mair we'll wan-der thro' the grove, by
2. mem'-ry aft will fond-ly brood, on yon burn-side, O'er haunts which we sae aft hae trod, by
3. far re-mov'd from ev'-ry care, 'boon yon burn-side, Thou bloom'st, my love, an an-gel fair, 'boon

*p*

*poco cres.*

1. yon burn-side; Ne'er a-gain the ma-vis' lay Will we hail at close of day, For we
2. yon burn-side; Still the walk wi' me thou'lt share, Tho' thy foot can nev-er mair Bend to
3. yon burn-side; And, if an-gels pit-y know, Sure the tear for me will flow, Who must

*poco cres.*

*poco rit.*

1. ne'er a-gain will stray doun by yon burn-side.
2. earth the gow-an fair, doun by yon burn-side.
3. lin-ger here be-low, doun by yon burn-side.

*poco rit.* *p* *rit.*

* R. A. Smith gives this song and air in his *Scottish Minstrel*, 1822. The air is Highland, and is one of the many versions of "Robi dohnn Gorrach":—Daft Robin.

# Now in her green mantle blythe Nature arrays.

MY NANNIE'S AWA'.*

Verses by BURNS.

*Andante con espressione.*

VOICE.

PIANO.

1. Now in her green man-tle blythe
2. The snawdrap and prim-rose our
3. Thou lav'-rock that springs frae the
4. Come Au-tumn, sae pen-sive, in

1. Na - ture ar - rays, And lis - tens the lamb - kins that bleat owre the braes, While
2. wood - lands a - dorn, And vi - o - lets bathe in the wect o' the morn; They
3. dews of the lawn, The shep - herd to warn of the grey - break - ing dawn, And
4. yel - low and grey, And soothe me wi' tid - ings o' Na - ture's de - cay; The

1. birds war - ble wel-come in il - ka green shaw; But to me it's de - light - less—my
2. pain my sad bo - som, sac sweet - ly they blaw, They mind me o' Nan - nie—and
3. thou mel - low ma - vis that hails the night - fa', Give o - ver for pi - ty—my
4. dark drea - ry win - ter, and wild driv - ing snaw, A - lane can de - light me—and

*cres.*

*rit.* | Last time.

1. Nan - nie's a - wa', But to me it's de-light-less, my Nannie's a - wa'!..
2. Nan - nie's a - wa', They mind me o' Nan-nie—and Nannie's a - wa'!..
3. Nan - nie's a - wa', Give o - ver for pi - ty—my Nannie's a - wa'!..
4. Nan - nie's a - wa'. A - lane can de - light me—and Nannie's a - wa'!..

*rit.*

* Burns wrote these verses in 1792. The heroine of the song is "Clarinda" (Mrs. MacLehose). Regarding the melody, George Farquhar Graham writes in *Wood's Songs of Scotland*, 1852; "The air we believe to be modern; yet we have not been able to trace it to any composer. Like many other airs it probably owes its present form to several individuals. It appears to have passed orally from one singer to another, until Mr. George Croall, music seller, Edinburgh, rescued it a few years ago from threatened oblivion."

K

# O, bonnie was yon rosy brier.*

Verses by Burns.

*Andante con moto.*

Air: "The wee, wee man."

VOICE.

PIANO.

*p*

*poco rit.*

con Ped.

*p*

1. O, bon - nie was yon ro - sy brier, That blooms sae far frae
2. All in its rude and prick - ly bow'r, That crim - son rose, how

*p*

1. haunt o' man, And bon - nie she, and oh! how dear! It
2. sweet and fair; But love is far a sweet - er flow'r A -

* John Findlay, in *Scottish Historical and Romantic Ballads*, vol. ii., 1808, considers this air to be possibly one of the most ancient of our legendary tunes. Burns' verses, "O bonnie was yon rosy brier," were written in the summer of 1795, and first published with the above air in George Thomson's Collection, vol. iii. The singular ballad, known as "The wee, wee man," was preserved by David Herd in his first volume of *Antient and Modern Scottish Songs*, issued in 1769. Its first appearance in conjunction with the air, is in Johnson's *Scots' Musical Museum*, vol. iv., No. 370.

1. shad - ed frae the eve - ning sun Yon rose - buds in the
2. mid life's thorn - y path o' care. The path - less wild and

1. morn - ing dew, How pure, a - mang the leaves sae green; But
2. wimp - ling burn, Wi' Chlo - ris in my arms, be mine; And

*cres.*

1. pur - er was the lov - er's vow, They wit - ness'd in the
2. I the warld nor wish nor scorn, It's joys and griefs a -

1. shade yes - treen.
2. like re - sign.

*poco rit.*

# O, can ye sew cushions?*

A NURSE'S LULLABY.

1. O, can ye sew cush - ions? And can ye sew sheets? And
2. I big - git the cra - dle Up - on the tree - top, And

1. can ye sing bal - loo - loo When the bairn greets? And
2. aye as the wind blew My cra - dle did rock. And

1. hee and baw, bird - ie, And hee and baw, lamb; And
2. hush - a - baw, ba - by, O ba - lil - li - loo, And

* This old traditional nursery song appears in Johnson's *Scots' Musical Museum*, vol. v., No. 444. It was communicated to the publisher of that work by Burns. The second verse is given by Stenhouse in the *Museum* Illustrations, p. 394.

1. hee and baw, bird - ie, My bon - nie wee lamb!
2. hee and baw, bird - ie, My bon - nie wee doo!

*Più mosso.*

Hee - o, wee - o, what wou'd I do wi' you? Black's the life that I lead wi' you; Mo - ny o' ye, lit - tle for to gi'e you

*Andante. ritard.*

Hee - o, wee - o, what wou'd I do wi' you?

## O, Charlie is my darling.

Verses by Lady NAIRNE.

O, Char-lie is my dar-ling, my dar-ling, my dar-ling! Char-lie is my dar-ling, The young Che-va-lier.

1. 'Twas on a Mon-day morn-ing Right
2. As he cam' march-in' up the street, The
3. Wi' High-land bon-nets on their heads, And
4. They've left their bon-nie Hie-land hills, Their
5. Oh! there were mon-y beat-ing hearts, And

---

* George F. Graham, in *The Songs of Scotland* (Messrs. Wood & Co., Glasgow), remarks that it has been the fate of this air to undergo several odd transformations. He considers that its present state (1850) may be due to some popular singer within the last forty years. Certainly, the air differs considerably from the one given in Johnson's *Museum* No. 428, and which was communicated to the Editor by Burns. Stenhouse says (Illustrations, p. 380) that "the *Museum* tune was 'modernized' by Mr. Clarke, and that the genuine version is the one given by Hogg in the *Jacobite Relics*, Ser. II., p, 92." The first verse and the chorus of "Charlie is my darling" seem to be old. They are included in the *Museum* song, but the four verses which follow differ entirely from Lady Nairne's spirited composition.

1. ear - ly in the year, When Char - lie came to our town, The
2. pipes play'd loud and clear; And a' the folks cam' rin - nin' out To
3. clay-mores bright and clear, They cam' to fight for Scot - land's right, And the
4. wives and bairn - ies dear, To draw the sword for Scot - land's lord, The
5. mon - y hope and fear; And mon - y were the pray'rs put up For the

1. young Che - va - lier.
2. meet the Che - va - lier.
3. young Che - va - lier.
4. gay Che - va - lier.
5. young Che - va - lier.

O, Char - lie is my dar - ling, my

dar - ling, my dar - ling, Char - lie is my dar - ling, The young Che - va - lier.

# Och, hey! Johnnie lad.

ROBERT TANNAHILL.

1. Och, hey! John-nie lad, Ye're no sae kind's ye should ha'e been; Och, hey! John-nie lad, Ye
2. Och, hey! John-nie lad, Ye're no sae kind's ye should ha'e been; Och, hey! John-nie lad, Ye
3. Och, hey! John-nie lad, Ye're no sae kind's ye should ha'e been; Och, hey! John-nie lad, Ye

1. did-na keep your tryst yestreen. I wait-ed lang be-side the wood, Sae wae au' wea-ry a' my lane;
2. did-na keep your tryst yestreen. I look-it by the whin-ny knowe, I look-it by the firs sae green, I
3. did-na keep your tryst yestreen. The ne'er a sup-per cross'd my craig, The ne'er a sleep has closed my een,

1. Och, hey! John-nie lad, Ye're no sae kind's ye should ha'e been!
2. look-it owre the spun-kie howe, And aye I thocht you wad ha'e been!
3. Och, hey! John-nie lad, Ye're no sae kind's ye should ha'e been!

* This tune is found in Bremner's *Collection of Reels and Country Dances*, 1764, under the name of "The lasses o' the Ferry." The old version of the song on which Tannahill's verses are based, is preserved in Herd's Collection, vol. ii., 1776. Robert Tannahill, one of Scotland's most talented poets, was born at Paisley, June 3rd, 1774. He committed suicide, May 17th, 1810.

# Och, och, mar tha mi!

### THE ISLAY MAIDEN.*

(A' CHURINNEAG ILEACH.)

*Moderato con espressione.*     Translated from the Gaelic by THOMAS PATTISON.

PIANO.

*poco rit.*

1. Och, och, mar tha mi! here so lone - ly, Des-pair has seized me and keeps his
2. When sleep-ing sweet - ly the rest are ly - ing, Wild dreams of an - guish my mind is
3. A - las! thy kind eye, so bright-ly shin - ing; Thy neck so come - ly, like ca-nach
4. Since thou hast left me, and with-out warn - ing, A - las! and tak - en a man for

*dim.*

1. hold; . . . O were I near thee in Is - lay on - ly, Be - fore tho'st
2. weav - ing; I'm like the swan that drops wound-ed,— dy - ing; My love ex-
3. blow - ing; Those e - bon eye - brows thy fore-head lin - ing; Thy cheeks like
4. gold! Had I been by thee, false wis-dom scorn - ing, Thy - self, my

*sf* *dim.*

*poco rit.*

1. tak - en that man for gold.
2. haunts me with bit - ter griev - ing.
3. ber - ries or row-ans glow - ing.
4. dear one, thou had'st not sold!

*poco rit.*     *p*     *rit.*
*a tempo.*

* From the *Celtic Lyre*, by permission of the Editor, Mr. Henry Whyte ("Fionn"). The Gaelic words and music of "The Islay Maiden" are ancient, and belong to Islay. The song was translated by the late Thomas Pattison, a gifted son of Islay, and appears in his interesting work, "Gaelic Bards." Mr. Pattison died when his work was passing through the press, 1866.

# O, could I be, love, in form of sea-gull.

## MY FAITHFUL FAIR ONE.*
### (Mo Run Geal Dileas.)

Translated from the Gaelic
by Henry Whyte (" Fionn ").

*Andantino con espressione.*

VOICE.

PIANO.

*p*     *rit.*

1. O, could I    be,    love, in · form    of    sea -    gull, That sails    so
2. O, could we    wan -    der where streams me -    an -    der, I'd ask    no
3. In    fo - reign    re -    gions I  liv'd    a    sea -    son, And none could
4. In    fe - ver'd'    an -    guish, when  left    to    lan -    guish, No  hu - man .
5. I'll  ne'er con -    tend    with    a  tree that    bends    not, Though on    its

*p*

1. free -    ly  up - on    the    sea,    I'd  vis - it    Is -    lay, for there a -
2. gran -    deur from  fo - reign    clime;    Where birds would  cheer    us,  and none would
3. see    there with thee  to    vie;    Thy  form so  slen -    der, thy words so
4. lan -    guage my thoughts could    tell;    I thought, my    dear -    ie! if thou wert
5. ten -    drils rich fruit should    grow;    If  thou for - sake    me,  I  won't  up-

*sf*

---

* From *The Celtic Lyre*, by kind permission of the Editor, Mr. Henry Whyte. Regarding this song Mr. Whyte sends us the following note: " This very popular lyric is said to have been written by Young MacLean, of Torlosk, Mull, Argyleshire, who as a tacksman visited Islay some time last century, where he was captivated by the charms of Isabel of Balinaby. He sought her hand, and she declining to give him a definite answer at the time, he gave way to melancholy, and was advised by his friends to go abroad, which he did. He refers to this circumstance in the song. Returning after an absence of nine months, he again sought the hand of the fair Isabel, but her parents prevented her accepting him. The refusal preyed so much upon him that his mind gave way, and he had to be confined in an asylum. While so confined he wrote *Mo run geal dileas* (My faithful fair one), and several other poems. Young MacLean died a raving lunatic."

1. bid - ing Is that sweet kind one I pine to see.
2. hear us, I'd kiss my dear one and call her mine.
3. ten - der, I will re - mem - ber un - til I die.
4. near me, To soothe and cheer me, I'd soon be well.
5. braid thee; The great - est ebb - tide brings full - est flow.

CHORUS.

My faith - ful fair one, my own, my rare one, Re - turn, my

fair one, O, hear my cry! For thee, my maid - en, I'm sor - row

lad - en; With - out my fair one I'll pine and die!

# Of a' the airts the wind can blaw.*

Verses by BURNS.

Air: "Miss Admiral Gordon's Strathspey."

*Andante con molto espressione.*

PIANO.

1. Of a' the airts the wind can blaw, I dear - ly like the west, For
2. O, blaw, ye west - lin winds, blaw saft A - mang the leaf - y trees, Wi'

1. there the bon - nie las - sie lives, The lass that I lo'e best; The wild woods grow, an' ri - vers row, And
2. gen - tle gale, frae muir and dale, Bring hame the la - den bees; And bring the las - sie back to me, "Wi'

1. mo - nie a hill be - tween; Baith day an' night my fan - cy's flight Is ev - er wi' my Jean. I
2. her twa watch - in' een;" Ae blink o' her wad ba - nish care, Sae love - ly is my Jean. What

* This tune is a transformation of "The lowlands o' Holland," by William Marshall, butler to the Duke of Gordon, about the middle of last century. He called it "Miss Admiral Gordon's Strathspey," and to it, in 1788, Burns wrote the above charming song. The "Jean" referred to was Mrs. Burns. William Marshall was born at Fochabers, Banffshire, in 1748. He seems to have possessed great musical ability, and to have employed much of his leisure time to the composition of Scottish airs and dance tunes. "The correctness of Marshall's ear was unrivalled, and his style of playing strathspeys and reels lively and inspiring, while his fine taste and peculiarly touching manner of executing the slow and more plaintive Scottish airs and melodies, delighted all who heard him." Marshall died in 1833, aged eighty-five. In 1781 Neil Stewart printed *A Collection of Strathspey Reels*, composed by Marshall, and in 1822 a collection of his *Airs and Melodies* was published by subscription. This volume contains 176 tunes, and was followed by a supplement of about 74 additional tunes.

*cres.*

1. see her in the dew - y flow'r, Sae love - ly, sweet, an' fair; I
2. sighs an' vows a - mang the knowes Hae past a - tween us twa! How

*cres.*

1. hear her voice in il - ka bird, Wi' mu - sic charm the air; There's
2. fain to meet, how wae to part, That day she gaed a - wa'! The

*poco rit.*

*f*

1. not a bon - nie flow'r that springs By foun - tain, shaw, or green; Nor
2. Pow'rs a - boon can on - ly ken, To whom the heart is seen, That

*poco rit.*

*poco rit.*

1. yet a bon - nie bird that sings, But minds me o' my Jean.
2. nane can be sae dear to me As my sweet love - ly Jean!

*f*

*poco rit.*

# O, Gilderoy was a bonnie boy.

## GILDEROY.*

*Maestoso.*

VOICE.

PIANO.

*mf*   *cres.*   *f*   *sf*

*con Ped.*

1. O, Gil - de - roy was a bon - nie boy; Had ros - es till his
2. Wi' mei - kle joy we spent our prime, Till we were baith six -
3. My Gil - de - roy, baith far and near, Was fear'd in il - ka
4. Gif Gil - de - roy had done a - miss, He micht ha'e ban - ish'd

*mf*

*cres.*

1. shoon;       His stock - ings were .. of silk - en soy, Wi'
2. teen;       And aft .. we pass'd .. the lang - some time A -
3. toun,       And bauld - ly bare .. a - way .. the gear O'
4. been;       Ah! what .. sair cru - - el - ty .. is this, To

*cres.*

* Gilderoy, or Gilruadh, *The Red-haired man*, a member of the Clan Gregor, was the leader of a band of desperate robbers who infested the Highlands of Perthshire about the beginning of the 17th century. He was hanged with ten of his followers at the Cross of Edinburgh in 1636. An early version of the ballad was published as a broadside about 1650, and again later on in a work entitled, *Westminster Drollery*; or, a *Choice Collection of the Newest Songs and Poems, both at Court and Theatres, by a Person of Quality*. London, 1671. D'Urfey prints ten verses of the ballad in his *Pills to Purge Melancholy*, 1719 (vol. v., p. 39), as "Gilderoy's Last Farewell. To a New Tune." The modern version is attributed to Lady Wardlaw, who died in 1727. The air is probably as old as the ballad. It appears in the second edition of Thomson's *Orpheus Caledonius*, 1733, vol. ii., p. 106.

1. gar - ters hang - ing donn. It was, I ween, a
2. mang the leaves sae green. Aft on the banks we'd
3. mony a Low - land loun. Nane e'er durst meet him
4. hang sic hand - some men! Had not their laws been

1. come - ly sicht, To see sae trim a boy; He
2. sit us there, And sweet - ly kiss and toy, Wi'
3. hand to hand, He was sae brave a boy; At
4. made so strict, I ne'er had lost my joy; Wi'

*cres.*

1. was . . my joy and heart's de - light, My hand - some Gil - de -
2. gar - lands gay wad deck . . my hair, My hand - some Gil - de -
3. length, wi' num - bers he . . . was ta'en, My hand - some Gil - de -
4. sor - row ne'er had wat . . my cheek For my dear Gil - de -

*cres.*

1. roy!
2. roy!
3. roy!
4. roy!

*sf*  *sf*  *p*  *rit.*

Ped.    Ped.    Ped.

# O! gin I were where Gadie rins.*

Verses by John Imlah.

1. O! gin I were where Ga - die rins, Where
2. O! gin I were where Ga - die rins, Where
3. O! gin I were where Ga - die rins, Where
4. O! gin I were where Ga - die rins, Where

1. Ga - die rins, where Ga - die rins, O! gin I were where Ga - die rins, By the
2. Ga - die rins, where Ga - die rins, O! gin I were where Ga - die rins, By the
3. Ga - die rins, where Ga - die rins, O! gin I were where Ga - die rins, By the
4. Ga - gie rins, where Ga - die rins, O! gin I were where Ga - die rins, By the

1. foot o' Ben - na - chie. I've roam'd by Tweed, I've roam'd by Tay, By
2. foot o' Ben - na - chie. When sim - mer cleads the var - ied scene, Wi'
3. foot o' Ben - na - chie. When win - ter winds blaw sharp and shrill, O'er
4. foot o' Ben - na - chie. Tho' few to wel - come me re - main; Tho'

* This melody comes from Aberdeenshire, and the first four lines of the song belong to the original verses. John Imlah was born in Aberdeen in 1799. He died in Jamaica in 1846. The Gadie is a river in Aberdeenshire.

1. bor - der Nith and High-land Spey; But dear - er far to me than they, The
2. licht o' gowd and leaves o' green, I fain wad be where aft I've been, At the
3. i - cy burn and sheet - ed hill, The in - gle neuk is glee-some still At the
4. a' I lov'd are dead, and gane; I'll back, tho' I should live a - lane, At the

1. braes o' Ben - na - chie! O! gin I were where Ga - die rins, Where
2. foot o' Ben - na - chie! O! gin I were where Ga - die rins, Where
3. foot o' Ben - na - chie! O! gin I were where Ga - die rins, Where
4. foot o' Ben - na - chie! O! gin I were where Ga - die rins, Where

1. Ga - die rins, where Ga - die rins, O! gin I were where Ga - die rins, By the
2. Ga - die rins, where Ga - die rins, O! gin I were where Ga - die rins, By the
3. Ga - die rins, where Ga - die rins, O! gin I were where Ga - die rins, By the
4. Ga - die rins, where Ga - die rins, O! gin I were where Ga - die rins, By the

*Last time.*

1. foot o' Ben - na - chie!
2. foot o' Ben - na - chie!
3. foot o' Ben - na - chie!
4. foot o' Ben - na - chie!

*rit. e dim.*

L

# O gin my love were yon red rose.

1st v. Traditional.   2nd v. by BURNS.
3rd v. by JOHN RICHARDSON.

*Andante affettuoso.*

VOICE.

PIANO.

*p*

*poco rit.*

con Ped.

*p*

*cres.*

1. O  gin  my  love  were  yon  red  rose,  That  grows  up - on  the
2. O  were  my  love  yon  li - lac  fair,  Wi'  pur - ple  blos - soms
3. O  were  my  love  yon  vi - o - let  sweet,  That  peeps  frae  neath  the

*p*

*cres.*

1. cas - tle  wa',  An'  I  my - sel'  a  drap  o'  dew,  Up -
2. to  the  spring;  An'  I  a  bud  to  shel - ter  there,  When
3. haw - thorn  spray;  An'  I  my - sel'  the  ze - phyr's  breath,  A -

*sf*

*colla voce.*

\* This air is old and of Highland origin. The first verse of the song is preserved in Herd's Collection, vol. ii., 1776.

1. on her blush - ing leaves to fa'. O! there wi' trem - bling
2. wea - ried on my lit - tle wing,— How wad I mourn when
3. maug its bon - nie leaves to play,— I'd fan it wi' a

1. love's un - rest, I'd plead my pas - sion a' the nicht; And
2. it was torn By au - tumn wild and win - ter rude! But
3. con - stant gale, Be - neath the noon - tide's scorch - ing ray; An'

1. kiss the bloom I gent - ly prest, Till fley'd a - wa' wi'
2. I wad sing, on wan - ton wing, When youth - fu' May its
3. sprin - kle it wi' fresh - est dews, At morn - ing dawn, and

Last verse.

1. morn - in's licht.
2. bloom re - new'd.
3. part - ing day.

# O, heard ye yon pibroch sound.

### GLENARA.*

Verses by THOMAS CAMPBELL.

*Adagio con molto espressione.*

Old Highland Funeral March.

PIANO.

1. O, heard ye yon pibroch sound sad in the gale, Where a band com-eth slow-ly with
2. In si-lence they reach'd o'er moun-tain and moor, To a heath, where the oak-tree grew
3. "I dreamt of my la - dy, I dreamt of her shroud," Cried a voice from the kins-man, all
4. In dust low the trai - tor has knelt to the ground, And the de - sert re-veal'd where his

1. weep - ing and wail; "Tis the Chief of Glen-ar - a la - ments for his dear, And her
2. lone - ly and hoar; "Now here let us place the grey stone of her cairn; Why
3. wrath - ful and loud; "And emp - ty that shroud and that cof - fin did seem; Glen -
4. la - dy was found; From a rock of the o-cean that beau - ty is borne, Now

1. sire and her peo - ple are call'd to her bier.
2. speak ye no word?" said Glen - ar - a the stern.
3. a - ra! Glen-a - ra! now rede me my dream!"
4. joy to the house of fair El - len of Lorn!

* A version of this melody is found in Thomson's Collection. In 1822 Thomson obtained permission from Thomas Campbell to publish the ballad.

# Oh! laddie with the golden hair.

## LADDIE WITH THE GOLDEN HAIR.*

### (Oigfhear a chùil-dualaich.)

Translated from the Gaelic by "Fionn" (Henry Whyte).

Moderato.

VOICE.

PIANO.

1. Oh! lad - die with the gold - en hair, In
2. Oh! would I were in yon - der glen Now
3. If dressed in silks or sa - tins rare, Al -

1. wa - vy ring - lets flow - ing; Oh! lad - die with the gold - en hair, Thy locks were my un -
2. roam - ing with my dear - ie; My heart would wake to joy a - gain, Tho' now 'tis sad and
3. though of low - ly sta - tion, I'd to thy state - ly halls re - pair, And face each proud re -

1. do - ing.
2. drear - y.
3. la - tion.

Thy beau - ty drew my heart to thee, But now I am de -
My locks un - tend - ed, loose - ly flow, My spi - rits are de -
The love we plight - ed in the glade I thought would fail us

1. ceiv - èd, The pro - mi - ses you gave to me My too fond heart be - liev - èd.
2. ject - ed; In vain I try the cause to know Why thou hast me ne - glect - ed.
3. nev - er; The knot we tied, the vows we made, I fear are loos'd for ev - er.

* From the *Celtic Lyre*, by kind permission of the Editor, Mr. Henry Whyte, Glasgow. This song owes its preservation to its own intrinsic merits, and its sweet but simple melody. The name of the author has never been disclosed, but it has been popular on the West Coast for at least the best portion of a century. The air seems to be a version of the Gaelic melody "Fal il o ro, fal il o." See p. 59.

# O, hearken, and I will tell you how.

MUIRLAND WILLIE.*

*Con spirito, molto energico.*

PIANO.

1. O, heark-en, and I will tell you how Young Muir-land Wil-lie cam'
2. On his gray yade as he did ride, Wi' dirk and pis-tol
3. "Now, woo-er, sin' ye're light-ed doun, Where do ye won, or
4. The maid-en blush'd, and bing'd fu' law, She had-na will to
5. The bri-dal day it cam' to pass, Wi' mon-y a blythe-some

1. here to woo, Tho' he could nei-ther say nor do, The
2. by his side, He prick'd her on wi' mei-kle pride, Wi'
3. in what toun? I think my doch-ter win-na gloom On
4. say him na, But to her dad-die she left it a', As
5. lad and lass; But sic a day there nev-er was, Sic

1. truth I tell to you. . . . . . But aye he cries, "What .
2. mei-kle mirth and glee, . . . . . Out owre yon moss, out
3. sic a lad as ye." . . . . . The woo-er he stepp'd
4. they twa could a-gree. . . . . . The lov-er gi'ed her
5. mirth was nev-er seen. . . . . . This win-some cou-ple

* This air appears in Mrs. Crockat's *Manuscript Music Book*, 1709. The complete ballad of thirteen verses was published by Ramsay in the *Tea-Table Miscellany*, 1724. It is there marked "Z," to denote that the Editor considered it to be of great antiquity. In 1725, Thomson printed both words and music in the *Orpheus Caledonius*, and, under the title of "Scotch Wedding," Watts included the song in the *Musical Miscellany*, 1729, vol. 4., p. 78.

1. e'er  be - tide,  Mag - gie I'se ha'e  to  be  my  bride,"  With a
2. owre  yon muir,  Till  he cam' to  her  dad - die's door,  With a
3. up  the house,  And  wow  but he  was  won - drous crouse,  With a
4. then  a kiss,  Syne  ran to  her dad - die and  tell'd  him this,  With a
5. strak  ed hands,  Mess  John  tied up  the  mar - riage bands,  With a

1. fal  da  ra,  fal  lal  da  ra,  la  fal  la  da  ra, la  da  ra
2. fal  da  ra,  fal  lal  da  ra,  la  fal  la  da  ra, la  da  ra
3. fal  da  ra,  fal  lal  da  ra,  la  fal  la  da  ra, la  da  ra
4. fal  da  ra,  fal  lal  da  ra,  la  fal  la  da  ra, la  da  ra
5. fal  da  ra,  fal  lal  da  ra,  la  fal  la  da  ra, la  da  ra

1. la! . . .
2. la! . . .
3. la! . . .
4. la! . . .
5. la! . . .

Verses 1 to 4.   After last verse.

# Oh! rowan tree, oh! rowan tree.

## THE ROWAN TREE.*

Verses by Lady NAIRNE.

1. Oh! row-an tree, oh! ro-wan tree, thou'lt aye be dear to me, En-twin'd thou art wi' mo-ny ties, O!
2. How fair wert thou in simmer-time, wi' a' thy clusters white; How rich and gay thy autumn dress, wi'
3. We sat aneath thy spreading shade, the bairnies round thee ran, They pu'd thy bon-nie berries red, and
4. Oh! there a-rose my father's pray'r, in ho - ly evening's calm, How sweet was then my mither's voice,

1. hame and in - fan - cy. Thy leaves were aye the first o'spring, thy flow'rs the simmer's pride; There
2. ber - ries red and bright. On thy fair stem were mo - ny names, which now nae mair I see,  But
3. neck - la - ces they strang. My mi - ther, O! I see her still, she smil'd our sports to see,  Wi'
4. in the mar-tyr's psalm. Now a' are gane! we meet nae mair, a - neath the row - an tree;  But

1. was nae sic a bon-nie tree in a' the coun - try side; Oh! row - an tree!
2. they're en - gra - ven on my heart,—for - got they ne'er can be! Oh! row - an tree!
3. lit - tle Jea - nie on her lap, wi' Ja - mie at her knee! Oh! row - an tree!
1. hal-low'd thoughts around thee twine o' hame and in - fan-cy, Oh! row - an tree!

* Lady Carolina Nairne was born at the house of Gask, Perthshire, in 1766. She was the daughter of Lawrence Oliphant, of Gask, a staunch Jacobite, who had followed Prince Charlie through the '45, and always spoke of King George as the Elector of Hanover. In 1806 she married Captain N. W. Nairne, a second cousin, and a son of one of the young Chevalier's adherents. He became Lord Nairne in 1824, and died in 1830. Lady Nairne survived him till 1845, when she died in her seventy-ninth year. No one was more shy of a literary reputation than Lady Nairne. Her best songs were contributed to R. A. Smith's Scottish Minstrel, 1822, under the nom de plume of B. B.—" Mrs. Bogan of Bogan," and so close did she guard her secret, that not even the Editor of that work was aware of the name and position of his contributor. For years her songs were introduced into collections of Scottish songs without any mention of the author's name. This, however, is now changed, and Lady Nairne has taken her place as a song writer beside Burns, Hogg, and Tannahill.

## Oh! why left I my hame?*

*Andante con espressione.*

Verses by R. Gilfillan.

1. Oh! why left I my hame? Why did I cross the deep? Oh! why left I the
2. Oh! here no Sab-bath bell A-wakes the Sab-bath morn, No song of rea-pers
3. There's a hope for ev-'ry woe, And a balm for ev-'ry pain, But the first joys of our

1. land Where my fore-fa-thers sleep? I sigh for Sco-tia's shore, And I
2. heard A-mang the yel-low corn; For the ty-rant's voice is here, And the
3. heart Come nev-er back a-gain. There's a track up-on the deep, And a

1. gaze a-cross the sea, But I can-na' get a blink O' my ain coun-trie!
2. wail of sla-ver-ie; But the sun of free-dom shines In my ain coun-trie
3. path a-cross the sea, But the wea-rie ne'er re-turn To their ain coun-trie!

* This air is an adaptation of " The Lowlands of Holland," by Peter McLeod, a talented amateur musician, who was born in 1797, and died near Edinburgh in 1859. McLeod published three collections of " Original Melodies," which show a decided ability for musical composition.

# O, I hae lost my silken snood.*

*Andante tranquillo.*

Air: "Twine weel the plaiden."

PIANO.

1. O, I hae lost my silk - en snood That tied my hair so yel - low; I've
2. He prais'd my een sae bon - nie blue, Sae li - ly-white my skin, O; And

1. gi'en my heart to the lad I lo'ed, He was a gal - lant fel - low. And
2. syne he prie'd my bon - nie mou', An' swore it was nae sin, O! But

1. twine it weel my bon - nie dow, And twine it weel the plaid - en; The
2. he has left the lass he loe'd, His own true love for - sak - en, Which

1. las - sie lost her silken snood In pu' - ing o' the brack - en.
2. gars me sair to greet the snood I lost a - mang the brack - en.

* Both Stenhouse and Graham err in stating that this song, with its melody, was first published by Napier in his *Selection of Scots' Songs*, the first volume of which was issued in Feb. 1790. The song and air are given in *The Musical Miscellany*, Perth, J. Brown, 1786, and again in the second edition of the same work, published by Elliot & Kay, London, in April, 1788, under the title of *Calliope; or, The Musical Miscellany*. In his *Select Melodies of Scotland*, George Thomson has marked the air with "A," to denote that he considered it to be of "remote antiquity." It was for this last mentioned work that Burns wrote his song beginning, "Farewell, thou stream, that winding flows," to the tune of "Twine weel the plaiden." Oswald has a tune in his collection with the title "The Lassie lost her silken snood," but it is entirely different from the one given above.

# O, I ha'e seen great anes.

### MY AIN FIRESIDE.*

Verses by Mrs. ELIZABETH HAMILTON, died *circa* 1817.

1. O, I ha'e seen great anes an' sat in great ha's, 'Mang lords an' 'mang la-dies a' cover'd wi' braws; But a sight sae de-light-ful I trow I ne'er spied, As the bon-nie blythe blink of my ain fire-side. My ain fire-side, my ain fire-side, O sweet is the blink o' my ain fire-side.

2. Nae false-hood to dread, and no ma-lice to fear, But truth to de-light me and friendship to cheer; Of a' roads to hap-pi-ness ev-er were tried, There is nane half sae sure as ane's ain fire-side. My ain fire-side, my ain fire-side, O sweet is the blink o' my ain fire-side.

3. When I draw in my stool on my co-sy hearthstane My heart loups sae light I scarce ken't for my ain; Care's down on the wind, it is clear out of sight, Past trou-bles they seem but as dreams o' the night. My ain fire-side, my ain fire-side, O sweet is the blink o' my ain fire-side.

* These verses are from Cromek's *Remains of Nithsdale and Galloway Song*, 1810, p. 46. The air is very old, and several versions of it exist under different names. The above version occurs in the third volume of Johnson's *Museum*, set to the old song, "Todlen Hame," the preservation of which we owe to Allan Ramsay's *Tea-Table Miscellany*. But the real old air known as "Todlen Hame," or rather "Todlen butt and todlen ben," published in the second edition of the *Orpheus Caledonius*, 1733, vol. ii., p. 94, has no connection with the melody adopted by Johnson, and which we give here with Mrs. Hamilton's beautiful verses.

# O, Kenmure's on and awa', Willie.

Border Jacobite Song.

1. O, Kenmure's on and a-wa', Wil-lie, O, Kenmure's on and a-wa', .... And 1. Ken-mure's lord's the brav-est lord That ev-er Gal-lo-way 1. saw. .... Suc-cess to Ken-mure's band, Wil-lie, Suc-

2. Here's Kenmure's health in wine, Wil-lie, Here's Kenmure's health in wine; .... There 2. ne'er was a coward o' Ken-mure's bluid, Nor yet o' Gor-don's 2. line. .... O, Ken-mure's lads are men, Wil-lie, O,

3. They'll live or die wi' fame, Wil-lie, They'll live or die wi' fame; .... But 3. soon wi' sound-ing vic-to-rie, May Ken-mure's lord come 3. hame. .... Here's him that's far a-wa', Wil-lie, Here's

* Burns sent this popular ballad and air to Johnson for his *Scots' Museum*. It is included in Cromek's *Remains of Nithsdale and Galloway Song*, 1810, and in Hogg's *Jacobite Relics*, Ser. II., 1821, with additional verses which are evidently spurious. William Gordon, Viscount of Kenmure, joined the Rebels in 1715. He was captured at Preston by the English army, and after being disgracefully treated, was beheaded in 1716.

1. cess to Ken-mure's band! . . . . There's no a heart that
2. Ken-mure's lads are men; . . . . Their hearts and swords are
3. him that's far a - wa'; . . . . But here's the flow'r that

*cres.*

1. fears a Whig, That rides in Ken - mure's band. . . . . .
2. met - tle true, And that their foes shall ken. . . . . .
3. I lo'e best, The rose that's like the snaw. . . . . .

*Verses 1 and 2.*　　　　　　　　*After last Verse.*

# O lay thy loof in mine, lass.*

Verses by Burns.
*Molto moderato.*

Air: "The Cordwainer's March."

1. O lay thy loof in mine, lass, In mine, lass, in mine, lass; And
2. O lay thy loof in mine, lass, In mine, lass, in mine, lass; And

1. swear on thy white hand, lass, That thou wilt be my ain. A
2. swear on thy white hand, lass, That thou wilt be my ain. There's

* Burns wrote these verses for Johnson's *Scots' Museum* in 1794. It is adapted to the old tune "The Cordwainer's March," which, in former times, was usually played before that ancient fraternity, at their annual procession on St. Crispin's Day. The tune is preserved in the second volume of Aird's *Selection of Scots' Airs*, published circa 1784.

1. slave to Love's un-bound-ed sway, He aft has wrought me mei-kle wae; But
2. mo-nie a lass has broke my rest, That for a blink I ha'e lo'ed best; But

1. now he is my dead-lie fae, Un-less thou be my ain. O
2. thou art queen with-in my breast, For ev-er to re-main. O

1. lay thy loof in mine, lass, In mine, lass, in mine, lass; And
2. lay thy loof in mine, lass, In mine, lass, in mine, lass; And

*poco rit.* Last time.

1. swear on thy white hand, lass, That thou wilt be my ain.
2. swear on thy white hand, lass, That thou wilt be my ain.

# O, Logie O' Buchan.*

Moderato.

PIANO.

Verses by Geo. HALKET, died 1756.

mf
cres.
mf

1. O,
2. Tho'
3. My
4. I

1. Lo - gie o' Bu - chan, O, Lo - gie the laird, They hae
2. San - dy has ow - sen, has gear, and has kye, An' a
3. dad - die looks sul - ky, and min - nie looks sour, They
4. sit on my creep - ie and spin at my wheel, An'

cres.

1. ta'en a - wa' Jam - ie that delv'd in the yard. Wha'
2. house an' a had - den, an' sil - ler for - bye, Yet I'd
3. gloom up - on Jam - ie be - cause he is puir, Tho' I
4. think on the lad - die that lo'es me so weel; He

cres.

cres.

*Mr. Patrick Buchan's note to this song is the following: "This inimitable song belongs to the 'North Countrie.' The Author was George Halket, Schoolmaster, for some time, at Rathen, and the author of 'Whurry Whigs awa',' man,' with several other esteemed Jacobite songs. He was a Jacobite out and out, so much so, that when the Duke of Cumberland was in the North, he offered a reward of one hundred guineas for his head, either dead or alive—so much offence had the effusions of his muse given to the then reigning powers. The hero of the piece was James Robertson, gardener at Logie, parish of Crimond, Aberdeenshire."—(Garland of Scotia, 1841.)

1. play'd on the pipe an' the vi - ol sae sma'; They hae
2. tak' my ain lad wi' a staff in his hand, Be -
3. lo'e them as weel as a daugh - ter should do, They are
4. had but ne sax - pence, he brak it in twa, An' he

1. ta'en a - wa' Jam - ie, the flow'r o' them a'. He said,
2. fore I'd ha'e him wi' his hous - es and land. He said,
3. no half sae dear to me, Jam - ie, as you. He said,
4. gl'ed me the hauf o't when he gaed a - wa'. But the

1. "Think na lang, las - sie, tho' I gang a - wa', For
2. "Sim - mer is com - in', cauld win - ter's a - wa'; An'
3. "Think na lang, las - sie, tho' I gang a - wa, For
4. sim - mer is com - in', cauld win - ter's a - wa, Then

1. I'll come an' see thee in spite o' them a'!"
2. I'll come an' see thee in spite o' them a'!"
3. I'll come an' see thee in spite o' them a'!"
4. haste ye back, Jam - ie, an' bide na a - wa'!

# O Lord, I sing Thy praises.

## HYMN OF PRAISE.*

### (Lavidh Molaidh.)

Translated from the Gaelic by Lachlan MacBean.

1. O Lord, I sing Thy prais - es Who art my strength and
2. For Thou, Thy glory show - ing, Mad'st me Thy beau - ty

1. stay, My Lead - er thro' life's ma - zes, To bring me to Thy way Thou
2. see; Thy love has been be - stow - ing New life and joy on me. Thou

1. didst not leave me stray - ing When I a - far would go, With heed - less foot - steps
2. grace and glo - ry giv - est, Thou art a sun and shield, Thou on - ly ev - er

1. play - ing Up - on the brink of woe!
2. liv - est, Thy words sal - va - tion yield.

* From *Songs and Hymns of the Scottish Highlands*, 1888, by the kind permission of the Editor, Mr. L. MacBean. This fine melody was obtained in the Highlands by Mr. MacBean, and published by him for the first time.

# O, love will venture in.*

Verses by BURNS.

*Molto andante.*

PIANO.

*p molto espres.*

*poco rit.*

con Ped.

*p*

1. O, love will ven - ture in where it daur - na weel be seen; O,
2. The prim - rose I will pu', the first - lin' o' the year, And
3. I'll pu' the bud - ding rose - bush when Phœ - bus peeps in view, For it's
4. The li - ly it is pure, an' the li - ly it is fair, And
5. The haw - thorn I will pu', wi' its locks o' sil - ler grey, Where,
6. I'll tie the po - sie round wi' the silk - en cord o' love, An' I'll

*poco rit.*

1. love will ven-ture in where wisdom ance has been; But I will down yon riv - er rove, a -
2. I will pu' the pink, the em-blem o' my dear; For she's the pink o' wo-man - kind, an'
3. like a band - my kiss o' her sweet bonnie mou'; The hy - a-cinth's for con-stan - cy, wi'
4. in her love-ly bo-som, I'll place the li - ly there; The dai - sy's for sim-pli-ci - ty, of
5. like an a - ged man, it stands at break o' day; The song-ster's nest with - in the bush I
6. place it in her breast, and I'll swear by a' a-bove, That to my lat - est breath o' life the

*poco rit.*

*cres.* *rit.*

1. mang the woods sae green, An' a' to pu' a po - sie to my ain dear May.
2. blooms with-out a peer; An' a' to be a po - sie to my ain dear May.
3. it's un-chang-ing blue, An' a' to be a po - sie to my ain dear May.
4. un - af-fect-ed air, An' a' to be a po - sie to my ain dear May.
5. win - na take a - way; An' a' to be a po - sie to my ain dear May.
6. band shall ne'er re - move: An' a' to be a po - sie to my ain dear May.

*cres.* *rit.*

* The verses were composed by Burns in 1792. In a letter to George Thomson, Oct. 19, 1794, the Poet says, "The air was taken down from Mrs. Burns' voice. It is well known in the West country, but the old words are trash." The old verses are published in Cromek's *Reliques of Robert Burns,* 1808.

M 2

# O, Mary, at thy window be.

### MARY MORISON.*

Verses by Burns.  
Air: "The Miller."

*Andante.*

VOICE.

PIANO.

*p con espress.*     *poco rit.*     *f* *sf* *pp*    *ten.*

*p*

1. O, Ma - ry, at thy win - dow be; It is the wish'd, the
2. Yes - treen when to the stent - ed string, The dance gaed thro' the
3. O, Ma - ry, canst thou wreck his peace, Wha for thy sake wad

*cres.*

1. tryst - ed hour; Those smiles and glan - ces let me see, That
2. licht - ed ha', To thee my fan - cy took its wing;— I
3. glad - ly dee? Or canst thou breake that heart of his, Whase

*cres.*

* Burns wrote this little poem in 1782 to the tune "Bide ye yet." This set has, however, been entirely superseded by "The Miller," a tune infinitely more suited to the verses.

1. make the mi - ser's trea - sure poor. How blythe - ly wad I
2. sat but nei - ther heard nor saw. Tho' this was fair and
3. on - ly faut is lov - ing thee? If love for love thou

1. bide the stoure, A wea - ry slave frae sun to sun, Could
2. that was braw, And you the toast o' a' the town, I
3. wilt na gi'e, At least be pi - ty to me shown, A

1. I the rich re - ward se - cure, The love - ly Ma - ry
2. sigh'd and said a - mang them a', Ye are na Ma - ry
3. thocht un - gen - tle can - na be The thocht o' Ma - ry

1. Mor - i - son.
2. Mor - i - son.
3. Mor - i - son.

poco rit.

# O mirk, mirk is the midnight hour.

### LORD GREGORY.*

Verses by BURNS.

Ancient Galloway Song.

1. O mirk, mirk is . . the mid - night hour, An'
2. O hard is thy heart, . Lord Gre - go - ry, An'

1. loud the tem - pest's roar; . . . . . A wae - fu'
2. flin - ty is thy breast; . . . . . Thou dart of

1. wan - d'rer seeks thy tow'r, Lord Gre - go - ry, ope thy
2. heav'n that flash - est by, O, wilt thou gi'e me

* Burns wrote this poem in 1793, and sent it to George Thomson for his *Collection of Original Scottish Airs*, vol. i., p. 38. The subject is founded on an old traditionary ballad called "The Lass o' Lochroyan." The air was first published in Pietro Urbani's *Selection of Scots Songs*, commenced circa 1792.

1. door! . . . . . . . . . . An ex - - ile frae her
2. rest? . . . . . . . . . . Ye must - - 'ring thun - ders
1. fa - - ther's ha', An' a' for lov - ing
2. from a - bove, Your will ing vic - tim
1. thee; At least some pi - - ty on me
2. see! But spare an' par - don my fause
1. shaw, If love it may na be! . . . . . . . . .
2. love, His wrangs to heav'n and me! . . . . . . . . .
p
sf
Ped.
sempre Ped.
f
cres.
dim. e rit.

# O, Mary, ye's be clad in silk.*

**Adagio con molto espressione.**

VOICE.

1. O, Ma-ry, ye's be clad in silk, And
2. For I have pledg'd my so-lemn troth Brave

PIANO.

1. dia-monds in your hair, Giu ye con-sent to be my bride, Nor
2. Ar-thur's fate to share, Au' he has giv'n to me his heart Wi'

1. think on Ar-thur mair. Oh, wha wad wear a silk-en gown, Wi' tears blind-ing their e'e, Be-
2. a' its vir-tues rare. The lang-est life can ne'er re-pay The love he bears to me; And

1. fore I'll break my true love's heart, I'll lay me down and dee.
2. e'er I'm forc'd to break my troth, I'll lay me down and dee.

* From Urbani's *Selection of Scots Songs, circa* 1792. These verses are a slightly altered version of the old song, "The Siller Crown." The air was composed by Miss Grace Corbett, of Edinburgh, when she was only eleven years old. Both the words and melody were copied into Johnson's *Museum,* vol. vi., song 585.

## O puirtith cauld.*

Verses by BURNS.
*Moderato.*

Air: "I had a horse."

VOICE.

PIANO.

1. O    puir - tith cauld and    rest - less love! Ye
2. This   warld's wealth when   I think ou't   Its
3. Her    e'en sae bon - nie    blue be - tray  How
4. O     wha can pru - dence think up - on,  Au'
5. How   blest the hum - ble   cot - tar's fate!  He

1. wreck my peace be - tween ye;    Yet   puir - tith a' .  I    could for - gi'e,  An' 'twere na for  my
2. pride, an' a' the lave o't;      Fie,  fie on sil - ly   cow - ard man, That he should be  the
3. she re - pays my pas - sion;     But   pru - dence is her  ower - word aye, She talks o' rank and
4. sic a las - sie by him?          O    wha can pru - dence think up - on,  Au'  sae in love as
5. woos his sim - ple dear - ie;    The   sil - ly bo - gle's wealth and state Can ne - ver make them

1. Jean - ie.
2. slave o't!
3. fash - ion.
4. I am?
5. eer - ie.

O   why should fate   sic   pleasure have, Life's dear - est bands un - twin - ing?   Or

why sae sweet a    flow'r as love De - pend on For - tune's shin - ing?

* The old comic verses, "I had a horse, and I had nae mair," appear in Herd's *Scots Songs*, vol. ii., 1776, under the title of "The Surprise." The air was published for the first time in Johnson's *Museum*, vol. ii. It is evidently the original tune to the song. Burns wrote his poem "O puirtith cauld" in 1793, for Thomson's Collection, where it appears, vol. i. p. 47. In a note to the song, Thomson remarks that "the heroine of this song was Miss Jean Blackstock."

# O, my love is like a red, red rose.*

*Andante con espressione.*

VOICE.

PIANO.

*p*

*poco rit.*

*p*

1. O, my love is like a red, red rose, That's new - ly sprung in June; O, my
2. Till a' the seas gang dry, my dear, And rocks melt wi' the sun, And

1. love is like a mel - o - die, That's sweet - ly play'd in tune. As
2. I will love thee still, my dear, While sands o' life shall run. But

* This is an old song, altered and extended for *The Scots' Museum* by Burns. Johnson gives two airs, neither of which is now sung to Burns' verses: the one invariably used is the one adopted here. It is a modern version of " Low down in the Broom," an old tune which seems to have been first published by Oswald, in his *Caledonian Pocket Companion,* under the title of " My love's in the Broom."

1. fair thou art, my bon - nie lass, Sae deep iu love am I; And
2. fare thee weel, my ou - ly love, And fare thee weel a - while, And

*poco rit.*     *a tempo.*

1. I will love thee still, my dear, Till a' the seas gang dry; Till
2. I will come a - gain, my love, Tho' 'twere ten thou - sand mile; Tho'

*poco rit.*

1. a' the seas gang dry, my dear, Till a' the seas gang dry, And
2. 'twere ten thou - sand mile, my love, Tho' 'twere ten thou - sand mile, And

*p a tempo.*

1. I will love thee still, my dear, Till a' the seas gang dry.
2. I will come a - gain, my love, Tho' 'twere ten thou - sand mile.

# O this is no my ain lassic.*

Air: "This is no my ain house."

*Con spirito.*

VOICE.

PIANO.

1. O this is no my ain las - sie, Fair tho' the las - sie be; O
2. O this is no my ain las - sie, Fair tho' the las - sie be; O
3. O this is no my ain las - sie, Fair tho' the las - sie be; O
4. O this is no my ain las - sie, Fair tho' the las - sie be; O

1. weel ken I my ain las - sie, Kind love is in her e'e. I
2. weel ken I my ain las - sie, Kind love is in her e'e. She's
3. weel ken I my ain las - sie, Kind love is in her e'e. A
4. weel ken I my ain las - sie, Kind love is in her e'e. It

* The old song of " This is no my ain house" was written by Ramsay prior to 1724. It is based upon a much older song beginning :—

O this is no my ain house.
My ain house, my ain house;
O this is no my ain house,
I ken by the biggin o't.
For bread and cheese are my door cheeks, etc.

(*See* Stenhouse's Illustrations, p. 206.) The air with its title appears in the Crockat MS. Music Book, 1709, and in Oswald's *Pocket Companion*, Bk. vii., commenced *circa* 1759. It is introduced into Aird's *Selection of Scotch Airs*, Bk. ii., 1782, and in *Calliope; or, The Vocal Enchantress*, 1788, it is given with verses beginning, " When the men a-courting came." Hogg also gives it in his *Jacobite Relics*, Ser. I., 1816, to Jacobitical verses which retain a portion of the old chorus. Burns wrote "O this is no my ain lassie" in July, 1795, for George Thomson's *Collection of Scottish Airs*, vol. ii.

1. see a form, I see a face. Ye weel may wi' the fair-est place, It
2. bon-nie bloom-in', straight, an' tall, An' lang has had my heart in thrall; An'
3. thief sae paw-ky, is my Jean, She'll steal a blink by a' un-seen, But
4. may es-cape the court-ly sparks, It may es-cape the learn- èd clerks; But

1. wants to me the witch-in' grace, The kind love that's in her e'e.
2. aye it charms my ve-ry saul, The kind love that's in her e'e.
3. gleg as light are lov-er's e'en, When kind love is in the e'e.
4. weel the watch-in' lov-er marks The kind love that's in her e'e.

O

this is no my ain las-sie, Fair tho' the las-sie be; O weel ken I my

*Last time.*

ain las-sie, Kind love is in her e'e.

# O, Sandy, why leaves thou thy Nelly?

## THRO' THE WOOD, LADDIE.*

ALLAN RAMSAY.

1. O, San - dy, why leaves thou thy Nel - ly to mourn? Thy pre - sence can ease me When nae - thing could please me; Now, dow - ie, I sigh on the banks of the burn, Or thro' the wood, lad - die, un - til thou re - turn.

2. The woods are now bon - nie, and morn - ings are clear, While lav' - rocks are sing - ing, And prim - ro - ses spring - ing; Yet none o' them pleas - es my eye or my ear, When thro' the wood, lad - die, ye din - na ap - pear.

3. Then stay, my dear San - dy, nae lang - er a - way, But quick as an ar - row Haste here to thy mar - row Wha's liv - ing in lan - gour till that hap - py day, When thro' the wood, lad - die, we'll dance, sing, and play.

---

\* This air occurs in Thomson's *Orpheus Caledonius*, 1725, to verses by Ramsay, beginning, "As early I walk'd on the first of sweet May"; McGibbon also included it in vol. ii. of his *Collection of Scots Tunes*, 1746. The song given above is published in the *Tea-Table Miscellany*, 1724. Dr. Blacklock supplied Johnson with what he considered to be the original verses to "Thro' the wood, Laddie;" they are given in vol. ii. of the *Museum*, Song 154.

# O waly, waly, up the bank.*

Moderato.

VOICE.

PIANO.

1. O  wa - ly, wa - ly,  up the bank, And wa - ly, wa - ly,  down the brae, And
2. O  wa - ly, wa - ly,  love be bon - nie Just a wee time while it's new; But
3. Now Ar - thur's seat shall  be my bed, The sheets shall ne'er be press'd by me; St.

1. wa - ly, wa - ly,  yon burn-side, Where I and my love wont to gae!  I lean'd my back  un -
2. when it's auld it  wax - es cauld, And fades a - way like morning dew.  O where-fore should I
3. An - ton's well shall  be my drink, Since my true love's for - sak - en me.  O, Mart'-mas wind, when

poco rit.

1. to an aik,  I thocht it was a  trust - y tree; But first it bow'd,  an' syne it brak',  Sae
2. busk my head,  Or where-fore should I  kame my hair? For my true love  has me for-sook,  An'
3. wilt thou blaw  An' shake the green leaves  aff the tree? O, gen - tle death,  when wilt thou come? For

1. my true love  did light - ly me.
2. says he'll nev - er  love me mair.
3. o' my life  I'm wea - rie.

p

sf ritard.

* This air is undoubtedly very ancient; Thomson has printed it in the first edition of the *Orpheus Caledonius*, issued in 1725. The entire ballad is given in the *Tea-Table Miscellany*, pt. ii. The song, "Adieu! adieu! all hope of bliss," in Gay's Opera *Polly*, 1729, is marked to be sung to the air "O waly, waly, up the bank." In Johnson's *Museum Illustrations*, p. 147, Stenhouse gives some interesting information regarding the age of the old verses. He concludes by saying, "There can be no doubt that this song is at least coeval with the reign of Mary, Queen of Scots, if not earlier." A curious version of both words and air is to be found in Christie's *Traditional Ballad Airs*, 1871, vol. ii., p. 158, under the title of "The Marchioness of Douglas."

# O weel may the boatie row.*

Allegretto ma non troppo.

VOICE.

PIANO.

*p*

*p*

*p*

1. O weel may the boat - ie row, And bet - ter may she
2. I cuist my lines in Lar - go Bay, And fish - es I got
3. O weel may the boat - ie row, That fills a hea - vy
4. When Saw - nie, Jock, and Ja - ne - tie Are up, and got - ten

*p*

1. speed! And weel may the boat - ie row That wins the bairns'
2. nine; There's three to boil, and three to fry, And three to bait the
3. creel, And cleads us a' frae head to feet And buys our par - ritch
4. lear, They'll help to gar the boat - ie row, And light - en a' our

* Robert Burns stated that "the author of this song, beginning 'O weel may the boatie row,' was a Mr. Ewen, of Aberdeen." It appears in Johnson's *Scots' Musical Museum*, vol. v., published about 1796. Since then, in almost all collections, the poem has been attributed to Mr. John Ewen, who was born in 1741, and died in 1821. In Mitchison's *Garland of Scotia*, 1841, we find the following note by Patrick Buchan: "This song has been erroneously ascribed to a Mr. Ewen, of Aberdeen, by many who should have known better; it was written at least a hundred years before honest John drew breath, and was called 'The Fisher's Rant of Fittie' (Foot Dea). The old song, or rather ballad, contains twice the number of verses as the present one, which was abridged by the late Mr. John Ewen, jeweller, for the purpose of being sung by a Mr. Wilson in the theatre of Aberdeen, where it became so popular, as to be published by James Chalmers in one of the Aberdeen papers."

1. bread!    The   boat - ie   rows,   the    boat - ie   rows,   The
2. line.    The   boat - ie   rows,   the    boat - ie   rows,   The
3. meal.    The   boat - ie   rows,   the    boat - ie   rows,   The
4. care.    The   boat - ie   rows,   the    boat - ie   rows,   The

1. boat - ie   rows   in - deed;     And   hap - py   be   the
2. boat - ie   rows   fu'   weel;     And   muc - kle   light - er
3. boat - ie   rows   in - deed;     And   hap - py   be   the
4. boat - ie   rows   fu'   weel;     And   light - some   be   her

1. lot   of   a'   That   wish - es   her   to   speed.
2. is   the   lade,   When   love   bears   up   the   creel.
3. lot   of   a'   That   wish   the   boat - ie   speed.
4. heart   that bears   The   mur - lain   and   the   creel!·

# O, wha's at the window, wha, wha?*

Verses by ALEXANDER CARLILE.

*Moderato.*

PIANO.

1. O, wha's at the win-dow, wha, wha? O wha's at the win-dow, wha, wha? Wha but
2. He's plight-ed his troth and a', and' a', Leal love to gi'e, and a', and a'; And

1. blythe Jamie Glen, He's come sax mile and ten, To tak' bon-nie Jeanie a-wa', a-wa', To
2. sae has she dune, By a' that's a-bune, For he lo'es her, she lo'es him, 'bune a', 'bune a', He

1. tak' bon-nie Jean-ie a-wa'. . . .
2. lo'es her, she lo'es him, 'bune a'. . . .

* This air is the composition of R. A. Smith, who was born at Reading in 1780. In 1823 he obtained the leadership of the psalmody at St. George's Church, Edinburgh. From 1820 to 1824 he published *The Scottish Minstrel* (6 vols.), a work containing several hundreds of the best Scottish songs. He died in 1829. In a letter to George Farquhar Graham, Carlile explains that the song, "O wha's at the window, wha, wha?" is modern, and written by himself, with the exception of the first line. This line belongs to an old nursery song, which Carlile remembered hearing his brother sing during his childhood. (See Wood's *Songs of Scotland.*) Allan Cunningham picked up Carlile's verses as a genuine antique, and published them in his notes to his Scottish Songs. The following is the first verse of a song printed in a work entitled *Ane Compendious Buik of Godlie Psalmes and Spirituall Sangis.* This volume is said to have been principally the work of three brothers, James, John, and Robert Wedderburn, of Dundee, who flourished about the middle of the sixteenth century. Unfortunately, very little is known of their lives, except the fact that they were staunch supporters of the Reformation.

O vho is at my windo'? quho, quho?
Go from my windo, go, go!
Quho callis thair so lyke a strangair,
Go from my windo, go, go!

3. There's mirth on the green, in the ha', the ha', There's mirth on the green, in the
4. It's no that she's Ja - mie's, a - va, a - va, It's no that she's Ja - mie's, a -

*p*  >

*cres.*

3. ha', the ha', There's laugh-ing, there's quaff-ing, There's jest - ing, there's daff - ing, And the
4. va, a - va, That my heart is sae eer - ie, When a' the lave's cheer-ie, But it's

*cres.*

3. fai - ther's the blyth-est of a', of a', And the fai - ther's the blyth - est of
4. just that she'll aye be a - wa', a - wa', It's just that she'll aye be a -

>

3. a'. . . . .
4. wa'. . . . .

*mf*

N 2

# O whistle, an' I'll come to you, my lad.*

*Con spirito.*

Air: "Whistle, and I'll come to ye."

VOICE.

PIANO.

*mf*      *p*

*mf*

1. O whis-tle, an' I'll come to you, my lad, O whis-tle, an' I'll come
2. O whis-tle, au' I'll come to you, my lad, O whis-tle, an' I'll come
3. O whis-tle, an' I'll come to you, my lad, O whis-tle, an' I'll come

*mf*

1. to you, my lad; Tho' fa-ther an' mo-ther an' a' should gae mad, O
2. to you, my lad; Tho' fa-ther an' mo-ther an' a' should gae mad, O
3. to you, my lad; Tho' fa-ther an' mo-ther an' a' should gae mad, O

* Burns wrote these verses for George Thomson's *Collection of Original Scottish Airs*; they appear in vol. ii., p. 94, issued in 1799. According to Stenhouse, the air was composed by John Bruce, a fiddle-player in Dumfries, about the beginning of last century. Shield introduced it in his comic opera, *The Poor Soldier*, produced at Covent Garden, 1783. The character, "Kathleen," sings verses to it commencing :—

"Since love is the plan
I'll love if I can,
But first let me tell you what sort of a man."

1. whis - tle, an' I'll come to you, my lad. But wa - ri - ly tent when you
2. whis - tle, an' I'll come to you, my lad, At kirk, or at mar - ket, where-
3. whis - tle, au' I'll come to you, my lad, Ay vow an' pro - test that ye

1. come to court me, An' come na un - less the back - yett be a - jee; Syne
2. e'er ye meet me, Gang by me as tho' that ye cared na a flie; But
3. care na for me, An' whiles ye may light - lie my beau - ty a wee; But

1. up the back - stile, an' let nae - bo - dy see, An' come as ye were na
2. steal me a blink o' your bon - nie black e'e, Yet look as ye were na
3. court nae a - ni - ther, tho' jo - kin' ye be, For fear that she wyle your

1. com - in' to me, An' come as ye were na com - in' to me.
2. look - in' at me, Yet look as ye were na look - in' at me.
3. fan - cy frae me, For fear that she wyle your fan - cy frae me.

# O where, tell me where.

## THE BLUE BELLS OF SCOTLAND.*

1. "O where, tell me where, is your High-land lad-die gone? O where, tell me where, is your High-land lad-die gone?" "He's gone wi' stream-ing ban - ners, where no - ble deeds are done; And it's oh! in my heart I . . . wish him safe at home."

2. "O what, las-sie, what does your High-land lad-die wear? O what, las-sie, what does your High-land lad-die wear?" "A scar - let coat and bon - net wi' bon - nie yel - low hair, And there's nane in the world can . . wi' my love com - pare."

3. "O what will you claim for your con-stan-cy to him? O what will you claim for your con-stan-cy to him?" "I'll claim a priest to wed us, and a clerk to say, 'A - men!' And I'll ne'er part a - gain from my bon - nie High-land - man."

---

\* These stanzas are from Johnson's *Museum*, vol. vi., No. 548 (1803); they are there set to an air now never sung. The popular, and seemingly modern, melody which we have adopted, seems to have been first printed by George Thomson in vol. iii., p. 135, of his *Collection of Original Scotish Airs*, 1801. In the latter Collection, the verses are marked as being "written for this work on the Marquis of Huntly's departure for the Continent with his regiment, in 1799, by Mrs. Grant." But Mrs. Grant's poem is merely an adaptation of the original old song given above.

# O, Willie's fair, and Willie's rare.*

*Andante espressivo, e maestoso.*

VOICE.

PIANO.

*mf*

1. O, Wil-lie's fair, and
2. Yes-treen I made my
3. Ye south-lan' winds, blaw
4. O! cam' ye by yon
5. She sought him east, she

*mf*  *poco rit. dim.*  *mf*

1. Wil-lie's rare, And Wil-lie's won-d'rous bon-nie; And Wil-lie hecht to
2. bed fu' braid, The night I'll mak' it nar-row; For a' the live-long
3. to the north, From where my love re-pair-eth; Con-vey a kiss frae
4. wa-ter-side? Pu'd ye the rose or lil-lie? Or cam' ye by yon
5. sought him west, She sought the braid and nar-row; Syne, in the clear-in'

*p*  *cres.*  *rit.*

1. mar-ry me, Gin e'er he mar-ried on-y, Gin e'er he mar-ried on-y.
2. win-ter night, I lie and dream of Yar-row, I lie and dream of Yar-row.
3. his dear mouth, And tell me how he far-eth, And tell me how he far-eth.
4. mea-dow green? Or saw ye my sweet Wil-lie? Or saw ye my sweet Wil-lie?
5. o' a craig, She found him droun'd in Yar-row, She found him droun'd in Yar-row.

*p*  *cres.*  *rit.*  *a tempo.*

Ped.

Last time.

*f*  *rit.*  *dim.*  *pp*

Ped.

* Verses 1, 2, 4 and 5 of this ancient ballad and its air appear in the *Orpheus Caledonius*, 1733, vol. ii., p. 110, and again in the *Tea-Table Miscellany*, Bk. ii., pt. iii. Verse 3 is from a version of the ballad rescued some years later.

# O, Willie brew'd a peck o' maut.*

Verses by BURNS.

1. O, Willie brew'd a peck o' maut, And Rob and Allan cam' to prie; Three blyther lads, that lee-lang night, Ye

2. Here are we met, three merry boys, Three merry boys, I trow, are we; And mony a nicht we've merry been, And

3. It is the moon—I ken her horn—That's blink-in' in the lift sae hie; She shines sae bright to wyle us hame, But!

4. Wha first shall rise to gang a-wa', A cuck-old, cow-ard loon is he! Wha last be-side his chair shall fa', He

* Of the origin of this song, Burns writes: "The air is Allan Masterton's, the song is mine. The occasion of it was this—Mr. William Nicol, of the High School, Edinburgh, being at Moffat during the Autumn vacation, honest Allan—who was at that time on a visit to Dalswinton—and I went to pay Nicol a visit. We had such a joyous meeting that Masterton and I agreed, each in our own way, that we should celebrate the business." Masterton's air appeared in the *Scots' Museum*, vol. iii., No. 291, issued 1790, but that set has been long since superseded by the one we give here. It is an improved version of Masterton's melody by some unknown hand. Masterton died about the end of last century.

1. wad - na found in Christ - en - die.
2. mon - y mae we hope to be!
3. by my sooth, she'll wait a wee!
4. is the king a - mang us three!

We are na fou', we're nae that fou', But just a wee drap in our e'e; The cock may craw, the day may daw', But aye we'll taste the bar - ley bree.

# O, Willie was a wanton wag.*

**Allegretto.**

VOICE.

1. O, Wil-lie was a wan-ton wag, The
2. He was a man with-out a clag; His
3. An' was not Wil-lie weel worth gowd? He

PIANO.

*mf*     *mf*

1. blith-est lad that e'er I saw; At bri-dals still he bore the brag, And car-ried aye the gree a - wa'. His
2. heart was frank without a flaw; And aye what-ev-er Wil-lie said, It still was had-den as a law. His
3. wan the love o' grate an'sma'; For af - ter he the bride had kiss'd, He kiss'd the lass-es haill-sale a'. Sae

*cres.*

1. doub-let was of Zet - land shag, And wow! but Wil - lie he was braw; An' at his shou-thers
2. boots they were made o' jag, When he went to the Weapon-shaw; Up - on the green nane
3. mer-r'ly round the ring they row'd When by the hand he led them a'; And kiss on kiss on

*cres.*

**Last time.**

1. hung a tag, That pleased the lass - es best of a'.
2. durst him brag, The fiend a ane a - mang them a'.
3. them be-stow'd, By vir - tue o' a stand - ing law.

*mf*

---

* These clever verses appeared in the *Tea-Table Miscellany*, pt. ii., *circa* 1725, signed with the initials "W. W." The air with the words was published in Thomson's *Orpheus Caledonius*, vol. ii., 1733. Mr. Chambers remarks of this song that "As a picture of health-enjoying youth, and high animal spirits, it is unsurpassed." The complete song is comprised of six verses. The initials in the *Tea-Table Miscellany* are said to denote William Walkingshaw, of Walkingshaw, in Renfrewshire, who lived about the latter end of the 17th century. In Johnson's *Scots Musical Museum*, "by Mr. Walkingshaw" was inserted on the authority of Burns. It appears, however, that there was no William in the family. David Laing considers that "W. W." means Wanton Willie, a sobriquet of Willie Hamilton, of Gilbertfield, a friend and correspondent of Allan Ramsay.

# On Ettrick banks.*

*Allegretto pastorale.*

1. On Et-trick banks ae
2. I said, my las - sie,
3. All day, when we ha'e
4. Syne, when the trees are

1. sim-mer's nicht, At gloam-in', when the sheep drove hame, I met my las-sie, braw and ticht, Came
2. will ye go' To the Highland hills, the Erse to learn? I'll baith gi'e thee a cow and ewe, When
3. wrought e-neuch, When win-ter frosts and snaws be-gin, Sune as the sun gaes west the loch, At
4. in their bloom, And gow-ans glent o'er il-ka field, I'll meet my lass a-mang the broom, And

1. wad-ing bare-foot a' her lane; My heart grew licht, I ran, I flung My arms a-bout her
2. ye come to the Brigg o' Earn. At Leith auld meal comes in, ne'er fash, And her-ring at the
3. nicht, when we sit doun to spin, I'll screw my pipes, and play a spring, And thus the wea-ry
4. lead her to my sim-mer shield, Then, far frae a' their scorn-fu' din, That make the kind-ly

1. lil-y neck, And kiss'd, and clasp'd her there fu' lang; My words they were na mon-y feck.
2. Broom-y Law; Cheer up your heart, my bon-nie lass, There's gear to win we nev-er saw.
3. nicht we'll end, Till the ten-der kid and lamb-time bring Our pleas-ant sim-mer back a-gain.
4. hearts their sport, We'll laugh and kiss, and dance and sing, And gar the long-est day seem short.

---

\* The first three verses of this beautiful song, with the pastoral melody, were inserted in Thomson's *Orpheus Caledonius*, vol. ii., 1733. Both proba-ly belong to a much earlier period, although their history cannot be traced. Verse 4 is from Ramsay's version of the song, printed in the *Tea-Table Miscellany*, pt. iv. The Ettrick is a river in Selkirkshire; it rises in the parish of the same name and after a winding course of some thirty miles, falls into the Tweed about three miles above Melrose.

# One day I heard Mary say.

## I'LL NEVER LEAVE THEE.*

Robert Crawfurd.

1. One day I heard Mary say, "How shall I leave thee? Stay, dearest Willie, stay; why wilt thou leave me? Ah! my fond heart will break, if thou should leave me; I'll live and die for thy sake, yet never leave thee!"

2. "Say, my own Mary, say, Has Willie deceiv'd thee? Did e'er her young heart betray, new love that has griev'd thee? O, my love ne'er shall stray, thou may believe me! I'll love thee, lad, night and day, and never leave thee!"

3. "Ah! leave thee, lad, How shall I leave thee? How that thought makes me sad! I'll never leave thee! Where would my Willie fly? why would he grieve me? Alas, my heart will die, if I should leave thee!"

* These verses were printed in the *Tea-Table Miscellany*, 1724, and, with the air, in the *Orpheus Caledonius*, 1733 (vol. ii., p. 2*). The melody is very old, and Sibbald (Chronicle of Scottish Poetry) considers it to have been the air to one of Wedderburn's Spiritual Ballads, about the year 1549. Wedderburn's work was printed in 1590 by Andro Hart, of Edinburgh, under the title of *Ane Compendious Booke of Godly and Spirituall Songs, collectit out of sundrie partes of the Scripture, with sundrie of other Ballates changed out of Prophaine Sanges*, etc. ; another edition was published in 1621, and in 1801 Sir John Graham Dalyell included the entire work in his volume of *Scotish Poems of the Sixteenth Century* (Edinburgh, Arch. Constable).

# Pibroch of Donuil Dhu.*

Verses by Sir WALTER SCOTT.

Air: "Piobaireach Donuil Duibh."

Con fuoco.

1. Pi - broch of Don - uil Dhu, Pi - broch of Don - uil, Wake thy wild voice a - new, summon Clan Co - nuil;
2. Come from the deep glen and moun-tain so rock - y, War-pipe and pen - non are at In - ver - lo - chy;
3. Leave un-at - tend - ed the flock with-out shel - ter, Leave the corpse un - interr'd, bride at the al - tar;
4. Come as the winds come when for - ests are rend - ed; Come as the waves come when na-vies are strand - ed;
5. Fast they come, fast they come, see how they gath - er! Wild waves the ea - gle plume, blended with heath - er!

1. Come a - way, come a - way, hark to the sum - mons, Come in your war ar - ray, gen - tles and com - mons!
2. Come, ev - 'ry hill-plaid, and true heart that wears one, Come, ev - 'ry steel blade, and strong arm that bears one!
3. Leave the deer, leave the steer, leave nets and bar - ges, Come with your fighting gear, broadsword, and tar - ges!
4. Fas - ter come, fas - ter come, fas - ter and fas - ter, Chief, vas-sal, page and groom, ten - ant and mas - ter!
5. Cast your plaids, draw your blades, forward each man set! Pi - broch o' Don - uil Dhu, knell for the on - set!

CHORUS.

1. Come a - way, come a - way, hark to the summons, Come in your war ar - ray, gen - tles and com - mons!
2. Come, ev - 'ry hill-plaid, and true heart that wears one, Come, ev - ry steel blade, and strong arm that bears one!
3. Leave the deer, leave the steer, leave nets and bar - ges, Come with your fighting gear, broadswords, and tar - ges!
4. Fas - ter come, fas - ter come, fas - ter and fas - ter, Chief, vas-sal, page and groom, ten-ant and mas - ter!
5. Cast your plaids, draw your blades, forward each man set! Pi - broch o' Don - uil Dhu, knell for the on - set!

* These verses were first published in *Albyn's Anthology*, vol. i., p. 89.   The tune was formerly known by the title of "Lochiel's March."

# Put off, and row wi' speed.[*]

Verses by ROBERT ALLAN.

Highland Boat Air.

1. Put off, put off, and row wi' speed, For now is the time and the hour of need; To oars, to oars, and trim the bark, Nor Scotland's Queen be a warder's mark! Yon light that plays round the cas-tle's mot Is on-ly the war-der's ran-dom shot; Put off, put off, and row wi' speed, For now is the time an' the hour o' need!

2. These pond'rous keys shall the Kel-pies keep And lodge in their ca-verns dark and deep; Nor shall Loch Lev-en's tow-ers or hall Hold thee, our love-ly Queen, in thrall; Or be the haunt of trai-tors, sold, While Scotland has hands and hearts so bold; Then steersman, steersman, on wi' speed, For now is the time an' the hour o' need!

3. Hark, hark! the a-lar-um bell hath rung, The war-der's voice hath trea-son sung! The e-choes to the fal-con-ets' roar, Chime sweet-ly to the dash-ing oar; Let tow-er, and hall, and battlements gleam, We steer by the light of the ta-per's beam; For Scotland and Ma-ry on wi' speed, For now is the time an' the hour o' need!

# Red, red is the path to glory!

## JOY OF MY HEART.*

Verses by Dr. Robert Couper, of Fochabers.

Air: "'Stu mo run."

Lento molto, ed espressivo.

1. Red, red is the path to glo-ry!
2. Turn, and see thy tar-tan plai-die

1. Thick you ban-ners meet the sky! O my Geor-die, death's be-fore ye!
2. Ris-ing o'er my break-ing heart! O my bon-nie Hie-land lad-die!

1. Turn and hear my bod-ing cry,
2. Wae was me, wi' thee to part! } Joy of my heart, Geor-die, A-gain,

joy of my heart, 'Stu mo Run!

* This song, with its melody, appears in Albyn's Anthology, vol. ii., 1818. In Smith's Scottish Minstrel we find that "Lady G. Gordon picked up this beautiful air in the Highlands. The verses were written by Dr. Couper, at her desire, on the Marquis of Huntly when in Holland." The complete poem consists of five verses. Robert Couper was born at Balsier, parish of Sorbir, Wigtonshire, in 1750. He resided some years in Virginia, America, but owing to the breaking out of the War of Independence, he returned to this country in 1776. He took his diploma as a surgeon in the College of Glasgow, and settled in Fochabers as Physician to the Duke of Gordon in 1788. He left Fochabers in 1806, and died in Wigton in 1818. He was M.D. and F.R.S.E.

192

## Roy's wife of Aldivalloch.*

Verses by Mrs. GRANT, of Carron, 1745–1814.

Air: "The Ruffian's Rant."

*Allegretto.*

Roy's wife of Al-di-val-loch, Roy's wife of Al-di-val-loch,

Wat ye how she cheat-ed me, As I cam' owre the braes o' Bal-loch?

* To this tune Burns also wrote a song, beginning, "Canst thou leave me thus, my Katy," but popular taste decided in favour of Mrs. Grant's verses, which have always held their ground. The air is Highland and probably very old. It appears in Bremner's *Collection of Scots Reels or Country Dances* (commenced 1757), and later, in Aird's *Selection of Scotch Airs* (1782), under the title of "The Ruffian's Rant."

1. She vow'd, she swore she wad be mine; She said she lo'ed me best of on-ie; But
2. But O, she was a can-ty quean Weel could she dance the High-land wal-loch; How
3. Her hair sae fair, her een sae clear, Her wee bit mou' sae sweet and bon-nie; To

1. O, the fic-kle, faith-less quean, She's ta'en the carle an' left her John-nie!
2. hap-py I, had she been mine, Or I been Roy of Al-di-val-loch!
3. me she ev-er will be dear, Tho' she's for ev-er left her John-nie!

Roy's wife of Al-di-val-loch, Roy's wife of Al-di-val-loch,

Da capo dal S.

Wat ye how she cheat-ed me, As I cam' owre the braes o' Bal-loch?

o

# Sad am I, and sorrow laden.

**FAREWELL!*** 

(SOIRIDH!)

*Lento sostenuto.*

VOICE.

PIANO.

1. Sad am I, and sor-row-
2. Ben of peaks the clouds that
3. Moun-tain bold! thy form sur-

1. la-den, For the maid I love so well; I a-dore thee, dear-est maid-en, But my
2. sev-er, Oft thy steeps have wea-ried me; Must I leave thy shade for ev-er? Then fare-
3. pass-es Ev'-ry ben that eye can see; Long may deer fre-quent thy pass-es, Near thee

1. thoughts I dare not tell. Why de-ny my heart is rend-ing For the fair one of the
2. well, fare-well to thee! Ev-'ry cor-rie, crag, and hol-low, Heath'-ry brae and flow'-ry
3. I would ev-er be. Sad am I, and sor-row-la-den, For the maid I love so

1. lea; Af-ter all my care-ful tend-ing She has now for-sak-en me.
2. dell, Now a-wak-en pangs of sor-row; But my thoughts I dare not tell.
3. well; I a-dore thee, dear-est mai-den, But my thoughts I dare not tell.

* By kind permission, from the *Celtic Lyre*. This is an old Hebridean air. The words were composed by a young Gael, from the Island of Jura, Argyllshire, when about to leave his native isle.

# Scots, wha ha'e wi' Wallace bled!*

Verses by BURNS.

*Maestoso.*

Air: "Hey, tutti tattie."

PIANO. *mf*

*mf*

1. Scots, wha ha'e wi' Wal - lace bled! Scots, wha Bruce has af - ten led!
2. Wha will be a trai - tor knave? Wha can fill a cow - ard's grave?
3. By op - pres - sion's woes and pains! By our sons in ser - vile chains!

*sf* *rit.* *dim.* *mf* *a tempo.*

1. Welcome to your go - ry bed, Or to vic - to - ry! Now's the day, an' now's the hour;
2. Wha sae base as be a slave? Let him turn and flee! Wha for Scotland's king and law,
3. We will drain our dear - est veins, But they shall be free! Lay the proud us - urp - ers low!

*ff*

*ff*

*poco rit.* *rit.*

1. See the front of bat - tle lour! See approach proud Edward's pow'r, Chains an' sla - ve - rie!
2. Free - dom's sword will strong - ly draw, Freeman stand, or free - man fa', Let him fol - low me!
3. Ty - rants fall in ev - 'ry foe! Li - ber - ty's in ev - 'ry blow! Let us do, or die!

*poco rit.* *rit. sf*

* Burns wrote these celebrated verses on 1st August, 1793. In a letter to George Thomson, the poet writes: "There is a tradition which I have met with in many places of Scotland, that it ('Hey, tutti tatti') was Robert Bruce's march at the Battle of Bannockburn." Little importance can be attached to a tradition of this description. In the earlier part of last century the air was sung to Jacobite verses, beginning, "Here's to the King, Sirs." It was to "Hey, tutti tatti" song slowly, that Lady Nairne wrote her beautiful song, "The Land o' the Leal." (See p. 85.) M'Gibbon prints the air in his *Scots Tunes*, Bk. III., 1755, as "Hey Tuti tatety."

o 2

# "Saw ye Johnnie comin'?" quo' she.*

*Andantino.*

VOICE.

1. "Saw ye John-nie com-in'?" quo' she,
2. "Fee him, fa-ther, fee him," quo' she,
3. "For weel do I lo'e him," quo' she,

PIANO.

1. "Saw ye John-nie com-in'? Saw ye John-nie comin'?" quo'she, "Saw ye John-nie com-in'?
2. "Fee him, fa-ther, fee him; Fee him, fa-ther, fee him," quo'she, "Fee him, fa-ther, fee him;
3. "For weel do I lo'e him; For weel do I lo'e him," quo'she, "For weel do I lo'e him;

1. Saw ye Johnnie comin'?" quo' she, "Saw ye Johnnie com-in' Wi' his blue bon-net on his head,
2. For he is a gal-lant lad-die, And a well-do-in', And a' the wark a-boot the house Gaes
3. Fee him, fa-ther, fee him," quo'she, "Fee him, fa-ther fee him; He'll haud the pleuch, thrash in the barn, And

1. And his doggie rinnin'?" quo' she, "And his doggie rinnin'?"
2. wi' me when I see him," quo' she, "Wi' me when I see him!"
3. crack wi' me at e'en," quo' she, "Crack wi' me at e'en."

* To this tune Burns wrote his beautiful poem, "Thou hast left me ever, Jamie." The old traditionary verses which we give above are from Herd's *Scots Songs*, 1776, vol. ii. They are given there under the title of "Fee him, father, fee him." The air is inserted in Aird's *Selection of Scotch, etc., Airs*, vol. ii., issued in 1782. The following is from G. Farquhar Graham's appendix to Wood's *Songs of Scotland*, vol. i., 1852. "We are aware that this song of the olden time has long been looked upon as belonging to the humorous class, and has been sung as such by the popular singers of the day. We confess, however, that we have never viewed it in this light. Manners and customs may have changed since the time the song was written, maidens may have become more reserved, duplicity, in some cases, may have taken the place of rustic simplicity, but human nature remains the same. . . . . Although the composer of the fine old melody to this song might not have been fully aware of the deep pathos which he had infused into it, yet he never could have so far mistaken his own intention, as to suppose he had written a *lively* air. This discovery was left to singers who came after him."

# Saw ye nae my Peggy?*

*Andante molto espressivo.*

VOICE.

PIANO.

1. Saw ye nae my Peg - gy,
2. O how Peg - gy charms me,
3. When I hope to gain her,

*p*

*rit.*

*con Ped.*

*sempre con Ped.*

1. Saw ye nae . . . my Peg - gy, Saw ye nae . . . my Peg - gy
2. Ev' - ry look . . . still warns me; Ev' - ry thought a - larms me,
3. Fate seems to . . . de - tain her; Cou'd I but . . . ob - tain her,

*rit.*    *a tempo, poco cres.*

1. Com - in' owre the lea? Sure a fi - ner crea - ture Ne'er was form'd by na - ture,
2. Lest she love nae me. Peg - gy doth dis - co - ver Nought but charms all ov - er,
3. Hap - py wou'd I be! I'll lie down be - fore her, Bless, sigh, and a - dore her,

*rit.*    *a tempo, poco cres.*

*rit.*     Last time.

1. So com - plete each fea - ture, So . . . di - vine is she!
2. Na - ture bids me love her; That's a law to me.
3. With faint looks em - plore her, Till . . she pi - ty me.

*rit.*    *sf rit. p*

Ped.

---

* Ramsay wrote new words beginning, "Come, lets hae mair wine in," to this air, and published them in *The Tea-Table Miscellany*, 1724. Of the verses given above, Burns wrote in his *Remarks on Scottish Song*: "This charming song is much older and, indeed, superior to Ramsay's verses, 'The Toast,' as he calls them." They appear, however, for the first time in Herd's *Ancient and Modern Scottish Songs*, 1769. The air is included in the first edition of the *Orpheus Caledonius*, 1725, with Ramsay's verses, and marked "To the Tune of Saw na ye my Maggie?" Thomson's version of the melody is very poor, and he has only slightly bettered it in the second edition of his work, in 1733. M'Gibbon's version, published in his *A Collection of Scots Tunes*, Bk. ii., 1746, as "Saw ye my Peggy?" is decidedly better; so also is the one inserted in vol. iii. of Aird's *Selection of Scotch, etc., Airs*, 1788. But we seem to be chiefly indebted to the *Scots Museum*, vol. i., 1787, for the modern and singable version of the tune "Saw ye nae my Peggy?" The air given above is almost identical with the first half of Johnson's setting.

# See afar yon hill Ardmore.

## THE PRAISE OF ISLAY.*
### (MOLADH NA LANDAIDH.)

Translated from the Gaelic by
THOMAS PATTISON.

1. See a - far yon hill Ard-more, Beat-ing bil - lows wash its shore; But its beau-ties bloom no more For me, now far from Is - lay.
2. Tho' its shore is rock - y, drear, Ear - ly doth the sun ap-pear On leaf - y brake and fai - low deer, And flocks and herds in Is - lay.
3. Ea - gles rise on soar - ing wing, Her - ons watch the gush - ing spring, Heath-cocks with their whirr-ing bring Their own de - light to Is - lay.
4. Bir - ken branch - es there are gay, Haw-thorns wave their sil - ver'd spray; Ev - 'ry bough the breez - es sway, A - wak - ens joy in Is - lay.
5. Ma - vis sings on ha - zel bough, Lin - nets haunt the glen be - low; O, may long their wild notes flow With mel - o - dies in Is - lay.

**CHORUS.**

O my Is - land! O my Isle! O, my dear, my na - tive soil! Nought from thee my heart can wile, That's wed with love to Is - lay.

---

* From *The Celtic Lyre*, by the kind permission of the Editor, Henry Whyte ("Fionn"). The Gaelic song is very old, and it is impossible to say who its author was. The translation is by the late Thomas Pattison, of Islay, who studied for the Church. He died in Glasgow in 1865, at the early age of 37.

# She's fair and fause.*

Larghetto.
Verses by Burns.

1. She's fair and fause that caus-es my smart, I lo'ed her meikle and lang;.... She's
2. Wha - e'er ye be that wo - man love, To this be nev - er blind;.... Nae

1. bro-ken her vow, she's bro-ken my heart, And I may e'en go hang!.... A
2. fer-lie it is, tho' fic-kle she prove, A wo-man has't by kind.... O

1. coof cam' in wi' rowth o' gear, And I ha'e tint my dear-est dear; But
2. wo-man love-ly, wo-man fair! An an-gel form's fa'n to thy share; 'Twad

1. wo-man is but warld's gear, Sae let the bonnie lass gang....
2. be ower mei-kle to gi'en thee mair— I mean an au-gel mind....

* This air is preserved by Oswald in his *Caledonian Pocket Companion*, vol. iv. It appears there under the title of "The Lads of Lieth." Some versions of this melody have D♯ instead of D♮ in bars 2, 3, 6, 7, 14 and 15. Burns wrote the verses "She's fair and fause" for the fourth volume of the *Scots Musical Museum*, issued 1792.

# Should auld acquaintance be forgot.

## AULD LANG SYNE.*

Verses partly traditional,
partly by Burns.

Moderato maestoso.

VOICE.

PIANO.

1. Should auld  acquaintance be  for-got, And
2. We twa  hae run a - bout the braes, An'
3. We twa  hae paid-elt  in  the burn Frae
4. And here's a hand, my trust - y fere, And
5. And sure - ly ye'll be your pint-stoup, And

1. nev - er brought to mind? Should auld  ac-quaint-ance be  for-got, And days o' lang  syne?
2. pu'd the gow - ans fine; We've wan-der'd mon-y a  wea - ry foot Sin'  auld  lang  syne.
3. morn-ing sun till dine; But seas be-tween us braid hae roar'd Sin'  auld  lang  syne.
4. gi'es a hand  o' thine; We'll tak'  a richt - gude-wil - lie-waught For  auld  lang  syne.
5. sure - ly I'll  be mine; We'll tak'  a cup  o' kind-ness yet For  auld  lang  syne.

For  auld  lang  syne, my dear, For  auld  lang  syne; We'll tak'  a cup o'

kind - ness yet, For  auld  lang  syne.

* This tune, according to Stenhouse, was formerly known under the name of " I fee'd a lad at Michaelmas." It was originally an old strathspey, and may be found in Bremner's *A Collection of Scots Reels* (commenced 1757), as "The Miller's Wedding," and in Alexander McGlashan's *A Collection of Strathspey Reels, with a bass for Violoncello or Harpsichord*, 1780, under the name of "The Miller's Daughter." The phrase "Auld lang syne" was known to Scotsmen long before the days of Burns. In James Watson's *Collection of Scots Poems*, 1711, pt. iii., we find a song of considerable dimension, the first verse of which we give. Mr. R. Chambers considers that this composition dates from the reign of Charles I. :—

Should old acquaintance be forgot,
    And never thocht upon ;
The flames of love extinguish'd,
    And freely past and gone ?

Is thy kind heart now grown so cold
    In that loving breast of thine,
That thou canst never once reflect
    On old long syne ?

Later on, Allan Ramsay produced a song on the same subject. It is to be found in Thomson's *Orpheus Caledonius*, 1725, p. 31, entitled, "Auld Lang Syne." The original air given by Thomson, McGibbon, and others is never sung now. Under the title of "O can ye labour lea, young man," an excellent version of the old tune, "I fee'd a lad," with three of the original verses, is preserved in Johnson's *Museum*, vol. iv., No. 394.

# Since all thy vows, false maid.*

Air: "Cromlet's Lilt."

1. Since all thy vows, false maid,
2. Have I not gra - ven our
3. Some gloo - my place I'll find,

1. Are blown to air, And my poor heart be-tray'd To sad des-pair,
2. Loves on ev - 'ry tree, In yon - der spread-ing groves, Tho' false thou be;
3. Some dole - ful shade, Where nei - ther sun nor wind E'er en - trance had;

1. In - to some wil - der-ness My grief I will ex-press, And thy hard -
2. Was not a so - lemn oath Plight - ed be - twixt us both, Thou thy faith
3. In - to that hol - low cave There will I sigh and rave, Be - cause thou

1. heart - ed - ness, O cru - el fair.
2. I my troth, Con - stant to be?
3. dost be - have So faith - less - ly.

* This traditionary ballad, which is preserved in Ramsay's *Tea-Table Miscellany*, pt. ii., refers to the love adventures of Chisholm of Cromlecks, in Perthshire, and Miss Helen Murray, a daughter of Stirling of Ardoch, commonly known, on account of her great beauty, as "Fair Helen of Ardoch." The incident, which took place during the reign of James VI., is too well known to repeat here. Both ballad and air are included in the second edition of Thomson's *Orpheus Caledonius*, vol. ii., 1733. Geddes chose the air for one of the hymns in the *Saints' Recreation*, compiled in 1673, and published in Edinburgh in 1683. This hymn is entitled "The Pathway to Paradise; or, The Pourtraiture of Piety."

# Since my loved one has gone.*

Gaelic verses translated by "Fionn" (HENRY WHYTE).    Air: "Mo nighean chruinn, donn."

*Andante con espressione.*

VOICE.

1. Since my loved one has gone I am drear - y!
2. Had I sheep on the hill I might woo thee;
3. Bear my love to the maid, Once so cheer - ful;

PIANO.

con Ped.

1. Since my loved one has gone, Who was pure as the swan; Here I'm sigh-ing all a - lone, Sad and
2. Had I sheep on the hill, By each fountain and rill, Then of thine own free will Thou wouldst
3. Bear my love to the maid, Whom I'll nev-er up-braid, For now she's low-ly laid Sad and

1. wear - y! Were I now with my love, Free-ly roam - ing; Were I now with my
2. choose me. Thou art now far a - way In Glen Iu - ray; Thou art now far a -
3. tear - ful. 'Tis an old carl, I hear, Wooed my maid - en; 'Tis an old carl, I

1. love, 'Neath the shade of the grove, To hear the coo - ing dove In the glcam - ing.
2. way— Sad by night and by day— While here I pine al - way, Naught can cure me!
3. hear, With his gold and his gear; And now he's left my dear, Sor-row - lad - en.

* From the *Celtic Lyre*, by kind permission of Mr. Henry Whyte, who sends us the following note: "The author of this old song is unknown. The Gaelic words were printed in a small collection of songs by James Munro, the Gaelic Grammarian, entitled, *An t-Ailleagan*, and published in 1830."

# Sing the praises o' my dearie.

Translated from the Gaelic of "Fionn," by
MALCOLM MACFARLANE, Elderslie.

Air: "Slàn gu'n till na Gaidheil ghasda."

*Allegretto.*

PIANO.

1. Sing the prais-es o' my dea-rie, Aye sae win-ning, blithe, and chee-rie; In her
2. Doun her grace-fu' shou-thers flow-ing, Her rich curls are gold-en glow-ing; Scarce her

1. pre-sence wha wad wea-rie? For her a' wad rich-es gie. She was rear'd a-mang the
2. foot-steps, light-ly go-ing, Bend the flow'-ret on the lea. Lik'd by il-ka ane comes

1. Hie-lans, Land o' crofts and sum-mer shie-lins; How it charms and warms the fee-lins When she
2. near her, And the lang-er kenn'd the dear-er; North or south there's nane can peer her; And she's

1. Gae-lic speaks tae me.
2. a' the warld tae me.

* From the *Celtic Lyre*, by kind permission. The original Gaelic verses to this air belong to the 17th century. We have here adopted
Mr. MacFarlane's translation of a new Gaelic song by Mr. Henry Whyte, entitled "A' mhaighdean àluinn."

# Sing couthilie, couthilie, merrie an' free.

## MY AIN HOOSE.*

Translated from the Gaelic of MALCOLM MACFARLANE
by ALEXANDER STEWART.

VOICE.

*Allegretto.*

PIANO.

*mf*

*p*

*mf*

1. Sing cou-thi-lie, cou-thi-lie, mer-rie an' free, O this is the oor o' sweet
2. A-yont by the fer-ry, whaur wood-lands are green, My can-ty cot-hoo-sie stan's
3. At fa' o' the gloam-in', when dark-ness is near, Oor hearth is sur-roond-ed wi'

1. so-lace to me, When wea-ried wi' toil-in' out owre the green lea, I
2. ti-dy an' clean; I en-vy nae laird in his cas-tle, I ween, I'm
3. daf-fin' an' cheer, The bair-nies are sing-in' sae licht-some an' clear, They're

1. tod-dle wi' glee to my ain hoose. The sod-ger may hie to a far for-eign shore, The
2. hap-py an bien in my ain hoose. My co-sy bit big-gin' it's dear a-boon a', Sur-
3. pleas-ant to hear in oor ain hoose. A-wa' wi' yer rich-es an' rank, wi' their glare, They're

* By kind permission of "An Comunn Gaidhealach," Glasgow. This air is evidently very old. It appears in Patrick MacDonald's *Collection of Highland Airs,* 1784, under the name of *Posadh peathar Iain bhain*—The wedding of fair John's daughter. The original song being unsatisfactory, Mr. Malcolm MacFarlane, of Elderslie, wrote new Gaelic verses to the melody at the request of Mr. Archibald Ferguson, Conductor of the Gaelic St. Columba Choir, Glasgow. For the excellent translation of these verses, Mr. Alexander Stewart, Polmont, was awarded a prize by "An Comunn Gaidhealach." The melody, with Gaelic and English verses, was first published in *The Celtic Monthly*—an excellent magazine, edited by Mr. John Mackay, Glasgow, which has been the means of bringing many old and rare Highland airs to public notice.

*cres.*

1. to - per de - light in the ale-house to roar, The mi - ser may rev - el in
2. roond-ed wi' dais - ies an' prim-ros - es braw, The hil - lock a - hint it's a
3. nae-thing but fol - ly an' phan-toms o' air; The ha' o' the Queen an' the

*sf* *cres.*

CHORUS.

*f*

1. count-ing his store; I hae plea-sure ga - lore in my ain hoose.⎫
2. bield frae the snaw When win-ter win's blaw roon my ain hoose.⎬ Sing cheer-i - lie, con - thi-lie,
3. lux - u - ries there Can nev - er com-pare wi' my ain hoose.⎭

*colla voce.* *f*

mer - rie an' free, O this is the cor of sweet so-lace to me; When wea-ried wi' toil-in' out

owre the green lea, I tod-dle wi' glee to my ain hoose.

*f*

# Smile na sae sweet, my bonnie babe.

## FINE FLOWERS IN THE VALLEY.*

*Andante.*

PIANO.

1. Smile na sae sweet, my bon - nie babe, (Fine flow'rs in the val - ley) An' ye
2. She's tak - en out her wee pen - knife, (Fine flow'rs in the val - ley) And
3. She's how - kit a grave by the licht o' the moon, (Fine flow'rs in the val - ley), And
4. As she was go - ing to the Church, (Fine flow'rs in the val - ley) She
5. O my sweet babe, an' thou wert mine, (Fine flow'rs in the val - ley), I wad
6. O mith - er, dear, when I was thine, (Fine flow'rs in the val - ley) Ye

1. smile sae sweet, ye'll smile me dead: (And the green leaves they grow rare - ly).
2. twin'd the sweet babe o' its life: (And the green leaves they grow rare - ly).
3. there she bur - ied her sweet babe: (And the green leaves they grow rare - ly).
4. saw a wee babe in the porch: (And the green leaves they grow rare - ly).
5. clead thee in the silk sae fine: (And the green leaves they grow rare - ly).
6. did na prove to me sae kin': (And the green leaves they grow rare - ly).

*Last time.*

*rit.*

* Stenhouse, in his note to this song in the *Scots' Musical Museum Illustrations*, p. 308, says: " This ancient and beautiful air, with the fragment of the ballad beginning, ' She sat down below a thorn' ['Smile na sae sweet' is the second verse], were both transmitted by Burns to Johnson for the *Museum*." Herd has inserted a few verses of what is evidently the same ballad in *Scots Songs*, 1776, vol. ii., p. 237. On p. 83 of vol. i. of the same work, there is an entirely different ballad entitled, " Fine flowers i' the valley," and beginning, " There was three ladies in a ha'." Stenhouse is of opinion that both ballads were sung to the same simple, plaintive melody.

# Sweet sir, for your courtesie.

### MY JO JANET.*

*Allegretto.*

PIANO.

*p*    *poco rit.*

*mf*

*mf*

1. Sweet sir, for your cour - te-sie, When ye come by the Bass, then, For the love you bear to me, Buy
2. Good sir, for your cour - te-sie, Com - ing thro' A - ber-deen, then, For the love ye bear to me, Buy
3. What if danc-ing on the green, And skip-ping like a mawk - ing, If they see my clout - ed shoon, Of

1. me a keek-ing glass, then. Keek in - to the draw - well, Jan - et, .. Jan - et, And
2. me a pair o' shoon, then. Clout the auld, the new are dear, Jan - et, .. Jan - et, Ac
3. me they will be tank - ing. Dance ay laigh, and dance at e'en, Jan - et, .. Jan - et, Syne

1. there you'll see your bon - nie sel', My jo Jan - et.
2. pair may gain you ha'f a year, My jo Jan - et.
3. a' their faut's will no be seen, My jo Jan - et.

*p*

* This song appears in Ramsay's *Tea-Table Miscellany*, 1724; we have omitted the last two verses. The air is probably very old; a version of it appears in the Skene MS., *circa* 1615-1620, "Long er onie old Man." Thomson inserted both song and air in the second edition of the *Orpheus Caledonius*, vol. ii., 1733.

# Sweet youth's a blithe and heartsome time.*

Verses by ALLAN RAMSAY.

Air: "Gin ye meet a bonnie lassie."

*Allegretto.*

VOICE.

PIANO.

1. Sweet youth's a blithe and
2. "Haith, ye're ill-bred," she'll

*p*    *rit.*    *a tempo.*

Ped.    Ped.

1. heartsome time; Then, lads and lass-es, while 'tis May, Gae pu' the gow-an in its prime, Be-
2. smi-ling say, " Ye'll wor-ry me, ye gree-dy rook !" Syne frae your arms she'll rin a-way And

1. fore it wi-ther and de-cay, And watch for min-utes o' de-light, When Jen-ny speaks be-
2. hide her-sel' in some dark neuk, Her laugh will lead ye to the place, Where lies the hap-pi-

*Last time.*

1. low her breath, And kisses, lay-in' a' the wyte On you if she kepp on-y straith.
2. ness ye want; And plainly tell ye to your face Nine-teen na-says are hauf a grant.

* This beautiful air is probably very old. We give two of the four verses written to it by Allan Ramsay, who has also adapted the air
to the song beginning, " Dear Roger, if your Jenny geck," in act I. of *The Gentle Shepherd*. Gay also introduced this melody in his Opera
*Achilles*, performed in 1733. Ramsay's complete poem, " Fy gar rub her o'er wi' strae," the first verse of which is traditional, is published
in the *Tea-Table Miscellany*, and with the air, in the *Orpheus Caledonius*, 1725, and in Watts' *Musical Miscellany*, vol. v., 1731.

# The Campbells are comin' *

*Allegro molto marcato.*

PIANO.

*p*

*8 mf*

The Camp-bells are com - in', O - ho, O - ho! The Camp-bells are com - in', O -

*mf*

*cres.*      FINE.

ho, O - ho! The Campbells are comin' to bonnie Loch Leven: The Campbells are comin', O - ho, O - ho!

*cres.*    *sf*

*mf*

1. Up - on the Lomonds I lay, I lay, Up - on the Lomonds I lay, I lay, I
2. The great Ar - gyle, he goes be - fore, He makes the cannons and guns to roar Wi'
3. The Camp-bells they are a' in arms, Their loy - al faith an' truth to show; Wi'

*mf*    *sf*

*cres.*

*cres.*        D.C. dal segno. 8

1. look - ed down to bon - nie Loch-Le-ven, And saw three bon - nie per - ches play.
2. sound o' trum - pet, pipe, and drum, The Camp-bells are com - in', O - ho, O - ho!
3. ban - ners rat - tling in the wind, The Camp-bells are com - in', O - ho, O - ho!

*cres.*    *sf*

* According to Stenhouse, these verses were written about 1715, on the breaking out of the rebellion. The air appears in Robert Bremner's *Collection of Scots Reels and Country Dances*, commenced 1757, and, later on, in Airds' *Selection of Scots Airs*, vol. i., 1782.

# The De'il cam' fiddlin' thro' the toun.

## THE DE'IL'S AWA' WI' THE EXCISEMAN.*

Verses by BURNS.
*Spiritoso.*

Air: "The Hempdresser."

VOICE.

PIANO.

*mf*

1. The De'il cam' fid - dlin'
2. We'll mak' our maut and
3. There's three - some reels, and

1. thro' the toun, And danc'd a - wa' wi' th' Ex - cise - man; And il - ka auld wife cried
2. brew our drink, We'll dance, and sing, and re - joice, man! And mon - y braw thanks to the
3. four - some reels, There's horn - pipes and strath-speys, man; But aye the best dance e'er

* Burns wrote these verses for Johnson's *Museum*, where they appear as song No. 399. The tune appears in Playford's *Dancing Master*, under the name of "The Hempdresser." Subsequently it became known by the name of "The Sun has loos'd his weary Team," from the first line of an old English song, which is given in the first volume of *Wit and Mirth; or, Pills to Purge Melancholy*, London, 1698. In the sixth and last volume of the same work, published in 1719, D'Urfey again prints the air to verses beginning, "Lorenzo, you amuse the town, and with your charms undo, Sir." The tune is evidently English, and is probably the original of the well known Scottish air, "Over the water to Charlie," published by Bremner in his *Collection of Scots Reels*, 1757.

1. "Auld Ma-houn, We wish you luck o' the prize, man!"
2. muck-le black De'il, That's danc'd a-wa' wi' the Ex-cise-man! } The De'il's a-wa', the
3. came to our land Was the De'il's a-wa' wi' the Ex-cise-man!

De'il's a-wa', He's danc'd a-wa' wi' th' Ex-cise - man! O

mon-y braw thanks to the muck-le black De'il, That's danc'd a-wa' wi' th' Ex-cise-man!

# The Isle of Mull.*

## An-t-Eilean Muileach.

Translated from the Gaelic by C. MacPhail.

VOICE.

PIANO.

*Molto andante.*

*mf*

*mf*          *poco rit.*          *mf*

con Ped.

1. The Isle of
2. Oh! fresh and
3. How plea - sant

*cres.*

1. Mull is of isles the fair - est, Of o - cean's gems 'tis the first and
2. fair are thy mea - dows bloom - ing, With fra - grant blos - soms the air per -
3. 'twas in the sweet May morn - ing, The ris - ing sun thy gay fields a -

*cres.*

*f*          *dim.*

1. rar - est; Green gras - sy is - land of spark - ling foun - tains, Of wav - ing
2. fum - ing; Where boy - hood's days I've oft spent in fool - ing, A - round Ben -
3. dorn - ing; The feath - er'd song - sters their lays were sing - ing, While rocks and

*f*          *dim.*

* From the *Celtic Lyre*, by permission of the Editor, Mr. Henry Whyte. who has kindly sent us the following note: "These verses, in praise of the Island of Mull, Argyllshire, were written by the late Daniel MacPhail, a native of that island, who died in 1887. He wrote several other Gaelic songs, which are popular in the Highlands. The melody belongs to much older, but inferior verses. Mr. MacPhail was resident in Newcastle when he wrote this poem.

*poco rit.*     *mf*

1. woods and high tow'r - ing moun - tains.    Tho' far from
2. Var - nick and Dur - ry - Cool - ing.    Where Lus - sa's
3. woods were with e - choes ring - ing.    But gone are

*cres.*

1. home, I am now a ran - ger In grim New - cas - tle a dole - ful
2. stream thro' the pools comes whirl - ing, Or o'er the clear peb - bly shal - lows
3. now all those joys for ev - er, Like bub - bles burst - ing on yon - der

*f*     *dim.*

1. stran - ger; The thought of thee stirs my heart's e - mo - tion, And deep - er
2. swirl - ing; The sil - v'ry sal - mon is there seen play - ing, And in the
3. riv - er; Fare - well, fare - well, to thy spark - ling foun - tains, Thy wav - ing

*poco rit.*

1. fix - es its fond de - vo - tion.
2. sun - beams his hues dis - play - ing.
3. woods and high tow'r - ing moun - tains.

*rit.*

# The Laird o' Cockpen.*

Verses by LADY NAIRNE.

Air: "When she cam' ben she bobbit."

VOICE.

1. The Laird o' Cock-pen, he's
2. Now doun by the dyke-side a
3. His wig was weel pouther'd as
4. He mount-ed his mare, an' he
5. Mis-tress Jean she was mak-in' the
6. An' when she came ben she
7. Dumb - found-ed was he, but nae
† 8. But noo that the Laird his
9. Neist time that the Laird and the

Moderato con spirito.

PIANO.

1. proud and he's great, His mind is ta'en up wi' the things o' the State; He
2. la - dy did dwell, At his ta - - ble head he thocht she'd look well; Mac
3. gude as when new, His waist - coat was white, his coat it was blue; He
4. rade can - ni - lie, An' rapp'd at the yett o' Cla - vers - ha' Lee. "Gae
5. el - der-flow'r wine; "What the de'il brings the Laird here at sic a like time?" She
6. bob - bit fu' low, And what was his er - rand he soon let her know; A
7. sigh did he gi'e; He mount - ed his mare, and he rade cau - ni - lie; An'
8. af - ten he thocht, as he gaed thro' the glen, "She was daft to re - fuse the Laird o' Cock-pen."
9. Led - dy were seen, They were gaun arm in arm to the Kirk on the green; Noo she

1. want-ed a wife his braw house to keep, But fa - vour wi' woo - in' was fashous to seek.
2. Cleish's ae doch - ter o' Cla-vers-ha' Lee, A pen - ny-less lass wi' a lang ped - i-gree.
3. put on a ring, a sword, an' cock'd hat, An' wha could re - fuse the Laird wi' a' that?
4. tell mis-tress Jean to come speed-i - ly ben, She's want - ed to speak wi' the Laird o' Cock-pen."
5. put off her a - pron, an' on her silk gown, Her mutch wi' red rib - bons, an' ga'ed a - wa' doun.
6. maz'd was the Laird, when the la - dy said "Na;" An' wi' a laigh curt - sie she turn - ed a - wa'!
7. af - ten he thocht, as he gaed thro' the glen, "She was daft to re - fuse the Laird o' Cock-pen.
8. ane I'll get bet - ter, its waur I'll get ten— I was daft to re - fuse the Laird o' Cock-pen."
9. sits in the ha' like a weel tap - pit hen, But as yet there's nae chickens ap - pear'd at Cock-pen!

# The lass o' Patie's Mill.*

Moderato.

Verses by Allan Ramsay.

PIANO.

1. The lass o' Pa - tie's Mill, .. So bon - nie, blythe, and gay, In
2. With - out the help of art, .. Like flow'rs that grace the wild, She
3. O, had I all that wealth .. Hope-toun's high moun - tains fill, In -

1. spite of all my skill, ... She stole my heart a - way! When
2. did her sweets im - part ... When - e'er she spoke or smil'd. Her
3. sur'd long life and health, .. And plea - sures at my will; I'd

1. ted - ding o' the hay, ... Bare - head - ed on the green, Love
2. looks they were so mild, ... Free from af - fect - ed pride, She
3. pro - mise and ful - fil. ... That none but bon - nie she, The

poco rit.

1. 'midst her locks did play, ... And wan - ton'd in her e'en. ...
2. me to love be - guil'd, .. I wish'd her for my bride. ..
3. Lass o' Pa - tie's Mill, .. Shou'd share the fame wi' me. ...

poco rit.

* Both air and words are published in Thomson's *Orpheus Caledonius*, 1725. It is one of the seven tunes foolishly attributed by the editor of that work to "David Rezzio." Ramsay's verses appear in *The Tea-Table Miscellany*, 1724. Ritson considers them "equal to any, and even in point of pastoral simplicity, superior to most lyric productions, either in the Scottish, or any other language." Stenhouse considers the air to date from the middle of the 16th century. (See *Museum Illustrations*, p. 20.) It is curious to note how differently the editors of the earlier Scottish song collections spell the name of the heroine of this song. Ramsay, and Thomson in the first edition of the *Orpheus Caledonius*, p. 1, spell the word "Patie." In the *Musical Miscellany*, vol. i., 1729, Watt has it "Peatie," whereas Adam Craig, in his *Choicest Scots Songs*, 1730, p. 24, "Pettie." In the second edition of his *Orpheus* in 1733, we find Thomson altering the title to "Peaty," and in the last volume of the *Miscellany*, Watt boldly heads the air, "Comely Patty."

# The lily of the vale is sweet.*

Verses by ALLAN RAMSAY.
*Moderato e molto tranquillo.*

Air: Miss Forbes' Farewell."

PIANO.

1. The li-ly of the vale is sweet, And sweet-er still the op'-ning rose; But
2. There will we walk at ear-ly dawn, Ere yet the sun be-gins to shine; At

1. sweet-er far my Ma-ry is Than an-y bloom-ing flow'r that blows, Whilst
2. eve oft to the lawn we'll tread, And mark that splen-did orb's de-cline. The

1. Spring her fra-grant blos-soms spreads, I'll wan-der oft by Ma-ry's side, And
2. fair-est, choic-est flow'rs I'll crop, To deck my love-ly Ma-ry's hair, And

1. whis-per saft the ten-der tale, By Forth, sweet Forth's me-an-d'ring tide.
2. while I live, I vow and swear, She'll be my chief, my on-ly care.

* This air appears in Gow's Repository, pt. iv., entitled "Miss Forbes' Farewell, by Mr. Isaac Couper, of Banff." It is another version of the old tune, " Twine weel the plaiden "; see p. 154.

# The love that I hae chosen.

### THE LOWLANDS O' HOLLAND.*

Lento.

VOICE.

PIANO.

*p con espressione.*    < *poco ritenuto.*

Ped.    Ped.    con Ped.

1. The love that I hae cho-sen Was
2. My love lies in the saut sea, And
3. There sall nae coif come on my head, Nae

1. to my heart's con-tent, The saut sea sall be fro- zen Be-fore that I re-pent; Re-
2. I am on the side, E-nough to break a young heart, Wha late-ly was a bride, Wha
3. kame come in my hair, There sall nae coal or can-dle licht Come in my bow-er mair; Nor

*mf*    *dim.*

1. pent it will I nev-er Un-til the day I dee, Tho' the Low-lands o' Hol-land Ha'e
2. late-ly was a bon-nie bride And plea-sure in her e'e, But the Low-lands o' Hol-land Ha'e
3. sall I hae a-ni-ther love Un-til the day I dee, For I nev-er lov'd a love but one, And

*mf*    *dim.*

[Last time.]

1. twinn'd my love and me.
2. twinn'd my love and me.
3. he's drown'd in the sea.

*poco rit.*    > *poco ritenuto.*

* A somewhat different version of this ballad is included in Herd's *Collection of Scots Songs*, 1776, vol. ii. The melody is probably very old, and is considered by Stenhouse, Graham, and others to be the foundation of William Marshall's popular tune, "Miss Admiral Gordon's Strathspey" (see p. 140). Mr John Glen, however, points out in his *Collection of Scottish Dance Music*, 1891, that the "Lowlands of Holland" was first published in 1788 in Johnson's *Museum*, vol. ii.; and that Marshall's "Miss Admiral" was printed as early as 1781 in Neil Stewart's *A Collection of Strathspey Reels* (etc.), composed by *Wm. Gordon*. But this does not prove that Marshall was unacquainted with the air prior to its being published by Johnson; and certainly the structure of the "Lowlands of Holland" is distinctly older than that of Marshall's tune. It has been suggested that Urbani adapted the air from Marshall's "Miss Admiral," but this is very improbable. Gow has a strathspey called "Major Graham of Inchbrakie, by Niel Gow," in his first *Collection*, 1784, which greatly resembles "The Lowlands o' Holland." In Christie's *Traditional Ballad Airs*, vol. ii., 1876, we find a tune entitled "The Lowlands o' Holland," which the editor of that work traces back to the middle of last century, but which has no connection with the melody given above. The air called the "Lowlands o' Holland," in Oswald's second *Collection*, is also entirely different.

# The mirk is gathering in the glen.*

### HIGHLAND CRADLE SONG.

Verses by K. R. MOFFAT.
*Andante tranquillo.*

Air: "Baba mo leancable."

PIANO.

*p*

*sempre con pedale.*

1. The mirk is gath-'ring in the glen, The shadows creep up to the brow o' the Ben, The
2. Now comes the bon-nie La-dy Moon, And on my ain bairnie she gent-ly looks doun, And

*sempre con pedale.*

1. sky, but now sae red, sae red, Grows dim be-fore the night's dull tread. The
2. smiles sae kind as if, sa'd she, "We'll watch the ba-by, you and me." Then

*poco rit.*

1. bird-ies a' ha'e gane to rest, Each lit-tle war-bler in his nest Has hid his head be-
2. shut these twa blue e'en, my dear, The moon and mith-er baith are here, We'll guard you weel, We'll

*poco rit.*
*p*

*After last verse.*

1. neath his wing, And closed his eye and ceased to sing.
2. guard you lang, And hush-a-bye will be our sang.

*p*
*rit.*

* A version of this melody occurs in Captain Fraser's, of Knockie, Collection of *Airs and Melodies peculiar to the Highlands of Scotland*, 1816.

# The Smiling Spring.

## DONNIE BELL.*

Verses by Burns.

*Allegretto vivo.*

VOICE.

PIANO.

1. The smil-ing Spring comes in re-joic-ing, And
2. The flow-'ry Spring leads sun-ny Sum-mer, And

*p* cres.　　*pp*　　*p*　　cres.

1. sur-ly Win-ter grim-ly flies; Now crystal clear are the fall-ing wa-ters, And bonnie blue are the
2. yel-low Au-tumn press-es near, Then in his turn comes gloomy Win-ter, Till smiling Spring a -

1. sunny skies. Fresh o'er the mountains breaks forth the morning, The ev'ning gilds the ocean's swell; All
2. gain ap-pear. Thus seasons danc-ing, life ad-vanc-ing, Old Time and Na-ture their changes tell, But

**Last time.**

1. creatures joy in the sun's re-turn-ing, And I re-joice in my bon-nie Bell.
2. nev-er rang-ing, still un-chang-ing, I a-dore my bon-nie Bell.

*f*　　*pp*

---

* Burns communicated this air and his verses to Johnson for his *Scots Musical Museum*, vol. iv. The air is probably from the Borderland.

# The news frae Moidart cam' yestreen.

## WHA'LL BE KING BUT CHARLIE?*

Verses by LADY NAIRNE.

*Spiritoso.*

VOICE.

PIANO.

1. The news frae Moi-dart cam' yes-treen, Will som gar mon-y
2. The High-land clans, wi' sword in hand, Frae John-o' Groats to
3. The Low-lands a', baith great an' sma', Wi' mon-y a lord and
4. Then here's a health to Char-lie's cause, An' be't com-plete an'

1. fer-lie, For ships o' war ha'e just come in, And land-ed Roy-al
2. Air-lie, Ha'e to a man de-clar'd to stand Or fa' wi' Roy-al
3. laird, Ha'e de-clar'd for Sco-tia's King and law, And spier ye wha, but
4. ear-ly, His ve-ry name our heart's-bluid warms; To arms for Roy-al

1. Char-lie!
2. Char-lie!
3. Char-lie!
4. Char-lie!

Come through the hea-ther, a-round him gath-er, Ye're a' the wel-com-er

* Captain Fraser, of Knockie, included this fine melody in his *Airs and Melodies peculiar to the Highlands of Scotland*, 1816. In a note to the air the Editor remarks, "This is a melody common to Ireland as well as to the Highlands of Scotland,—but having been known in this country since the 1715, as one of the incentives to rebellion; if originally Irish, some of the troops or partisans engaged for Charles from that country might have brought it over, but the melody is simple and beautiful, assimilating itself very much to the style of either." (Note No. 156.) The incident of which the song treats, is the landing of Prince Charles Edward Stuart, on the 25th July, 1745. The Prince was accompanied by seven followers. They landed at Borodale, a farm belonging to the Clanranald, and lying close to the shore of Lochnanuagh, Moidart. The air, with Lady Nairne's verses, is given in Smith's *Scotish Minstrel*, vol. vi., 1824.

ear - - ly, A - round him cling wi' a' your kin, For wha'll be King but

Char - lie? Come through the hea-ther, a - round him gath-er, Come Ron-ald, come Don-ald, come

a' the-gith-er And crown your right-fu', law-fu' King! For wha'll be King but

Char - lie?

# The pawky auld carle cam' owre the lea.

## THE GABERLUNZIE MAN.*

Air: "Bung your eye."

Con spirito.

VOICE.

PIANO.

*p*     *f*     *dim.*

*p*

1. The paw-ky auld carle cam' owre the lea, Wi' mon-y guid-e'ens and
2. "O wow," quo' he, "were I as free As first when I saw
3. Be-tween the twa was made a plot; They raise a wee be-
4. She gaed to where the beg-gar lay; The strae was cauld, he
5. "Since nae-thing's a-wa' as we can learn, The kirn's to kirn, the

1. days to me, say-ing, "Guid-wife, for your cour-te-sie, Will ye
2. this coun-trie, How blythe and mer-ry wad I be! And
3. fore the cock, And wil-i-ly they shot the lock, And
4. was a-way, She clapt her hands, cry'd, "Wal-a-day, For
5. milk to yirne, Gae butt the house, and wake my bairn, And

* This excellent old ballad, from which we have chosen five verses, is preserved in the *Tea Table Miscellany*, 1724. It is there signed "J," and has been thought by many—Percy among others—(see his *Reliques*, vol. ii., Bk. I.)—to be the composition of James V., whose custom it was to wander about the country in disguise. This is, however, extremely improbable. Mr. R. Chambers remarks that "there is not the faintest assimilation of the style of this song to the manner of any of the 'makkers' of the early part of the 16th century." Mr. Chambers considers it possible that "The Gaberlunzie Man," "Maggie Lauder," "Muirland Willie," "Willie was a wanton wag," "My Jo Janet," and a few other songs, all of which can be traced back to the period immediately preceding Allan Ramsay, were the compositions of one author—an *earlier Burns*, who has chosen to remain for ever unknown (see *Songs of Scotland prior to Burns*, p. 179). The air to which the ballad is set in the *Orpheus Caledonius*, 1725, and in Watt's *Musical Miscellany*, vol. v., 1731, is now entirely forgotten; it is in 3 time, and has a compass of almost two octaves. Chritic gives an entirely different air in his *Traditional Ballad Airs*, vol. ii., 1881, and remarks, that after the publication of the ballad in Herd's *Collection* in 1776, the air "Muirland Willie" was used. Stenhouse makes a similar remark in the *Museum Illustrations*, but both these authors probably meant the tune "Bung your eye," which in many ways greatly resembles "Muirland Willie." "Bung your eye" was first published by Robert Ross in *A Choice Collection of Scots Reels, etc.*, 1780, and two years later, by James Aird in *A Selection of Scotch, etc., Airs*, vol. i.

*cres.*

1. lodge    a    sil-ly    puir    man?"    . . . .    The    nicht    was    cauld,    the
2. I    wad    nev-er    think    lang."    . . . .    He    grew    can-    ty,
3. fast    to the    bent are    they    gane.    . . . . .    Up    in    the    morn    the
4. some    of our    gear will    be    gane!"    . . . .    Some    ran    to    cof-    fer,
5. bid    her come    quick-    ly    ben."    . . . .    The    ser-    vant    gaed    to

*cres.*

1. carle    was    wat,    And    doun    a-yont    the    in-gle    he    sat;    My
2. she    grew    faiu,    But    lit-    tle    did    her    min-    ny    ken,    What
3. auld    wife    raise,    And    at    her    ease    pat    on    her    claise;    Syne
4. some    to    kist,    But    nought    was    stown    that    could    be    miss'd;    She
5. where the    lass    lay,    The    sheets    were cauld,    she    was    a-    way;    And

1. daught-ers    shou-thers    he    'gan    to    clap,    And    cad-ge-ly    rant    and
2. thir    slee    twa    to-gith-er    were    say-in',    When    woo-ing they    were    sae
3. to    the    kit-    chen    ben    she    gaes,    To    spier    for the    sil-ly    auld
4. danc'd    her    lane,    cry'd    "Praise    be    blest!    I've lodg'd    a    leal    puir
5. fast    to    her    guid-    wife    she    say,    "She's    aff    wi' the    auld beg-gar

1. sang!    . . . . .
2. thrang.    . . . . .
3. man.    . . . . .
4. mau!"    . . . . .
5. man!"    . . . . .

*f*

# The stars are burning cheerily, cheerily.

## TURN YE TO ME.*

Verses by CHRISTOPHER NORTH,
Born at Paisley, 1785, died 1854.

Air: "Horo Mhairi dhu."

1. The stars are burn - ing
2. The waves are danc - ing

*Andante con moto.*

*pp molto legato.*

*sempre con pedale.*

1. cheer - i - ly, cheer - i - ly, Ho - ro, Mhai - ri dhu, turn ye ... to me; The
2. mer - ri - ly, mer - ri - ly, Ho - ro, Mhai - ri dhu, turn ye ... to me; . The

1. sea - mew is moan - ing drear - i - ly, drear - i - ly, Ho - ro, Mhai - ri dhu,
2. sea - birds are wail - ing wear - i - ly, wear - i - ly, Ho - ro, Mhai - ri dhu,

* This melody was first published in *Albyn's Anthology*, 1816, vol. i. The following is Campbell's note to the song: "The above stanza [in Gaelic] is the only one the Editor took down from the singing of Misses Anne and Janet McLeod, of Guesto, Skye. The melody is supposed to be ancient. The verses were composed to Mrs. McPherson, of Ostaig, by a female maniac, several years ago, who sung them, it is said, in so sweetly wild a manner, as to thrill the listener with pleasing terror." The poem, which is usually called "The Sea-mew," was written by John Wilson (Christopher North). We have Mr. Malcolm Lawson's permission to use his version of the air. It appears in *The Songs of the North*, of which collection Mr. Lawson is the musical Editor. It differs considerably from Alexander Campbell's version.

*rit.*                          *a tempo.*

1. turn ye . . . to me.    Cold is the storm-wind that ruf-fles his breast, But
2. turn ye . . . to me.    Hush'd be thy moan-ing, lone bird of the sea,     Thy

*rit. colla voce.*        *a tempo.*

*sempre con Ped.*

*p*                                        *rit.*              *a tempo.*

1. warm are the down-y plumes lin-ing his    nest.    Cold blows the
2. home on the rocks is a shel-ter to    thee.    Thy house is the

*p*                              *rit.*              *a tempo.*

*poco rit.*

1. storm there,    soft falls the    snow, . . Then,    Ho - - ro Mhai - ri dhu,
2. au-gry wave,    mine but the    lone - ly grave,    Ho - - ro Mhai - ri dhu,

*poco rit.*

*con Ped.*

1. turn ye . . . to me.
2. turn ye . . . to me.

*pp*                                      *molto rall.*

2

# The weary pund o' tow.*

Verses partly by BURNS.

The wea-ry pund, the wea-ry pund, The wea-ry pund o' tow; I think my wife will end her life Be-fore she spin her tow!

1. I bought my wife a skane o' lint, As gude as e'er did grow; And a' that she has made o' that Is a puir pund o' tow!
2. There sat a bot-tle in a bole Be-yond the in-gle low; And ay she took the ti-ther souk To drouk the stou-rie tow!
3. Quo' I, for shame, ye dir-ty dame, Gae spin your tap o' tow! She took the rock and wi' a knock, She brak it owre my pow!
4. At last her feet,—I sang to see't! Gaed fore-most owre the knowe; And or I wad a-ni-ther jad, I'll wal-lop in a tow!

* This tune and title occur in Oswald's *Caledonian Pocket Companion*, Bk. viii. Burns wrote the words for Johnson's *Scots Musical Museum*, vol. iv., 1792. They are an improved version of the traditional verses.

# The wind is fair.

### FAREWELL TO FIUNARY! *
### Soraidh slàn le Fionn-Airidh!

Translated from the Gaelic of
Dr. McLeod (" Caraid nan Gaidheal "),
by Archibald Sinclair.

*Molto andante, maestoso.*

VOICE.

PIANO.

*mf*

1. The wind is fair, the day is fine, Swift - ly,
2. A thou - sand, thou - sand ten - der ties— Ac - cept this
3. With pen - sive steps I've of - ten stroll'd Where Fin - gals
4. I've of - ten paused at close of day Where Os - sian
5. 'Tis not the hills nor wood-ed vales A - lone my
6. O, must I leave these hap - py scenes? See, they

*cres.*    *ff*    *p rit.*

1. swift - ly runs the time; The boat is float-ing on the tide That wafts me off from Fiun - a - ry.
2. day my plaintive sighs; My heart with-in me al-most dies At thought of leav - ing Fiun - a - ry.
3. cas - tle stood of old, And listen'd while the shepherds told The le - gend tales of Fiun - a - ry.
4. sang his mar-tial lay, And view'd the sun's de-part-ing ray, When wand'ring o'er Dun Fiun - a - ry.
5. joy - less heart be-wails, A mourn-ful group this day re-mains With - in the manse of Fiun - a - ry.
6. spread the flap-ping sails, A-dieu, a-dieu! my na-tive plains; Farewell, fare - well to Fiun - a - ry!

*cres.*    *ff*    *p rit.*

**Chorus.**

*mf*      *cres.*

Ei - rich ag— us tiu-gainn O,   Ei - rich ag - us tiu - gainn O,   Ei - rich
(pronounced Ay - reech agh - us choo-king O)

*mf*      *cres.*

*f*    *p decres.*    *rit.*

ag - us tiu - gainn O,   Fare-well, fare - well to Fiun - a - ry!

*f*    *p decres. rit.*

* From the *Celtic Lyre*, by the kind permission of the Editor, Mr. Henry Whyte ("Fionn"), who sends us the following note: "The Manse at Fiunary, Argyleshire, was long the home of the MacLeods. The song, 'Farewell to Fiunary,' was written by the elder Dr. MacLeod, known as *Caraid nan Gaidheal*, the Highlander's Friend, on the occasion of his leaving home to enter the Glasgow University. His leave-taking is beautifully described by his son, Dr. Norman MacLeod, in his 'Reminiscences of a Highland Parish.' The air is much older than the song, belonging originally to a song by Allan MacDougal, better known as *Ailean Dall*, or Blind Allan, who was born in Glenco, 1750. The original song, *Irinn drinn a horô*, is a lyric of merit, but it never obtained the popularity of 'Fiunary.'" To this we have only to add that in the sixth volume of the *Scottish Minstrel*, issued in 1824, R. A. Smith published a somewhat different version of the air with verses by Morehead, entitled, "Farewell to Funery." With the exception of v. 5, Mr. Sinclair's excellent translation is almost identical with the song in the *Scottish Minstrel*.

# The winter it is past.*

*Andante molto espressivo.*

VOICE.

1. The win - ter it is
2. The rose up - on the
3. My love is like the
4. All you that are in

PIANO.

*sempre Ped.*

1. past, and the simmer's come at last, And the small birds sing on ev - - 'ry
2. brier, by the wa - ters run-ning clear, May have charms for the lin - net or the
3. sun that in the sky doth run, For ev - er so con - stant and
4. love, and can - not it re - move, I pi - ty the pains you en -

1. tree; The hearts of these are glad, but mine is ve - ry
2. bee; Their lit - tle loves are blest, their lit - tle hearts at
3. true; But his is like the moon that wan-ders up and
4. dure; For ex - pe - rience makes me know your hearts are full of

*cres.* *rit.* *dim.*

1. sad, For my true love is part - ed from me. . . . . . . .
2. rest, But my true love is part - ed from me. . . . . . . .
3. down, And ev - ry month it is new. . . . . . . .
4. woe, A woe that no mor - tal can cure. . . . . . . .

*f cres.*

* This air appears in Oswald's *Caledonian Pocket Companion*, Bk. vii., under the same title. The song was contributed by Burns to Johnson's *Museum*, vol. ii., 1788; its author is unknown. In Christie's *Traditional Ballad Airs*, vol i., 1876, we find another version of the ballad, entitled, "The winter's gone and past," and set to an entirely different air, which the author says is well known in the counties of Banff and Aberdeen. Dean Christie also remarks that the hero of the song was a highwayman of the name of Johnston, who was executed about the middle of last century for the many robberies he committed in Curragh of Kildare, Ireland. † In some editions C ♯.

# There grows a bonnie brier=bush.*

*Andante.*

*Verses partly by* LADY NAIRNE.

VOICE.

PIANO.

*p con molto espressione.*

1. There grows a bon-nie bri-er-bush in
2. He's com-in' frae the North that's to
3. The bri-er-bush was bon-nie ance in

1. oor Kail-yaird, And white are the blos-soms on't, in oor Kail-yaird; Like
2. fan-cy me, He's com-in' frae the North that's to fan-cy me; ∧
3. oor Kail-yaird, The bri-er bush was bon-nie ance in oor Kail-yaird; ∧

*poco rit.* *a tempo.*

1. wee bit white cock-ades for our loy-al Hie-land lads; And the
2. fea-ther in his ban-net, a rib-bon at his knee; He's a
3. blast blew owre the hill that gaed A-tholl's flow'rs a chill; And the

*poco rit.* *a tempo.*

1. lass-es lo'e the bonnie bush in oor Kail-yaird.
2. bon-nie Hie-land lad-die, and you'll na be he!
3. bloom's blawn aff the bonnie bush in oor Kail-yaird!

*poco rit.*

* This air was communicated to Johnson by Burns for the *Scots Museum.* We adopt three of the six verses given by R. A. Smith in his *Scotish Minstrel,* 1822. They are the composition of Lady Nairne, and, like Burns' song in the *Museum,* are founded on the fragment of an old traditional song which seems to have been popular about the middle of last century.

# The women are a' gane wud.*

Spirituoso.

PIANO.

1. The wo-men are a' gane wud, ... O that he had bid-den a - wa'! ... He's
2. My wife she wears the cock-ade, ... She kens 'tis the thing that I hate; ... There's
3. The wild Hieland lads did pass, ... The Yetts wide o - pen did flee; ... They

1. turn'd their heads, the lad, ... And ru - in will bring on us a'. ... I
2. ane too prin'd on her maid, ... And baith will tak' their own gait. ... I've
3. eat the ve - ry hoose bare, ... And spier'd nae leave o' me. ... But

1. aye was a peace - a - ble man, .. My wife she did douce-ly be - have; .. But
2. liev'd a' my days in the strath, . Now To - ries in - fest me at hame; .. And
3. when the red - coats gaed bye, .. D'ye think they'd let him a - lane? .. They

* The older version of this song is in 9 time, which, on the whole, suits the restlessness and annoyance depicted in the verses better than
the more regular setting in 6 rhythm. As, however, the latter version seems to have become more popular—probably because it is more singable
—we have adopted it here. The verses we have taken from R. A. Smith's *Scotish Minstrel*, 1822, vol. iv., p. 41. Smith gives the air in 9 time.

1. now do a' that I can . . . . She's just as wild as the lave. . . .
2. tho' I tak' no part at a', . . . . Baith sides do gie me the blame. . .
3. aye the loud-er did cry, . . . . "Prince Char-lie will sune get his ain." . . .

The wo-men are a' gane wud, . . . O that he had bid-den a-wa'! . . . He's turn'd their heads, the lad, . . . . And ru-in will bring on us a'! . . .

232

## The yellow=hair'd laddie.*

* This air, Stenhouse informs us, is found in Mrs. Crockat's Manuscript Music-Book, 1709. The song is preserved in *The Tea-Table Miscellany*, pt. ii., issued *circa* 1725, as "The auld Yellow-hair'd Laddie." Ramsay wrote verses to the same air commencing, "In April, when primroses paint the sweet plain," and published them in *The Tea-Table Miscellany*, pt. L., 1724; a year later Thomson inserted Ramsay's poem with the air in the first edition of the *Orpheus Caledonius*, after which the melody seems to have become very popular. We find Watts, Adam Craig, McGibbon, and many others, including it in their collections.

*sempre Ped.*

1. aye . . . she milk - ed and aye . . . . she sang, The
2. win - - na bught in tho' I . . . . . shou'd die, O,
3. but - ter and cheese . . . . and a' . . . . shou'd sour, I'll

1. yel - low hair'd lad - die shall be my gude - man; And
2. yel - low hair'd lad - die, be kind . . . . to me; They
3. crack and kiss wi' my love ae . . . . ha'f hour; It's

1. aye . . . . she milk - ed, and aye . . . . she sang, The
2. win - - na bught in tho' I . . . . . shou'd die, O,
3. ae . . . . ha'f hour and we's e'en mak' it three, For the

1. yel - low hair'd lad - die shall be my gude - man.
2. yel - low hair'd lad - die, be kind . . . . to me.
3. yel - low hair'd lad - die my hus - band shall be.

# There's nought but care on ev'ry hand.

### GREEN GROW THE RASHES, O!*

Verses by BURNS.

Allegretto.

VOICE.

PIANO.

*mf*

*mf*

1. There's nought but care on ev'-ry hand, In ev'-ry hour that pass-es, O; What
2. Gie me a can-nie hour at e'en, My arms a-bout my dear-ie, O; An'
3. For you sae douse wha sneer at this, Ye're nought but sense-less ass-es, O, The
4. Auld Na-ture swears the love-ly dears, Her no-blest work she class-es, O, Her

*mf*

1. sig - ni - fies the life o' man, An' 'twere na for the lass - es, O!
2. warld - ly cares, and warld - ly men May a' gae tap - sal - tee - rie, O!
3. wis - est man the warld e'er saw, He dear - ly lo'ed the lass - es, O!
4. pren - tice han' she tried on man, An' then she made the lass - es, O!

* Mr. R. Chambers considers this tune to be one of the oldest which have been handed down to us. It appears in the MS. Lute-Book of Sir Gordon Straloch, compiled between 1627 and 1629, as "Green greus ye rasses, A dannce." Another version of it is preserved in the same MS. as "I kist her while she blusht." Both airs are given in Laing's *Additional Illustrations* to Johnson's *Museum*, p. 138, from which the following is taken: "The MS. from which these tunes are given, is a small oblong 8vo., and has the following title:—' AN PLAYING BOOKE FOR THE LVTE, wherin ar contained many Currents and other musical things. *Musica mentis medicina mœsta.* AT ABERDEIN, Notted and collected by Robert Gordon. In the yeere of our Lord 1627. In februare.' At the end is this colophon, 'Finis huic libro impositus Anno D. 1629. Ad finem Decemb. In Straloch.'" In vol. ii. of *Ancient and Modern Scottish Songs* (1776), Herd prints an old song beginning:

"Green grows the rashes, O,
Green grows the rashes, O,
A feather bed is no sae saft
As a bed amang the rashes, O," etc.

But it is impossible to say whether these are the original verses or not belonging to the air. All we know is, that as far back as can be traced, the tune has been known under the title of "Green grows the rashes, O." although in Bremner's *Collection of Scots Reels*, circa 1757, it is given as "The Grant's Rant." In McGibbon's *Collection of Scots Tunes*, bk. i., 1742, an entirely different melody is given as "Green grows the Rashes."

1. Green grow the rash - es, O! Green grow the rash - es, O! The
2. Green grow the rash - es, O! Green grow the rash - es, O! The
3. Green grow the rash - es, O! Green grow the rash - es, O! The
4. Green grow the rash - es, O! Green grow the rash - es, O! The

1. sweet - est hours that e'er I spent Were spent a - mong the lass - es, O!
2. sweet - est hours that e'er I spent Were spent a - mong the lass - es, O!
3. sweet - est hours that e'er I spent Were spent a - mong the lass - es, O!
4. sweet - est hours that e'er I spent Were spent a - mong the lass - es, O!

Chorus.

Green grow the rash - es, O! Green grow the rash - es, O! The

sweet - est hours that e'er I spent Were spent a - mong the lass - es, O!

# There was a lad was born in Kyle.*

Verses by BURNS.

Air: "O an' ye were deid, guidman."

*Allegretto vivo.*

VOICE.

PIANO.

1. There was a lad was
2. Our mon-arch's hind-most
3. The gos - sip keek - it
4. He'll hae mis - for - tunes
5. But sure as three times

1. born in Kyle, But what - na day or what - na style, I doubt it's hard - ly
2. year but ane Was five and twen - ty days be - gun, 'Twas then a blast o'
3. in his loof, Quo' she, wha lives will see the proof, This wa - ly boy will
4. great an' sma', But ay a heart a - boon them a'; He'll be a cre - dit
5. three mak' nine, I see by il - ka score an' line, This chap will dear - ly

1. worth the while To be sae nice wi' Ro - bin.
2. Jan - war win' Blew han - sel in on Ro - bin.
3. be nae cool, I think we'll ca' him Ro - bin. For Ro - bin was a ro - vin' boy, A
4. till us a' We'll a' be proud o' Ro - bin.
5. like our kin, So leeze me on thee, Ro - bin.

rant - in', ro - vin', rant - in', rovin', Ro - bin was a ro - vin' boy; O ran - tin', ro - vin' Ro - bin.

* This old traditional melody dates probably from as far back as the earlier part of the 16th century; it was used by the Reformers as a hymn tune. Oswald has included it in his *Caledonian Pocket Companion* (commenced 1759), vol. iv. It originally consisted of one strain only, the second being adapted from a variation composed by McGibbon, and published in his *Scots Tunes*, Bk. III., 1755, as "Watson's Scots' Measure." Burns wrote his song in 1784. It is a description of the incidents attending his birth. Burns was born on the 25th of January, 1759.

# There was a lass and she was fair.*

Verses by BURNS.

Air: "Willie was a wanton wag."

*Allegretto.*

VOICE.

PIANO.

1. There was a lass, and she was fair, At
2. But hawks will rob the ten - der joys That
3. He gaed wi' Jean - ie to the tryste, He
4. The sun was sink - ing in the west, The

1. kirk and mar - ket to be seen, When a' the fair - est maids were met, The fair - est maid was
2. bless the lit - tle lint-white's nest; And frost will blight the fair - est flow'rs, And love will break the
3. danc'd wi' Jean - ie on the down; And lang e'er wit - less Jean - ie wist, Her heart was tint, her
4. birds sang sweet in il - ka grove; His cheek to hers he fond - ly press'd, And whis-per'd thus his

1. bon - nie Jean. And aye she wrought her mammie's wark, And aye she sang sae mer - ri - lie; The
2. sound - est rest. Young Rob - bie was the braw - est lad, The flow'r and pride o' a' the glen; And
3. peace was stown. As in the bo - som o' the stream The moonbeam dwells at dew - y e'en; So
4. tale o' lo'e: "O Jean - ie fair, I lo'e thee dear; O canst thou think to fan - cy me? Or

*cres.* *f*

1. blith - est bird up - on the bush Had ne'er a light - er heart than she.
2. he had owsen, sheep, and kye, And wan-ton nai-gies nine or ten.
3. trembling, pure, was tender love With - in the breast o' bon - nie Jean.
4. wilt thou leave thy mammie's cot, And learn to tent the farms wi' me?"

*cres.* *f*

---

* George Thomson adapted these verses to the tune, "Willie was a wanton wag," and inserted them in his Collection. Burns wrote the verses in 1793. The heroine of the song was Miss Jane McMurdo, daughter of John McMurdo, Esq., Chamberlain to the Duke of Queensberry. The air, "Willie was a wanton wag," was first published in the second edition of Thomson's *Orpheus Caledonius*, 1733, vol. ii, p. 60.

# There was anes a May.

## WERE NA MY HEART LICHT I WAD DEE.*

Verses by LADY GRIZEL BAILLIE.

1. There was anes a May, and she lo'ed na men; She big-git her bon-nie bow'r
2. When bon-nie young John-nie cam' owre the sea, He said he saw nae-thing sae
3. He had a wee las-sie that lo'ed na me, Be-cause I was twice as
4. And were I but young for thee as I hae been, We should hae be gal-lop-ing

1. doun in yon glen; But now she cries, dule and a-well-a-day! Come
2. bon-nie as me; He haight me baith rings and mon-ie braw things; And
3. bon-nie as she; She rais'd sick a po-ther 'twixt him and his mo-ther, That
4. doun in yon green, And link-in' out o'er the li-ly-white lea; And

1. doun the green gate, and come here a-way!
2. were na my heart licht I wad dee.
3. were na my heart licht I wad dee.
4. wow, giu I were but young for thee!

* This song, with its air, appears in Thomson's *Orpheus Caledonius*, 1725, p. 40, under the title of, " Were ne my Hearts light I wad Dye."
Later on, Allan Ramsay inserted it in the fourth part of the *Tea-Table Miscellany*. The complete ballad consists of ten verses. Lady Grizel
Home, by whom it was written, was the daughter of Sir Patrick Home, afterwards Earl of Marchmont; she was born at Redbraes Castle in
1665. In 1692 she married George Baillie, of Jarviswood; she died in the 81st year of her life, in 1746.

# Three score o' nobles rade up the King's ha'.

## GLENOGIE.*

*Moderato.*

VOICE.

1. Three score o'  no - bles rade
2. "Haud your tongue, doch - ter, there's
3. "There is,  Glen - o - gie,  a
4.   Then to Glen - fel - dy's,—but
5.   Pale and  wan  was  she when Glen-

PIANO.

*mf*  *cres.*  *sf*  *p*  *mf*

con Ped.  *sempre con Ped.*

1.  up   the King's ha',   But  bon - nie  Glen - o - gie's  the flow'r o' them  a'!  Wi'
2. bet - ter  than  he,"  "O   say  na  sae, mith - er,  for that can - na  be;  Tho'
3. let - ter  for thee,  O  there is,  Glen - o - gie,  a  let - ter for  thee!"  The
4. sma' mirth  was  there,  And  bon - nie  Jean's mith - er  was  tear - in' her  hair;  "Ye're
5. o - gie gaed  ben,  But  ro - sy  red  grew she  when - e'er  he  sat  doun;  She

1. his milk-white steed and his  bon - nie  black e'e,  "Glen - o - gie, dear mither, Glen - o - gie for  me!"
2. Doumlie is great-er and  rich - er  than he,  Yet  if  I maun tak' him, I'll cer - tain - ly  dee."
3. first line he look'd at  a  licht lauch lauched he,  But  ere he had read thro't, tears blinded his  e'e.
4. wel-come, Glen - o - gie, ye're  wel-come!" quo' she,  "Ye're welcome, Glen-o-gie, your Jea-nie to  see."
5. turn-ed  a - wa', wi' a  smile  in  her e'e,  "O  din - na fear, mither, I'll may be no  dee!"

*rit.*

*Last time.*

*mf*  *cres.*  *sf*  *p*

* The first printed version of this ancient ballad and air is found in R. A. Smith's *The Scotish Minstrel*, 1822-24, vol. iv., p. 78. Smith's version contains eight verses. The incident which furnished the theme of the ballad is thus described by Buchan in his *Ancient Ballads*, vol. i., p. 319. "When the intestine troubles and broils of the North disturbed the public peace so much, in 1562, the Queen's presence was thought necessary to put a stop to some of them, and for this purpose she appeared in the North among her friends and foes. Jane, daughter of Baron Meldrum and laird of Bothelule, in Aberdeenshire, was one of Queen Mary's favourites, with whom she occasionally dined at the house of Fetternear, where the Queen resided for a few days; and, having chanced to espy Sir George Gordon, of Glenlogie, as he rode through the village of Banchory, fell desperately in love with him, and, that he might know her case, she despatched a letter to him for this purpose, but he, for a while, made light of the same, which came to the lady's ears, and threw her into a violent fever. Her father's chaplain, no doubt bred at the court of Cupid, undertook the correspondence, and was more successful. She was afterwards married to Sir George, the object of her wishes, in her fifteenth year."

## Thy cheek is o' the rose's hue.*

Verses by RICHARD GALL, 1776–1801.

Air: "My only jo and dearie, O."

*Moderato.*

VOICE.

PIANO.

*p*

*con Ped.*

*p*

*p*

1. Thy cheek is o' the ro - se's hue, My on - ly jo and
2. The bird - ie sings up - on the thorn, It sang o' joy fu'
3. When we were bairn - ies on yon brae, And youth was blink - in',
4. I ha'e a wish I can - na tine, 'Mang a' the cares that

1. dear - ie, O; Thy neck is like the sil - er dew, Up -
2. cheer - ie, O, Re - joic - ing in the sim - mer morn, Nae
3. bon - nie, O, Aft we would daff the lee - lang day, Our
4. grieve me, O; A wish that thou wert ev - er mine, And

* Richard Gall, the author of this beautiful song, was brought up as a joiner, but later on, entered the printing office of Mr. Ramsay, Edinburgh. He died in his 25th year. The above song was written at the request of Mr. Thomas Oliver, publisher, Edinburgh. Mr. Oliver heard the air sung in the pantomime of Harlequin Highlander, at the Circus. He was so struck with it that it dwelt upon his mind. The only part of the words he recollected were:—

"My love's the sweetest creature
That ever trode the dewy grass;

Her cheeks they are like roses
Wi' the opening gowans wet between."

Gall's song, with the air, was included in the sixth and last volume of Johnson's *Scots Musical Museum*, 1803. Christie gives an air in his *Traditional Ballad Airs*, vol. i., 1876, entitled "Cow the gowan," which resembles "Thy cheek is o' the rose's hue." This melody was obtained by the Dean's grandfather, from Singing Jamie, a blind mendicant, well known in the Buchan district towards the close of last century.

cres.

1. on the bank sae brier - ie, O. Thy teeth are o' the
2. care to mak' it eer - ie, O. Ah! lit - tle kens the
3. joys fu' sweet and mon - ie, O. Aft wad I chase thee
4. nev - er mair to leave thee; O. Then I wad dawt thee

cres.

p

1. i - vor - y; O, sweet's the twin - kle o' thine e'e, Nac
2. sang - ster sweet, Aught o' the cares I hae to meet, That
3. owre the lee, And round a - bout the thorn - y tree, Or
4. night and day, Nac i - ther warld - ly care I'd ha'e, Till

poco rit.

1. joy, nae plea - sure blinks on me, My on - ly jo and
2. gars my rest - less bo - som beat, My on - ly jo and
3. pu' the wild flow'rs a' for thee, My on - ly jo and
4. life's warm stream for - gat to play, My on - ly jo and

poco rit.

1. dear - ie, O.
2. dear - ie, O.
3. dear - ie, O.
4. dear - ie, O.

p rit.

# To the Lords o' Convention.

### BONNIE DUNDEE.*

*Allegro spirituoso.*

Verses by Sir WALTER SCOTT.

PIANO. *mf*

*mf >*

*cres.*

1. To the Lords o' Con - ven - tion 'twas Cla - ver - house spoke, "Ere the
2. Dun - dee he is mount - ed, he rides up the street, The
3. There are hills be - yond Pent - land, and lands be - yond Forth, Be there
4. Then a - wa' to the hills, to the lea, to the rocks, Ere I

1. King's crown go down there are crowns to be broke; Then each Ca - va - lier who loves
2. bells they ring back - ward and drums they are beat, But the pro - vost (douce man) said, "Just
3. lords in the south, there are chiefs in the north, There are brave Duin - ne - was - sels, three
4. own a u - surp - er I'll crouch wi' the fox; And trem - ble, fause Whigs, in the

*cres.*

1. hon - our and me, Let him fol - low the bon - nets o' Bon - nie Dun - dee."
2. e'en let it be, For the town is weel rid o' that de'il o' Dun - dee."
3. thou - sand times three, Will cry, "Hie, for the bon - nets o' Bon - nie Dun - dee!"
4. midst o' your glee, Ye hae no seen the last o' my bon - nets and me!

*f*

Come

*f*

*f*

---

* Sir Walter Scott's song consists of eleven verses; it was written in 1825, and first published in "The Doom of Devorgoil," 1830. In vol. v., p. 17, of D'Urfey's *Pills*, 1719, there is a song entitled "Jockey's escape from Dundee," and set to a version of the old air "Adew, Dundee." (*See* p. 7.) The following is the chorus of D'Urfey's verses; it is probably the fragment of some song belonging to a period much older than that in which D'Urfey flourished.

Come fill up my Cup, come fill up my Can,    |    Come open the Gates, and let me go free,
Come saddle my Horse, and call up my Man,    |    And shew me the way to Bonny Dundee.

The above melody is evidently quite modern, and is given in *Lyric Gems of Scotland*, 1856, as the composition of an unknown author.

fill up my cup, come fill up my can, Come sad-dle my hor-ses and

call out my men; Un - hook the West - port and let us gae free, For its

up wi' the bon-nets o' Bon - nie Dun-dee!

# 'Twas on a simmer's afternoon.

## THE LASS O' GOWRIE.*

Verses by Lady Nairne.
Moderato assai.

Air: " O'er young to marry yet."

VOICE.

PIANO.

*p*

*rit.*

*p*

*p*

1. 'Twas on a sim-mer's af-ter-noon, A wee be-fore the
2. I prais'd her beau-ty loud an' lang, Then round her waist my
3. Saft kiss-es on her lips I laid, The blush up-on her

1. sun gaed down, My las-sie, wi' a braw new gown, Cam'
2. arms I flang, Au' said, "My dear-ie, will ye gang To
3. cheeks soon spread; She whis-per'd mod-est-ly, and said, "I'll

* This air is derived from an old Scottish Strathspey, preserved by Bremner in his *Collection of Scots Reels or Country Dances*, 1757, as "O'er young to marry yet"; Gow prints an embellished version of it in his *A Second Collection of Strathspey Reels*, etc., 1788, as "Loch Erroch Side, a Strathspey. Composed by Niel Gow & his second Wife." The Carse of Gowrie lies between Perth and Dundee, and is one of the most fertile spots in Scotland.

*poco rit.*      *p a tempo.*

1. owre the hills to Gow - rie. The rose - bud tinged wi'
2. see the Carse o' Gow - rie? I'll tak' ye to my
3. gang wi' ye to Gow - rie." The auld folks soon gaed

1. morn - ing show'r, Blooms fresh with - in the sun - ny bow'r; But
2. fa - ther's ha', In yon green field be - side the shaw; I'll
3. their con - sent, Syne for Mess John they quick - ly sent, Wha

1. Ka - tie was the fair - est flow'r That ev - er bloom'd in
2. mak' you la - dy o' them a', The braw - est wife in
3. tied them to their heart's con - tent, And now she's La - dy

1. Gow - rie.
2. Gow - rie."
3. Gow - rie!

# 'Twas within a mile o' Edinburgh town.

Moderato e grazioso.

Verses adapted from Thomas D'Urfey.

1. 'Twas with - in a mile of Ed-in - burgh town, In the ro - sy time o' the
2. Young Jock-ie was a wag that nev-er wad wed, Tho' lang he had fol-low'd the
3. But when he vow'd he wad mak' her his bride, Tho' his flocks and herds were na

1. year; Sweet flow - ers bloom'd, and the grass was down, And each
2. lass; Con - tent - ed she earn'd and eat her brown bread, And
3. few, She gi'ed him her hand, and a kiss be - side, And

poco rit.

cres.

* This air is the composition of James Hook. It is a good example of a melody written in the "Scots style." Hook was born at Norwich, 1746, and died in 1827. The original version of the poem is found in *Wit and Mirth; or, Pills to Purge Melancholy*, vol. i., 1698, under the title of "A Scotch Song," the first verse of which is:—

'Twas within a Mile o' Edinborough Town,
In the Rosie time of the year when the Grass was down;
Bonnie Jockey Blith and Gay,
Said to Jenny making Hay,
Let's sit a little (Dear), and prattle;
'Tis a sultry Day.

The song is attributed to D'Urfey, the air to which it is set is English, and bears some resemblance to "Come with me a-rushing," preserved in Queen Elizabeth's Virginal Book. Hook's composition quickly became popular; it is included in many Scottish musical works issued during the latter half of last century, and among others, in *The Musical Miscellany*, Perth, 1786.

1. shep - herd woo'd his dear. Bon - nie Jock-ie, blythe and gay,
2. mer-ri - ly turn'd up the grass. Bon - nie Jock-ie, blythe and free,
3. vow'd she'd ev - er be true. Bon - nie Jock-ie, blythe and free,

1. kiss'd young Jen - nie mak-ing hay; The las - sie blush'd, and, frown-ing, cried, "Na,
2. Won her heart right mer-ri - ly; Yet still she blush'd, and, frown-ing, cried, "Na,
3. Won her heart right mer-ri - ly; At kirk she no more frown-ing cried, "Na,

*poco rit.* *a tempo.*

1. na, it win - na do, I can - na, can - na, win - na, win - na,
2. na, it win - na do, I can - na, can - na, win - na, win - na,
3. na, it win - na do, I can - na, can - na, win - na, win - na,

*rall. e colla voce.* *a tempo.*

1. mau - na buc - kle to!"
2. mau - na buc - kle to!"
3. mau - na buc - kle to!"

*mf*   *poco rit.*

# 'Twas in that season of the year.

### ROSLIN CASTLE.*

Verses by RICHARD HEWITT.

Air : "House of Glams."

*Larghetto con molto espressione.*

PIANO.

con Ped.

1. 'Twas in that sea - son of the year, When all things gay and sweet ap-pear, That
2. A - wake, sweet muse! the breath-ing spring With rap - ture warms; a - wake and sing! A -
3. O come, my love! thy Co - lin's lay With rap - ture calls, O come a - way! Come,

con Ped.

1. Co - lin, with the morn-ing ray, A - rose and sung his ru - ral lay. Of
2. wake and join the vo - cal throng, Who hail the morn - ing with a song. To
3. while the muse this wreath shall twine A - round that mod - est brow of thine. O

mf

rit.       p a tempo.

1. Nan - cy's charms the shep-herd sung, The hills and dales with Nan - cy . . rung; And
2. Nan - cy raise the cheer-ful lay, O bid her haste and come a - way; In
3. bi - ther haste, and with thee bring That beau - ty bloom-ing like the . . spring, Those

rit.       a tempo.

poco rit.

1. Ros - lin Cas - tle heard the swain, And e - choed back the cheer - ful strain.
2. sweet - est smiles her - self a - dorn, And add new gra - ces to the morn.
3. gra - ces that di - vine - ly shine, And charm this ra - vish'd breast o' thine.

f poco rit.

* This air appears on p. 18 of M'Gibbon's *Scots Tunes*, Bk. II., 1746, as the "House of Glams." It has been wrongly attributed by many to Oswald, although never claimed by that clever composer of Scottish melodies. The song is published in Herd's *Scots Songs*, 1776, vol. i.; and, with the air, in *St. Cecilia ; or, the Lady's and Gentleman's Harmonious Companion*, Edinburgh, 1779 ; and again in *The Musical Miscellany*, issued at Perth in 1786. Richard Hewitt was a native of Cumberland. He was educated by Dr. Blacklock, whose amanuensis he was for some years. He died in 1764.

# We'll meet beside the dusky glen.

Verses by ROBERT TANNAHILL.

1. We'll meet be-side the dus-ky glen, on yon burn - side, Where the bush-es form a co-sie den, on yon burn - side; Tho' the broom-y knowes be green, Yet there we may be seen; But we'll meet, we'll meet at e'en, down by yon burn - side.

2. I'll lead thee to the birk-en bow'r, on yon burn - side, Sae sweet-ly wove wi' woodbine flow'r, on yon burn - side; There the ma-vis we will hear, And the black-bird sing-in' clear, As on my arm ye lean, down by yon burn - side.

3. The plant-in' taps are ting'd wi' gowd, on yon burn - side, And gloam-in' draws her fog-gy shroud, o'er yon burn - side; Far frae the noi-sy scene, I'll thro' the fields a - lane, There we'll meet, my ain dear Jean! down by yon burn - side.

* This melody is another version of "The bonnie brier-bush"; it was first published by R. A. Smith. In addition to our note on p. 229, it may be mentioned that the air "The brier-bush," is a variation of an old tune published in Oswald's *Pocket Companion*, under the title of "For the lak of gold I lost her, O,"—a tune which in many ways greatly resembles the old melody, "I love my love in secret." (*See* p. 126.)

## Were J but able to rehearse.

### THE EWIE WI' THE CROOKIT HORN.*

Verses by John Skinner.

Air: "Carron's Reel."

1. Were I but a - ble
2. I nev - er need-ed
3. And cauld or hun - ger
4. But yet last ouk, for
5. I socht her sair up -
6. O gin I had the
7. O had she died o'
8. But thus, puir thing, to
9. O a' ye bards be -

1. to re - hearse My ew - ie's praise in pro - per verse, I'd sound it forth as
2. tar nor keil To mark her up - on hip or heel; Her crook - it horn - ie
3. nev - er dang her, Wind or wet could nev - er wrang her; Ance she lay an
4. a' my keep - in' (Wha can speak it with - out greet - in'?) Vil - lains cam' when
5. on the morn, An' doun a - neath, a buss o' thorn, I got my ew - ie's
6. loun that did it, I hae sworn as weel as said it, Tho' the warld should
7. crouk, or cauld, As ew - ies do when they grow auld, It wad - na been, by
8. lose her life Be - neath a blui - dy vil - lain's knife; I'm real - ly fley't that
9. north King-horn, Ca' up your mu - ses, let them mourn, Our ew - ie wi' the

* This is a Highland dance-tune, a somewhat different version of which is published in Angus Cumming's *Collection of Strathspeys or old Highland Reels*, 1780, as "Carron's Reel, or U Choria Chruim"; it is also included in Robert Ross' *Scots Reels*, 1780, and in Gow's *Collection of Strathspey Reels*, 1784. The "Ewie wi' the crookit horn" is the whiskey-still with its spiral apparatus. We give here the genuine melody with the flattened seventh, the characteristic of Scotish bagpipe music. The Rev. John Skinner was born at Balfour, in the parish of Birse, Aberdeenshire, in 1721. In 1742 he settled at Longside, near Peterhead, as Pastor of the Episcopal Church. He ministered there until his death in 1807. Two years after his death a little book was published entitled *Amusements of leisure hours; or, poetical pieces by the late Reverend John Skinner*, Edinburgh, 1809. This work contains an interesting sketch of the Author's life. Burns greatly admired Skinner's genius as a song writer. He alludes to "Tullochgorum" as "this first of songs" and "masterpiece." *See Reliques*, p. 281. Skinner probably wrote his "Ewie wi' the crookit horn" not later than 1780, and there is strong reason to believe that the air was composed about the same date.

1. loud and fierce As ev - er pi - per's drone could blaw.
2. did as weel To ken her by a - mang them a'.
3. ouk and lan - ger Furth a - neath a wreath o' snaw.
4. I was sleep - in', Staw my ew - ie, horn an' a'!
5. crook - it horn, . . But my ew - ie was a - wa! } The
6. a' for - bid it, I wad gi'e his neck a thraw.
7. mon - y fauld, Sae sair a heart to nane o's a'.
8. our guide - wife Will nev - er win a - boon't a - va.
9. crook - it horn Is frae us stown, and fell't an' a'!

ew - ie, wi' the crook - it horn! Wha had kent her might ha'e sworn

Sic a ewe was nev - er born, Here - a - bout, or far a - wa'!

con brio.

f          dim.          p

# Wha the de'il ha'e we gotten for a king?

### THE WEE, WEE GERMAN LAIRDIE.*

* One of the most virulent of Jacobite ballads. It appears in Cromek's *Reliques of Nithsdale and Galloway Song*, 1810, p. 117. The air, which was contributed by Burns to the *Scots Museum*, vol. v., 1796, with new verses entitled, "O May, thy morn was ne'er so sweet," seems to bear striking resemblance to "When the King came o'er the water" (published in M'Gibbon's *Scots Tunes*, Bk. III., 1755), or, as it is sometimes called, "Lady Keith's Lament," a tune which the Irish claim under the title of "The Boyne Water." Another version of the air is given in Mr. Lachlan McBean's *Songs and Hymns of the Scottish Highlands*, as "O Theid Sinn." Hogg has included the song in his *Jacobite Relics*, Ser. I., 1819. In a note to it on p. 263 he writes: "This is one of the most spirited songs existing, and a great favourite all over Scotland. . . It is sung to many different tunes in different districts of the kingdom: but the one to which it is here set was composed by me a number of years bygone, and it having been sung so often to it, I found that all over the south country any other would have been reckoned spurious. I have, however, added the best original one I could find, which, though perhaps scarcely so good a tune as the former, is more in character." It is needless to remark that Hogg's own tune has been quite forgotten—indeed, we doubt if it was ever known at all, and that the old setting is now universally used. Another interesting version of the air, "What the D'il," is given in *Traditional Tunes*, Collected and Edited by Frank Kidson, Oxford, 1891, under the title of "The Dowie Dens of Yarrow." It was contributed to Mr. Kidson's work by Mrs. Calvert, of Gilknockie, in Eskdale. "Mrs. Calvert originally obtained it on the braes of Yarrow from her grandmother, who was the celebrated Tibbie Shiel, the humble friend of Sir Walter Scott and James Hogg."

1. del - vin in his kail yaird - ie. He was sheugh - in' kail, and
2. dib - bled them in his yaird - ie. He has pu'd the rose o'
3. dib - bled in his yaird - ie. An' if a stock ye
4. bark and howl in Ger - man. Then keep thy dib - ble

1. lay - in' leeks Wi' - out the hose and but the breeks, An'
2. Eng - lish loons, An' broke the harp o' Ir - ish clowns; But our
3. daur to pu', Or haud the yok - in' o' a plough, We'll
4. in thy hand, Thy spade put in thy yaird - ie, For

1. up wi' his beg - gar duds he cleeks, This wee, wee Ger - man
2. this - tle taps will jag his thumbs, This wee, wee Ger - man
3. brak your scep - tre owre your mou', Thou wee, bit Ger - man
4. wha the de'il now claims thy land, But a wee, wee Ger - man

1. laird - ie!
2. laird - ie!
3. laird - ie!
4. laird - ie!

# Wha wadna be in love wi' bonnie Maggie Lauder?

## MAGGIE LAUDER.*

Verses by FRANCIS SEMPLE, born *circa* 1615, died 1685.

1. Wha wad - na be in love Wi' bon - nie Mag - gie Lau - der; A pi - per met her gaun to Fife, An' spier'd what was't they ca'd her. Right
2. "Mag - gie," quo' he, "by my bags, I'm fid - gin' fain to see thee; Sit doun by me, my bon - nie bird, In troth, I win - na steer thee. For
3. "Then," quo' Meg, "hae ye your bags, An' is your drone in or - der? If ye be Rob, I've heard o' you, Live you up - on the Bor - der? The
4. To his bags he flew wi' speed, A - bout the drone he twist - ed; Meg up and wal - lop'd owre the green, For braw - ly could she frisk it. "Weel
5. "Weel you've play'd your part," quo' Meg, "Your cheeks are like the crim - son; There's nane in Scot - land plays sae weel, Sin' we lost Hab - bie Sim - son. I've

* Although probably belonging to a much older date, this fine song first appears in Herd's *Collection of Scottish Songs*, vol. ii., 1776. It is attributed to Francis Semple, of Beltrees, Renfrewshire, on the not very reliable authority of his grandchildren. The author of the air is unknown, but it seems to have been sung in London about the beginning of the 18th century. We have not been able to find it in any collection of Scottish music prior to Adam Craig's *A Collection of the Choicest Scots Tunes*, p. 34, a work issued in 1730. Some years later, M'Gibbon published it with variations composed by himself, in his *Scots Tunes*, Bk. I., p. 16. 1742. Gay introduced it in his opera *Achilles*, published 1733. "Anster" is the town of Anstruther, Fifeshire. Habbie Simson was the celebrated piper of Kilbarchan, whose memory and merits are preserved in an excellent elegy composed by Robert Semple (the father of Francis Semple), and published in Watson's *A Choice Collection of Comic and Serious Scots Poems*, pt. i., p. 32, issued in 1706.

*poco rit.* . . . .

1. scorn - ful - ly she an - swer'd him, "Be - gone, you hal - lan sha - ker! Jogg
2. I'm a pi - per to my trade, My name is Rob the Ran - ter, The
3. lass - es a', baith far and near, Have heard o' Rob the Ran - ter; I'll
4. done!" quo' he, "Play up!" quo' she; "Weel bobb'd," quo' Rob the Ran - ter; "'Tis
5. liv'd in Fife, baith maid an' wife, These ten years and a quar - ter; Gin

*poco rit.* . . . .

f

*poco rit.*

1. on your gate, you blad - der - skate, My name is Mag - gie Lau - der."
2. lass - es loup as they were daft, When I blaw up my chan - ter."
3. shake my foot wi' right gude will, Gif you'll blaw up your chan - ter."
4. worth my while to play, in - deed, When I ha'e sic a dan - cer."
5. ye should come to Au - ster fair, Speir ye for Mag - gie Lau - der."

*colla voce.*

*poco rit.*

*Allegro con brio.*

f

*sf*

# Wha wadna fecht for Charlie?

Maestoso.

Air: "Will ye go and marry Kettie."

VOICE.

PIANO.

1. Wha wad - na fecht for Char - lie? Wha wad - na draw the sword?
2. Rouse, rouse, ye kilt - ed war - riors, Rouse, he - roes of the North!
3. See, north - ern clans ad - vanc - ing! Glen - gar - ry and Loch - iel!

1. Wha wad - na up and ral - ly At the roy - al Prin - ce's word?
2. Rouse, join your chief - tain's ban - ners— 'Tis your Prince that calls you forth!
3. See, bran - dish'd broad - swords glanc - ing!— High - land hearts are true as steel!

1. Think on Sco - tia's an - cient he - roes, Think on fo - reign foes re - pell'd,
2. Shall we base - ly crouch to ty - rants, Shall we own a fo - reign sway?
3. Now our Prince has rais'd our ban - ner, Now tri - um - phant is the cause,

* From James Hogg's *Jacobite Relics*, Ser. II., 1821. The air was first published in Neil Stewart's *A Collection of the Newest and Best Reels or Country Dances*, 1761, as, "Will ye go & marry Kettie?" and in Angus Cumming's *A Collection of Strathspeys or Old Highland Reels*, 1780, as "Mulchard's Dream, or Bruarthar Feare Mulachaird"; Gow names it "Marry Ketty" in his *Second Collection*, 1788.

1. Think on glo - rious Bruce and Wal - lace, Who the proud u - sur - pers quell'd.
2. Shall a roy - al Stuart be ban - ish'd While a stran - ger rules the day?
3. Now the Scot - tish li - on ral - lies— Let us strike for Prince and laws!

CHORUS.

Wha wad - na fecht for Char - lie? Wha wad - na draw the sword?

Wha wad - na up and ral - ly At the roy - al Prin - ce's word?

# Whar' hae ye been a' day?

## MY BOY TAMMIE.*

Verses by HECTOR MACNEILL.

1. Whar' ha'e ye been a' day,
2. An' whaur gat ye that young thing,
3. What said ye to the bon - nie bairn,
4. I held her to my beat-in' heart, My
5. Has she been to the kirk wi' thee,

1. My boy Tammie? An' whar' ha'e ye been a' day, My boy Tammie? I've been by burn and
2. My boy Tammie? An' whaur gat ye that young thing, My boy Tammie? I gat her doun in
3. My boy Tammie? What said ye to the bon-nie bairn, My boy Tammie? I prais'd her e'en, sae
4. young, my smiling lammie; I held her to my beatin' heart, My young, my smiling lammie. I ha'e a house, it
5. My boy Tammie? Has she been to the kirk wi' thee, My boy Tammie? O, she's been to the

1. flow'ry brae, Meadow green and mountain grey, Courtin' o' this young thing, Just come frae her mammie.
2. yonder howe, Smiling on a broom-y knowe, Herding ae wee lamb and yowe, For her puir mammie.
3. lovely blue, Her dimpled cheek an' cher-ry mou', An' pree'd it aft as ye may trow!—She said she'd tell her mammie!
4. cost me dear, I've walth o' plen-ish-ing an' gear, Ye'se get it a', wer't ten times mair, Gin ye will leave your mammie.
5. kirk wi' me, An' the tear was in her e'e, For O! she's but a young thing, Just come frae her mammie!

* Hector Macneill's beautiful verses first appeared in an Edinburgh magazine called *The Bee*, in 1791. Mr. G. F. Graham, in Wood's *Songs of Scotland*, vol. i., 1852, shows that the melody is evidently a comparatively modern transformation of the tune, "Muirland Willie" (see p. 150). In the *Museum Illustrations*, No. 502, Mr. Stenhouse gives two verses of an old song which he had often heard sung by old people in his boyhood. The following is one of the verses:—

Is she fit to soop the house, my boy Tammie?
Is she fit to soop the house, my boy Tammie?

She's just as fit to soop the house as the cat to tak' a mouse;
And yet she's but a young thing, just come frae her mammie.

# What ails this heart o' mine?

Verses by Miss Susanna Blamire.

Air: "My dearie, an' thou dee."

* A version of this ancient melody appears in the MS. Lyra-Viol Book of the celebrated Dr. John Leyden, *circa* 1695–1700, and in the *Orpheus Caledonius*, vol. ii., 1733, to verses by Crawfurd beginning, "Love never more shall give me pain." But Thomson's "set" of the melody differs considerably from the one given above, which seems to be more modern. Miss Blamire was born at Cardew Hall, Cumberland, in 1747. She seems to have been of an affable, lively disposition, and beloved by all who knew her. She died at Carlin in 1794.

s 2

# What's a' the steer, Kimmer?

*Allegro con spirito.*

VOICE.

PIANO.

*mf*

1. What's a' the steer, Kim-mer? What's a' the steer? Char - lie he is land - ed, And
2. I'm glad to hear't, Kim-mer, I'm glad to hear't, I ha'e a gude braid clay - more, And

1. haith he'll soon be here; The win' was at his back, Carle, The
2. for his sake I'll wear't; Sin Char - lie he is land - ed, We

1. win' was at his back, I care - na, sin' he's come, Carle, We were na worth a plack.
2. hae nae mair to fear, Sin Char - lie he is come, Kimmer, We'll hae a jub' - lee year!

*cres.*

*sf*

*cres.*

* This air is published in R. A. Smith's *Scotish Minstrel*, vol. ii., 1822. The words bear considerable similarity to verses published in Cromek's *Reliques of Nithsdale and Galloway Song*, p. 113, beginning, "What news to me, Carlin?" About 1825, through the singing of Miss Stephens, afterwards Countess of Essex, "What's a' the steer, Kimmer?" became very popular.

# What's this dull town to me?

ROBIN ADAIR.*

Andantino.

VOICE.

PIANO.

*poco rit.*

1. What's this dull
2. What made th' as -
3. But now thou'rt

1. town to me? Ro - bin's not near; What was't I wish'd to see?
2. sem - bly shine? Ro - bin A - dair; What made the ball so fine?
3. cold to me, Ro - bin A - dair; But now thou'rt cold to me,

1. What wish'd to hear? Where's all the joy and mirth Made this town heav'n on earth?
2. Ro - bin was there. What when the play was o'er, What made my heart so sore?
3. Ro - bin A - dair. Yet he I lov'd so well, Still in my heart shall dwell;

*cres.*

1. O, they're all fled wi' thee, Ro - bin A - dair.
2. O, it was part - ing with Ro - bin A - dair.
3. Oh, I can ne'er for - get Ro - bin A - dair.

* This is the modernised version of the old Celtic air. Regarding it, Mr. Colin Brown remarks in *The Thistle*, p. 167: "It belongs to a class of gems which bear the impress of remote antiquity. Few of such peerless beauty can be found in music, so simple in construction, and so full of power and pathos. The Celtic name of this air is *Ceud mile fàilte, Eilean mo rùn*—A hundred thousand welcomes, island of my love. It belongs alike to the ancient Sons of Ireland and Scotland." Verses beginning, "You're welcome to Paxton, Robin Adair," were formerly sung to the air of "Robin Adair"; a good version of them is given in Sime's *Edinburgh Musical Miscellany*, vol. ii., 1793. The Irish name of the tune is "Aileen Aroon," and under this title Gow prints it in his *Second Repository*.

# When all the birds in Gaelic sang.

### An uair bha Gàilig aig na h-eòin.

Translated from the Gaelic of J. MacCuaraig
by Lachlan MacBean.

1. When all the birds in Gae-lic sang, Milk lay like dew up-on the lea; The
2. was no dis-cord, war or strife, For none were wrong'd and none op-press'd; But
3. pi - ty, and good-will were spread A-mong the peo - ple ev'-ry-where; From

1. heath - - er - in-to hon-ey sprang, And ev'-ry-thing was
2. ev' - - ry-one just led the life, And did the things that
3. where the morn-ing ri-ses red To where the eve - - ning

1. good and free.
2. pleased him best.
3. shin - eth fair.

* By kind permission, from *Songs and Hymns of the Scottish Highlands*, edited by Lachlan MacBean. The Gaelic verses were probably written at the close of the last century; they are entitled " Linn an aigh."—The happy age.

# When I think on this warld's pelf.

## "SHAME FA' THE GEAR AND THE BLATHRIE O'T!" *

1. When I think on this warld's pelf And the lit-tle share I ha'e
2. Joc-kie was the lad that held the pleuch, But now he's got gowd and
3. Jen-ny was the lass that muck-it the byre, But now she's clead in her
4. But all this ne'er shall daun-ton me, Sae lang as I keep my

1. o't to my-self; And how the lass that wants it is
2. gear e - neuch, He thinks nae mair o' me that
3. silk - en at-tire; And Jock - ie says he lo'es her, and
4. fan - cy free; The lad that's sae in - con - stant, he

1. by the lads for - got, May the shame fa' the gear and the blath - rie o't!
2. wears the plai-din' coat, May the shame fa' the gear and the blath - rie o't!
3. me he has for - got, May the shame fa' the gear and the blath - rie o't!
4. is na worth a groat, May the shame fa' the gear and the blath - rie o't!

"Shame fa' the gear and the bladry o't" is an old Scottish proverb. Kelly, in *Scots Proverbs*, 1721, says that it "is the turn of an old Scottish song, spoken when a young handsome girl marries an old man upon account of his wealth." A seemingly more modern version of the song is published in Yair's *Charmer*, 1749. In *Reliques*, p. 210, Burns prints a song containing the same proverb in the last line of each verse. This song, the Poet remarks, "was the earliest song I remember to have got by heart. When a child, an old woman sung it to me, and I picked it up, every word, at first hearing." The air is included in McGibbon's *Scots Tunes*, Bk. III., 1755, as "De'el take the gear & the bladrie o't."

# When life was gay.*

Gaelic Tune: "Robi donn gòrach."

Molto andante.

VOICE.

PIANO.

1. When life was gay an'
2. Nae bird - ie sing - in'
3. But sin' the dear - est

1. hope was young, Nae cares to ... mak' me ee - rie, O; By ..
2. frae the tree Was hauf sac ... blythe, sae gay as me; Till ..
3. bliss o' man That wyles our ... way sae drear - ie, O; The ..

poco cres.

dim.

1. birk - en - shaw I sat an' sung, An' tun'd my pipe fu'
2. tost up - on life's trou - bled sea, I tra - vers'd lang an'
3. braw - est lass in a' the lan' Smiles on me kind an'

poco cres.

dim.

poco rit.

1. cheer - ie, O.
2. wear - ie, O.
3. cheer - ie, O.

poco rit.

p

poco rit.

* This is one of the many versions of an old Gaelic air, known as "Robi donn gòrach," and published by Gow in his first *Collection of Strathspey Reels*, as "Robie donna gorach, Daft Robin, an old Highland song." Alluding to this air, which, in the *Museum* is set to the old song, "Todlen Hame," Mr. Stenhouse remarks that it "has been wrought into a variety of modern tunes; such as 'Armstrong's Farewell'; 'Robidh donna gorrah'; 'The Days o' Langsyne'; 'Lude's Lament'; 'The Death of the Chief,' etc.," *Museum Illustrations*, No. 275. To this list may be added, "Nae mair we'll meet"; "My ain Fire-side"; and "Na laithean a dhaoim; or, The Gay Days of Yore." The verses which we have adopted in this work, are reprinted by permission from Mr. R. Maver's *Genuine Scottish Melodies*.

# When o'er the hill the eastern star.

Verses by Burns.

**MY AIN KIND DEARIE, O.**

_Allegretto._

PIANO.

_poco rit._

1. When o'er the hill the east-ern star Tells bught-in'-time is near, my jo; And
2. In mirk-est glen, at mid-night hour, I'd rove, an' ne'er be co-rie, O; If
3. The hun-ter lo'es the morn-ing sun, To rouse the moun-tain deer, my jo; At

1. ow-sen frae the fur-row'd field Re-turn sae dowf and wea-ry, O! Down
2. thro' that glen I gaed to thee, My ain, my ain kind dea-rie, O! Al-
3. noon the fish-er seeks the glen, A-long the burn to steer, my jo; Gi'e

1. by the burn where scent-ed birks Wi' dew are hang-ing clear, my jo; I'll meet thee on the lea-rig, My
2. tho' the night were ne'er sae wild, And I were ne'er sae wea-rie, O, I'd meet thee on the lea-rig, My
3. me the hour o' gloa-min' gray, It mak's my heart sae chee-rie, O, To meet thee on the lea-rig, My

1-3. ain, my ain kind dea-rie, O!

_poco rit._

* This air is to be found in Bremner's *Scots Reels*, 1757, as "My ain kind Dearie"; and also in Bk. III. of Oswald's *Caledonian Pocket Companion*, 1751. Later on, the tune seems to have become known as "The Lee Rigg," from some old verses sung to it, beginning, "Will ye gang owre the Lee-rig, my ain kind dearie, O?" In Angus Cumming's *Collection of Strathspeys*, 1780, it is given as "The Wedding; or, San Rire va Vannich," and in Aird's *Selection of Scotch, etc., Airs*, vol. i., 1782, as "The Lee Rigg." A tune occurs in Gow's *Second Collection of Strathspey Reels*, 1788, which the author of that work names "Old Lee Rigg, or Rose Tree," but it is entirely different from "My ain kind dearie." Burns' poem was written in 1792 for Thomson's Collection.

# When trees did bud.

### DOUN THE BURN, DAVIE.*

Verses by CRAWFURD.

*Allegretto.*

PIANO.

*con Ped.*

*sempre con Ped.*

1. When trees did bud, and fields were green, And broom bloom'd fair to see; When
2. Now Da - vie did each lad sur - pass That dwelt on this burn - side; And
3. As down the burn they took their way, And thro' the flow' - ry dale; His

1. Ma - ry was com - plete fif - teen, And love laugh'd in her e'e. Blithe Da - vie's blinks her
2. Ma - ry was the bon - niest lass, Just meet to be a bride. Her cheeks were ro - sy
3. cheek to hers he aft did lay, And love was aye the tale. With, "Ma - ry, when shall

*cres.*

1. heart did move To speak her mind thus free; "Gang doun the burn, . . .
2. red and white, Her een were bon - nie blue; Her looks were like the
3. we re - turn, Sic plea - sure to re - new?" Quoth Ma - ry, "Love, I

*cres.*

*rit.*

1. Da - vie, love, And I will fol - low thee."
2. morn - ing bright, Her li s like drop - ping dew.
3. like the burn, And I will fol - low you."

*colla voce.* *rit.* *p* *rit.*

* This air, with Crawfurd's verses, appeared in the *Orpheus Caledonius*, 1725, p. 50; it is one of the seven tunes foolishly ascribed by the author of that work to "David Rezzio." The version of the tune in the first edition of the *Orpheus Caledonius* differs greatly from that published in the second edition, 1733. M'Gibbon's version in *Scots Tunes*, Bk. I., 1742, differs again from either of those in the *Orpheus*. The air seems to owe its present singable condition to some arranger belonging to the latter half of last century; it is to be found in the *Musical Miscellany*, Perth, 1786, a work issued more than a year prior to the first volume of the *Scots Museum*. An improved version of the last verse of Crawfurd's poem, from the pen of Burns, is here adopted.

# Where are the joys I have met in the morning?*

Verses by BURNS.

Air: "Saw ye my father?"

*Adagio.*

PIANO.

1. Where are the joys I have met in the morn - ing, That danc'd to the
2. Is it that sum - mer's for - sak - en our val - leys, And grim sur - ly
3. Fain would I hide what I fear to dis - cov - er, Yet long, long too

1. lark's ear - ly song?
2. win - ter is near?
3. well have I known;

Where is the peace that a -
No, no; the bees hum - ming
All that has caused this

*f rit.*

*p*

*cres.* ——— *p molto rit. e dim.*

1. wait - ed my wand - 'ring At ev' - ning the wild woods a - mong?
2. round the gay ros - es, Pro - claim it the pride of the year.
3. wreck in my bo - som Is Jen - nie, fair Jen - nie, a - lone.

*cres.* *p molto rit. e dim.*

* The old verses seem to have been first published in Herd's Collection of *Scottish Songs, Ancient Ballads,* etc. (1st ed. 1769), under the title of "The Grey Cock," and, with the air, in *Vocal Music; or, The Songster's Companion,* 1772. The air is also to be found in *Straight & Skillern's Country Dances for 1773,* a work issued about October, 1772, and in *The Universal Magazine* for January, 1773. In the latter volume it is entitled, "A favourite Scotch Song." Chappell's suggestion that Hook composed the melody is extremely improbable. Burns wrote the song, "Where are the joys," in September, 1793, for George Thomson's Collection. In a letter to Thomson he refers to the tune as "one of my greatest favourites" (see letter No. 42 of Dr. Currie's *Complete Works of Robert Burns,* 1800).

# When wild war's deadly blast.

### THE SOLDIER'S RETURN.*

Verses by BURNS.

Air: "The Mill, mill, O."

*Andantino con moto.*

1. When wild war's dead - ly blast was blawn, And gen - tle peace re
2. At length I reach'd the bon - nie glen Where ear - ly life I
3. She gaz'd— she red - den'd like a rose— Syne pale as an - y
4. The wars are o'er, and I'm come hame, And find thee still true

1. turn - - ing, Wi' mon - y a sweet babe fa - ther - less, And
2. sport - - ed; I pass'd the mill and tryst - in' thorn, Where
3. li - - ly; She sank with - in my arms, and cried, "Art
4. heart - - ed; Tho' poor in gear, we're rich in love, And

* This air appears in Mrs. Crockat's *Manuscript Music Book*, 1709, but it evidently belongs to a much earlier period; its first appearance in print is in Thomson's *Orpheus Caledonius*, 1725. Watts gives a peculiar version of it in his *Musical Miscellany*, vol. vi., 1731. The old indelicate song, "Beneath a green shade, i fand a fair maid," is supposed to be the composition of Allan Ramsay; it was first published in the *Tea-Table Miscellany*, 1724, and must have been very popular, as it is included in almost every collection of Scottish songs up to the end of last century. Its last appearance seems to be in *The Caledonian Musical Repository*, 1806, where a version of Burns' "The Soldier's Return" is also given. Burns' poem was written in the spring of 1793, for George Thomson's Collection, vol. i.

1. mony a wi - dow mourn - - ing. I left tho lines and
2. Nan - cy oft I court - - ed. Wha spied I but my
3. thou my ain dear Wil - - lie?" "By Him who made yon
4. mair we'se ne'er be part - - ed." Quoth she, "My grand - sire

1. tent - ed field, Where lang I'd been a lodg - - - er, My
2. ain dear maid, Down by her mo - ther's dwell - - - ing! And
3. sun and sky, By whom true love's re - gard - - - ed, I
4. left me gowd, A mail - in plen - ish'd fair - - - ly; Then

1. hum - ble knap - sack a' my wealth, A poor but hon - est sod - - ger.
2. turn'd me round to hide the flood That in my e'e was swell - - ing.
3. am the man! and thus may still True lov - ers be re - ward - ed.
4. come, my faith - ful sod - ger lad, Thou'rt wel - come to it dear - - ly."

## "Why weep ye by the tide, ladye?"

### JOCK O' HAZELDEAN.*

Ballad by Sir WALTER SCOTT.

Air: "Willie and Annet."

*Moderato.*

1. "Why weep ye by the tide, la - dye? Why weep ye by the
2. "Now let this wil - ful grief be done, And dry that cheek so
3. "A chain o' gold ye sall not lack, Nor braid to bind your
4. The kirk was deck'd at morn - ing - tide, The ta - pers glim - mer'd

1. tide? . . . I'll wed ye to my young - est son, And
2. pale; . . . Young Frank is chief of Er - ring - ton, And
3. hair; . . . Nor met - tled hound, nor man - aged hawk, Nor
4. fair; . . . The priest and bride - groom wait the bride, And

* From *Albyn's Anthology*, vol. i., 1816, for which collection Sir Walter Scott wrote the ballad. A version of the melody occurs in the Leyden Manuscript, under the title of "The Bony brow." Scott's song was founded on the old ballad of "Jock o' Hazelgreen," a version of which is given by Buchan, in his *Ancient Ballads and Songs of the North of Scotland*. In his note to "The glancing of her apron," *Museum Illustrations*, p. 384, Stenhouse points out that the tune of "Jock o' Hazeldean" is merely the old simple air of "Willie and Annet," a florid version of which is given in Playford's *Choice Ayres*, Bk. II., London, 1679, with verses by Thomas D'Urfey, beginning, "In January last, on Munnonday at Moru." The manuscript, known as the Leyden MS., belonged to the celebrated Dr. John Leyden. It is written in tablature for the Lyra-viol, and in 1847 George F. Graham made a transcript of it for the Advocates Library in Edinburgh. Its date is uncertain, but from internal evidence, it cannot be older than 1605. It contains a number of Scottish tunes, which have been referred to in this volume.

*cres.*

1. ye    sall    be    his    bride;    And    ye    sall    bo    his
2. lord    of    Long - ley    Dale.    His    step    is    first    in
3. pal - frey    fresh    and    fair;    And    you    the    fore - most
4. dame    and    knight    were    there;    They    sought    her    baith    by

*cres.*

*rit.*

1. bride,    la - dye,    Sae    come - ly    to    be    seen!"—    But
2. peace - ful    ha',    His    sword    in    bat - tle    keen!"—    But
3. o'    them    a',    Shall    ride    our    for - est    queen!"—    But
4. bow'r    and    ha'    The    la - dye    was    not    seen!—    She's

*colla voce.*    *rit.*

*a tempo.*

1. aye    she    loot    the    tears    down    fa',    For    Jock    o'    Ha - zel - dean.
2. aye    she    loot    the    tears    down    fa',    For    Jock    o'    Ha - zel - dean.
3. aye    she    loot    the    tears    down    fa',    For    Jock    o'    Ha - zel - dean.
4. o'er    the    bor - der    and    a - wa'    Wi'    Jock    o'    Ha - zel - dean!

*a tempo.*

*mf*

*poco rit.*

# Wi' a hundred pipers.*

*Allegro energico.*

Verses by LADY NAIRNE.

PIANO.

*mf*

*mf*

1. Wi' a hun - dred pi - pers an' a', an' a', Wi' a hun - dred pi - pers an'
2. Oh! our sol - ger lads look'd braw, look'd braw, Wi' their tar - tan, kilt, au'
3. The Esk was swol - len sae red, sae deep; But side by side the

*mf*

*cres.*

1. a', an' a', We'll up an' gie them a blaw, a blaw, Wi' a
2. a', an' a', Wi' ban - nets, fea - thers, an' glitt'r - in' gear, An'
3. brave lads keep, Twa' thou - sand swam to fell Eng - lish ground, An'

*cres.*

*mf*

1. hun - dred pi - pers an' a', an' a'! O, it's owre the Bor - der, a -
2. pi - brochs sound - in' sweet an' clear. Will they a' re - turn to their
3. danc'd them dry to the pi - broch's sound. Dum - foun - der'd the Eng - lish

*mf*

* This song refers to Prince Charlie's capture of Carlisle in November, 1745. The Prince entered Carlisle seated on a white charger, and preceded by one hundred pipers. In the retreat some two thousand Highlanders crossed the Esk at Longtown. The river was in flood, and took them nearly breast high. On reaching the opposite side, the pipers struck up, and the daring Highlanders danced reels and strathspeys till they were dry again. The air, which is evidently modern, was first issued with Lady Nairne's verses about the year 1852 by Messrs. Wood & Co., Edinburgh, as a single song, with symphonies and accompaniment by Elizabeth Rainforth; a few years later it was secured by Messrs. Paterson & Sons, Edinburgh, for the second edition of the *Lays from Strathearn*, 1857. Whence Miss Rainforth obtained the air is unfortunately not known, but there is little doubt that it was composed to Lady Nairne's song. Miss Rainforth was a Soprano vocalist, who resided in Edinburgh about 1851-56; she was born in London in 1814, and died in Redland, Bristol, in 1877.

1. wa', a - wa', It's owre the Bor - der, a - wa', a - wa', We'll
2. ain dear glen? Will they a' re - turn, oor Hie - land men? Se - cond-
3. saw, they saw, Dum - foun - der'd they heard the blaw, the blaw! Dum -

*cres.*                    *f*                                    CHORUS.

1. on and we'll march to Car - lisle ha', Wi' its yetts, its cas - tle, an' a', an' a'.
2. sicht - ed San - dy look'd fu' wae, An' mi - thers grat when they march'd a - way.  } Wi' a
3. founder'd they a' ran a - wa', a - wa', Frae the hun - dred pi - pers an' a', an' a'.

*cres.*                    *f*                                         *f*

hun - dred pi - pers an' a', an' a', Wi' a hun - dred pi - pers an' a', an' a'! We'll

up an' gie them a blaw, a blaw, Wi' a hun - dred pi - pers an' a', an' a'!

# Where ha'e ye been a' the day?*

Air: "Highland Laddie."

**Poco vivace.**

VOICE.

PIANO.

1. Where ha'e ye been a' the day,
2. When he drew his gude braid-sword,
3. Geor-die sits in Char-lie's chair,

1. Bon-nie lad-die, High-land lad-die? Saw ye him that's far a-way, Bon-nie lad-die,
2. Bon-nie lad-die, High-land lad-die, Then he gave his roy-al word, Bon-nie lad-die,
3. Bon-nie lad-die, High-land lad-die, But I think he'll no bide there, Bon-nie lad-die,

1. High-land lad-die? On his head a bon-net blue, Bon-nie lad-die, High-land lad-die,
2. High-land lad-die; Frae the field he ne'er wad flee, Bon-nie lad-die, High-land lad-die,
3. High-land lad-die; Char-lie yet shall mount the throne, Bon-nie lad-die, High-land lad-die,

*cres.*

*After last verse.*

1. Tar-tan plaid and High-land trews, Bon-nie lad-die, High-land lad-die.
2. Wi' his friends wad live or dee, Bon-nie lad-die, High-land lad-die.
3. Weel ye ken it is his own, Bon-nie lad-die, High-land lad-die.

* The three stanzas which we give belong to a long and very coarse Jacobite ballad, published by George Thomson and James Hogg. The Ettrick Shepherd, in his *Jacobite Relics*, includes the air to verses first published in *Remains of Nithsdale and Galloway Song*, 1810, p. 122, beginning :—

> Princely is my luver's weed,
> Bonnie laddie, Highland laddie;
> His veins are fu' o' princely blude,
> My bonnie Highland laddie.

In a note to this song on p. 337, he writes: " The ' Highland Laddie ' is from Cromek, and is said by Allan Cunningham to have been copied from the mouth of a young girl, who learned it from an old woman, who was a Roman Catholic. There are six different airs designated, 'Highland Laddie.' This is the oldest. It was sung to a very old song, beginning :—

> I canna get my mare ta'en,
> Bonnie laddie, Highland laddie;
> Master had she never nane,
> My bonnie laddie, Highland laddie."

Hogg was correct in his remark that the air, which we give above, is the oldest " Highland Laddie "; it is a modification of a very old tune published in Playford's *The English Dancing Master; or, plaine and easie rules for the dancing of country dances, with the tune to each dance*, 1651, under the title of " Cockle-Shells."

# "Will ye gang to the Hielands, Leezie Lindsay?" *

Air: "Lizzie Lindsay."

Moderato.

VOICE.

PIANO.

1. "Will ye gang to the
2. "To gang to the
3. "O, Leez - ie, lass,
4. She has kilt - ed her

cres.

1. Hie - lands, Lee - zie Lind - say? Will ye gang .. to the Hie - lands wi'
2. Hie - lands wi' you, sir, I din - na ken how that may
3. ye maun ken lit - tle, If sae .. ye din - na ken
4. conts o' green sa - tin, She has kilt - - ed them up to her

cres.

1. me? . . . . . . Will ye gang to the Hie - lands, Lee - zie Lind - say, My
2. be; . . . . . . For I ken na the land that ye live in, Nor
3. me; . . . . . . For my name is Lord Ron - ald Mac - Dou - ald, A
4. knee; . . . . . . And she's off wi' Lord Ron - ald Mac - Dou - ald, His

Ped.

1. bride and my dar - ling to be." . . . . . .
2. ken I the lad I'm ganu wi'." . . . . . .
3. chief - tain o' high de - gree." . . . . . .
4. bride and his dar - ling to be. . . . . . .

Ped. Ped. *

* We have adopted Buchan's version of the air. The song is old, and *seems* to be a fragmentary version of the ballad given by Aytoun from Kinloch's MSS., under the title of "Donald of the Isles," and since published in many collections as "Lizzie Lindsay." The air with the first verse of the song was communicated to the *Scots Musical Museum*, vol. v., by Burns; it does not appear in print prior to the publication of Johnson's work.

T 2

## Will ye go to the ewe-bughts, Marion?*

*Andante con espressione.*

VOICE.

PIANO.

1. Will ye go to the ewe-bughts,
2. O Ma-rion's a bon-nie
3. I've nine milk ewes, my
4. Sae put on your par-lins,

1. Ma-rion, And weir in the sheep wi' me? The sun shines sweet, my Ma-rion, But
2. lass, And the blythe blinks in her e'e; And fain wad I mar-ry Ma-rion, Gin
3. Ma-rion, A cow and a braw-ny quey; I'll gi'e them a' to my Ma-rion, Just
4. Ma-rion, And kyr-tle o' cram-as-ie, And when the sun sinks, Ma-rion, I'll

1. nae half sae sweet as thee, The sun shines sweet, my Ma-rion, But nae half sae
2. Ma-rion wad mar-ry me, And fain wad I mar-ry Ma-rion, Gin Ma-rion wad
3. on her bri-dal-day, I'll gi'e them a' to my Ma-rion, Just on her
4. come west and see thee, And when the sun sinks, Ma-rion, I'll come west

*Last time only.*

1. sweet as thee.
2. mar-ry me.
3. bri-dal-day.
4. and see thee.

*molto ritard.* *p a tempo.* *rit. sf p*

---

\* This song is probably very old, and the author unknown. It appears in Ramsay's *Tea-Table Miscellany*, 1724, marked with the letter "Q," to denote that it is an old song with additions. In the *Orpheus Caledonius*, vol. ii., 1733, Thomson gives an air bearing some resemblance to the one now generally sung. It is difficult to say whether this is the original tune or not. Ritson (*Scottish Songs*, 1794, vol. i.) includes "Will ye go to the ewe-bughts, Marion?" in a list of songs, the exact age of which he considers very doubtful. The complete poem consists of eight verses; we have slightly altered the third line of verse 4.

# Wilt thou be my dearie?*

Verses by BURNS.
*Andante con moto.*

Air: "Suttor's Daughter; or, Nighean a ghreisich."

VOICE.

PIANO.

1. Wilt thou be my dea - rie? When
2. Las - sie, say thou lo'es me,

*poco rit. . . . a tempo.*

1. sor - row wrings thy gen-tle heart, O, wilt thou let me cheer thee? By the treasures of my soul,
2. Or, if thou wilt not be my ain, Say thou'lt not re - fuse me; If it win-na, can-na be,

*colla voce.*

*poco rit.*

1. That's the love I bear thee! I swear and vow that on - ly thou Shall ev - er be my dea - rie;
2. Thou, for thine, may choose me. Let me, las - sie, quickly dee, Trust - ing that thou lo'es me;

*colla voce.*

*After last verse.*

1. On - ly thou, I swear and vow, Shall ev - er be my dea - rie!
2. Let me, las - sie, quick - ly dee, Trust - ing that thou lo'es me.

---

* This is an old strathspey tune, known by the name of "The Suttor's Daughter." It appears in Alexander M'Glashan's *A Collection of Strathspey Reels, with a Bass for the Violoncello or Harpsichord,* 1780, and in Gow's *A Collection of Strathspey Reels,* 1784; an earlier version of it occurs in Neil Stewart's *A Collection of the Newest and Best Reels,* 1761, as "Shoe Maker's daughter." Burns' verses were written for the fifth volume of Johnson's *Scots Musical Museum,* which was issued shortly after the Poet's death.

278

# Ye banks and braes.

HIGHLAND MARY.*

Verses by Burns.

Air: "Katherine Ogie."

*Lento con molto espressione.*

VOICE.

1. Ye
2. How
3. Wi'

PIANO.

1. banks, and braes, and streams a-round The cas-tle o' Mont-
2. sweet-ly bloom'd the gay green birk, How rich the haw-thorn's
3. mo-nie a vow, and lock'd em-brace, Our part-ing was fu'

1. gom-e-rie, Green be your woods, and fair your flow'rs, Your
2. blos--som, As un-der-neath their fra-grant shade I
3. ten--der; And pledg-ing aft to meet a-gain, We

* The air of "Katherine Ogie," with the ballad beginning:—

As I went furth to view the plain
Upon a morning early,
While May's sweet scent did chear my brain
From flowers which grew so early,

probably dates from the middle of the 17th century. It was sung by John Abell, Gentleman of the Chapel Royal, at his concert in Stationers' Hall in 1680, and shortly afterwards appeared as a single-sheet song. The claim which Mr. W. Chappell puts forward in *Popular Music of the Olden Time*, for the tune being English, has been well met by Mr. John Glen, of Edinburgh. In the excellent preface to the *Glen Collection of Scottish Dance Music*, Mr. Glen points out that as early as 16-7, the air was published by John Playford, in his *Apollo's Banquet*, as "a Scotch Tune." Burns wrote the song, "Ye banks and braes," in 1792. The affecting story of Highland Mary is too well known to repeat here. The word *Ogie* in the Celtic, means *little or young*.

1. wa - ters nev - er drum - - lie! There sim - mer first un -
2. clasped her to my bo - - som! The gold - en hours, on
3. tore our - selves a - sun - - der; But, oh! fell death's un -
dim.
dim.
1. fauld her robes, And there the lan - gest tar - - ry! For
2. an - gel wings, Flew o'er me and my dear - - ie; For
3. time - ly frost, That nipp'd my flow'r sae ear - - ly! Now
cres.
f
p
poco rit. e dim.
1. there I took the last fare - well O' my sweet High - land Ma - ry!
2. dear to me as light and life, Was my sweet High - land Ma - ry!
3. green's the sod, and cauld's the clay, That wraps my High - land Ma - ry!
cres.
f
colla voce.

# Ye banks and braes o' bonnie Doon.*

Verses by BURNS.

*Andante, con tenerezza.*

Air: "The Caledonian Hunt's Delight."

VOICE.

PIANO.

*p* *con molto espressione.*

*con Ped.*

*p*

1. Ye banks and braes o' bon - nie Doon, How
2. Oft ha'e I rov'd by bon - nie Doon, To

*sempre con Ped.*

1. can ye bloom sae fresh and fair; How can ye chant, ye
2. see the rose and wood - bine twine; And il - ka bird sang

* In a letter to George Thomson, dated Nov. 1794, Burns writes: "There is an air, 'The Caledonian Hunt's Delight,' to which I wrote a song that you will find in Johnson, 'Ye banks and braes o' Bonnie Doon'; this air, I think, might find a place among your hundred, as Lear says of his knights. Do you know the history of the air? It is curious enough. A good many years ago, Mr. James Miller, writer in your good town, a gentleman whom possibly you know, was in company with our friend Clarke; and, talking of Scottish music, Miller expressed an ardent ambition to be able to compose a Scots tune. Mr. Clarke, partly by way of a joke, told him to keep to the black keys of the harpsichord, and preserve some kind of rhythm, and he would infallibly compose a Scots air. Certain it is, that, in a few days Mr. Miller produced the rudiments of an air, which Mr. Clarke, with some touches and corrections, fashioned into the tune in question." (See Currie's *Works of Robert Burns*, 1800.) Miller's air was first published in Gow's *A Second Collection of Strathspey Reels*, 1788, as "The Caledonian Hunt's Delight," and with Burns' verses, in the *Museum*, vol. iv., 1792. The beautiful poem is a second version of the song composed in 1787, "Ye flowery banks o' bonnie Doon," and although in many respects inferior to the first, it has almost entirely superseded it. "The Caledonian Hunt's Delight" is another Scottish air, which Mr. Chappell, in *Popular Music of the Olden Time* claims as English, on the ground that it resembles "Lost is my quiet," an air published in Dale's Collection of English Songs (undated, but probably *circa* 1785-90). For a decisive answer to this absurd statement we must refer the reader to Mr. Glen's interesting preface to the *Glen Collection of Scottish Dance Music*, Edin., 1891.

*dim.*

1. lit - tle birds, And I sae wea - ry, fu' o' care! Ye'll
2. o' its love, And fond - ly sae did I o' mine! Wi'

*cres.*

1. break my heart, ye warb - ling birds, That
2. light - some heart I pu'd a rose, Fu'

*ritard. . . . . . . . . . u tempo.*

1. wan - ton through the flow' - ry thorn; Ye mind me o' de -
2. sweet up - on its thorn - y tree; But my fause lov - er

*dim.*

1. part - ed joys, De - part - ed, nev - er to re - turn!
2. stole my rose, And ah! he left the thorn wi' me!

# Young Jamie lo'ed me weel.

## AULD ROBIN GRAY.*

Ballad by LADY ANNE LINDSAY.

1. Young Ja-mie lo'ed me weel, and
2. My fa-ther could-na work, my
3. My fa-ther urged me sair, my
4. O sair did we greet, and

1. sought me for his bride, But sav - ing a crown he had nae-thing else be - side; To
2. mi-ther could-na spin, I toil'd day and night, but their bread I could-na win; Auld
3. mi-ther did-na speak, But look'd in my face till my heart was like to break; So
4. mei-kle did we say, We took but ae kiss and we tore our-selves a - way; I

1. make the crown a pound, my Ja-mie gaed to sea, And the crown and the pound were
2. Rob maintain'd them baith, an' wi tears in his e'e Said, "Jeanie, for their sakes, O
3. they gi'ed him my hand, my heart it was at sea, And auld Ro-bin Gray is
4. wish I were dead—but I'm no like to dee; Oh! why do I live to

* Lady Anne Lindsay, the eldest daughter of the Earl of Balcarres, was born in December, 1750. In 1772 she wrote her celebrated ballad to an apparently old tune, which Burns (*Reliques*, p. 273) says was formerly called " The Bridegroom greets when the sun gangs down," and which, we may mention, is either the original, or another version of the airs " My love's in Germanie," and " Hame, hame, hame." This setting, however, has been entirely superseded by the one given above, which was composed by an English clergyman of the name of William Leeves, Rector of Wrington, in Somersetshire. Mr. Leeves first published his air, adapted to Lady Anne's verses, in a little book entitled, *Six Sacred Airs or Hymns, intended as a Sunday-evening's Recreation.* London. S. Birchall, 1812, in the preface of which the author asserts his claim to the melody, and alludes to its surreptitious appearance in print. Certainly the reverend gentleman had reason to complain, as his air was pirated by more than one publisher at an early date. Twenty-four years before the issue of the little book alluded to, it was printed in *Calliope; or, the Vocal Enchantress*, where the old tune is also given, and again in 1788 in the second volume of *The Vocal Magazine.* The first appearance of the ballad in print was in Herbert Croft's novel of *Love and Madness*, 1780. Lady Anne died in 1825; she only acknowledged the authorship of " Auld Robin Gray " towards the close of her life.

*mf*  *poco a*

1. baith for me. He had na been gane a week but on-ly twa, When my
2. mar - - ry me." My heart it said nay— I look'd for Ja-mie back, But the
3. gude-man to me. I had-na been a wife a week but on-ly four, When
4. say, wae's me! I gang like a ghaist, and I care-na to spin, I

*poco. cres.*  *p con espress.*

1. fa-ther brak' his arm, and our cow was stown a-wa'; My mi-ther she fell sick, and
2. wind it blew high, and the ship it was a wrack. The ship it was a wrack, why
3. sit-ting sae mournful-ly ae night at the door, I saw my Ja-mie's wraith— I
4. dare-na think o' Ja - mie, for that wad be a sin! But I'll do my best a

*ritard.*

*rit.*

1. Ja - mie at the sea, And auld Ro-bin Gray cam' a-court-in' me.
2. did - na Ja-mie dee? And why do I live to say, wae's me!
3. could-na think it he, Till he said, "I'm come back to mar-ry thee!"
4. gude - wife to be, For auld Ro-bin Gray is a kind man to me!

# With the Loorgeen, O hee.*

Verses translated from the Gaelic
by M. MacFarlane.

Boat Song.

Air: "Leis an Lurgainn."

VOICE.

1. With the Loor-geen, o hee, With the
2. Is - lay loom - ing, o hee, In the
3. Skip - per bel - lows, o hee, To his
4. Crowd her sails on, o hee, And tho'

PIANO.

Allegretto.

p legato.

p

con Ped.

1. Loor-geen, o ho, In the gray dusk of eve, O'er the waves let us go. . . . .
2. gloam - ing, o ho, Our ship's com - pass set we, And our lights we did show. . . .
3. fel - lows, o ho, "Steady! cour - age take ye, Tho' a tem - pest should blow. . . .
4. gales come, o ho, Light as sea - gull will she O'er the heav - ing waves go. . . .

1. On the o - cean, o hee, Waves in mo - tion, o ho, Naught but clouds could we
2. A - ros pass - ing, o hee, 'Twas ha - rass - ing, o ho, The strong bil - lows to
3. Look a - head, mates, o hee, Without dread, mates, o ho, Those that dan - ger would
4. Bil - lows lash - ing, o hee, Wa - ters crash - ing, o ho, With - out blench - ing we

sempre Ped.

Last time.

1. see, O'er the blue sea be - low. . . .
2. see, High as mast - head to flow. . . .
3. flee, Let them sneak down be - low." . . .
4. see, There be stout hearts on board. . . .

p

* From *The Celtic Lyre*, by kind permission of the Editor, Mr. Henry Whyte. This is a popular boat-song, frequently sung by rowers,
keeping time with their oars. It belongs to the West Coast of Scotland.

# GLOSSARY.

## A

A', all.
Aback, away, aloof.
Abeigh, at a shy distance.
Abeit, albeit.
Aboon, above, up.
Abread, abroad, in sight.
Ae, one.
Aff, off; Aff-loof, unpremeditated.
Afore, before.
Aft, oft.
Aften, often.
Agley, off the right line; wrong.
Aiblins, perhaps.
Ain, own.
Airt, corner, direction.
Aiver, an old horse.
Aizle, a hot cinder.
Ajee, ajar, half open.
Akwart, awkward.
Alake, alas.
Alane, alone.
Amaist, almost.
Amang, among.
Ambry, cupboard.
An', and; if.
Ance, once.
Ane, one.
Aneut, over against.
Anither, another.
Asklent, asquint; aslant.
Asse, ashes.
Asteer, abroad; stirring.
Athart, athwart.
Aught, possession.
Auld lang syne, olden time, days of other years.
Auld, old.
Ava, at all.
Awa', away.
Awee, a short time.
Awfu', awful.
Awn, owing.
Ayont, beyond.

## B

Ba', ball.
Backets, ash-boards.
Bad, bade.
Baide, endured, did stay.
Bairn, a child.
Baith, both.
Bane, bone.
Bang, to beat; to strive.
Bardie, diminutive of bard.
Barefit, barefooted.
Barley - bree, beer, sometimes whiskey.
Barmie, or, like barm.
Bateh, a crow, a gang.
Baudrons, a cat.
Bauld, bold.
Bawbee, a half-penny.
Bawk, bank.
Bawsand, a white spot on the forehead of a horse.
Be, to let be; to give over; to cease.
Bear, barley.
Beastie, diminutive of beast.
Beet, to add fuel to fire.
Beld, bald.
Belyve, by and by.

Ben, into the spence or parlour; a spence.
Benlomond, a noted mountain in Dumbartonshire.
Bent, field.
Beuk, a book.
Bicker, a kind of wooden dish; a short race.
Bide, bear; endure; remain.
Bie, or Bield, shelter.
Bien, wealthy; plentiful.
Bigg, to build.
Biggin, building; a house.
Biggit, built.
Bigonet, a linen cap.
Bill, a bull.
Bing, to bow, curtsey.
Bing, a heap of grain, potatoes, &c.
Bink, a bench beside the fire.
Birk, birch.
Birken - shaw, Birchen - wood-shaw, a small wood.
Birkie, a young fellow.
Birled, to share; to toss up.
Bit, crisis; nick of time.
Bizz, a bustle; to buzz.
Bladderskate, an indiscreet talker.
Blastie, a shrivelled dwarf; a term of contempt.
Blastit, blasted.
Blate, bashful; sheepish.
Blathrie, talking nonsense.
Blaud, a flat piece of anything; to slap.
Blaw, to blow; to boast.
Bleer, blear, inflame.
Bleert and blin', bleared and blind.
Bleezing, blazing.
Blether, to talk idly; nonsense.
Bleth'rin, talking idly.
Blink, a little while; a smiling look; to look kindly; to shine.
Blinker, a term of contempt.
Blinkin', smirking.
Bluart, the bilberry.
Bluid, blood.
Bodle, a small gold coin.
Bogles, spirits, hobgoblins.
Bole, hole; recess.
Bonnie, or Bonny, handsome; beautiful.
Bonnock, a kind of thick cake of bread; a small jannock, or loaf made of oatmeal.
Borrows town, the county town.
Bothy, a private whiskey-still.
Bourtree, the elder-bush or tree.
Bousing, drinking.
Bow-kail, cabbage.
Bowt, bended; crooked.
Brackens, ferns.
Brae, a declivity; the slope of a hill.
Braid, broad.
Brak, broke.
Brash, a sudden illness.
Brats, coarse clothes, rags; children.
Braw, fine, handsome.
Brawly, or brawlie, very well; finely; heartily.
Braxie, smoked flesh of sheep which die on the hills.
Breastit, did spring up or forward.

Breckan, fern.
Breef, an invulnerable or irresistible spell.
Breeks, breeches.
Breut, smooth.
Brewin, brewing.
Brie, juice, liquid.
Brig, a bridge.
Brisket, the breast, or bosom.
Brither, a brother.
Brogue, a hum; a trick.
Broo, broth; liquid; water.
Broose, broth; a race at country weddings, who shall first reach the bridegroom's house on returning from church.
Bruilzie, a broil, a fight.
Brulyie, see Bruilzie.
Brume or broom, a kind of shrub.
Brunstane, brimstone.
Brunt, did burn, burnt.
Brust, to burst; burst.
Bught, a pen in which the ewes are milked.
Bughtin-time, the time of collecting the sheep in the pens to be milked.
Burdies, diminutive of birds.
Burgonet, a helmet.
Burn, water; a rivulet.
Burnie, diminutive of burn.
Busk, dress; v. to dress.
Buskie, bushy.
Buskit, dressed.
Buss, bush.
Buss, shelter.
Bussle, a bustle; to bustle.
But, with; without.
Butt an' ben, the country kitchen and parlour.
Byde, remain; wait.
Byke, a bee-hive.
Byre, a cow-stable; a sheep-pen.

## C

Ca', to call; to name; to drive.
Ca't, or ca'd, called; driven; calved.
Cadgely, cheerfully.
Cadger, a carrier.
Cadie, or Caddie, a person; a young fellow.
Caff, chaff.
Caird, a tinker.
Cairn, a loose heap of stones.
Callan, a boy.
Caller, fresh; sound; refreshing.
Canach, a species of long grass.
Canie, or cannie, gentle; mild; cautious; dexterous.
Cankered, angry.
Cannilie, dexterously; gently.
Cantie, or cany, cheerful; merry.
Careerin, cheerfully.
Carle, an old man.
Carlin, a stout old woman.
Carry (the), the firmament.
Cartes, cards.
Cauldron, a cauldron.
Cank an keel, chalk and red clay.
Cauld, cold.
Caup, a wooden drinking-vessel.
Chanter, a part of a bagpipe.
Chap, a person, a fellow; a blow.

Chaup, a stroke; a blow.
Checkit, cheeked.
Cheep, a chirp; to chirp.
Chiel, or cheel, a sly fellow.
Chimla, or chimlie, a fire-grate; a fire-place.
Chimla-lug, the fireside.
Chockin', choking.
Chow, to chew, cheek-for-chow; side by side.
Clachan, a small village about a church; a hamlet.
Clag, a fault or failing.
Claise, or claes, clothes.
Claith, cloth.
Claithing, clothing.
Claivers, nonsense; not speaking sense.
Clarkit, wrote.
Clash, an idle tale, the story of the day.
Clatter, to tell idle stories; an idle story.
Claught, snatched at, laid hold of.
Clavers, idle stories.
Cleed, to clothe.
Cleed, clothes.
Cleckit, having caught.
Clinkin', jerking; clinking.
Clishmaclaver, idle conversation.
Clock, to hatch; a beetle.
Clockin, hatching.
Clootie, an old name for the Devil.
Clout, patch.
Cluds, clouds.
Coaxin, wheedling.
Coble, a fishing boat.
Cockernony, a lock of hair tied upon a girl's head; a cap.
Coft, bought.
Cog, a wooden dish.
Coggie, diminutive of cog.
Coif, cap; head-dress.
Coof, a blockhead; a ninny.
Coost, cast.
Coot, the ankle or foot.
Corbies, a species of the crow.
Cotter, the inhabitant of a cot-house or cottage.
Couls, coals.
Couthie, kind; loving.
Cove, a cave.
Cowp, to barter; to tumble over; a gang.
Cowpit, tumbled.
Cozie, snug.
Cozily, snugly.
Crabbit, crabbed; fretful.
Crack, conversation; to converse.
Crackin, conversing.
Craft, or croft, a field near a house (in old husbandry).
Craig, throat.
Craiks, incessant cries or calls; a bird.
Cramasie, crimson.
Cranreuch, hoar frost.
Crap, a crop; to crop.
Craw, the crowing of a cock; a rook.
Creel, a basket; to have one's wits in a creel, to be crazed; to be fascinated.
Creepie-stool, or cutty-stool, the stool of repentance.

Crood, to coo.
Croon, a hollow and continued moan; to hum a tune.
Crooning, humming.
Crouse, cheerful; courageous.
Crousely, cheerfully; courageously.
Crowdie, a composition of oatmeal and boiled water, sometimes from the broth of beef mutton, &c.
Crummock, a cow with crooked horns.
Cuif, a blockhead, a ninny.
Cuist, cast.
Cunimock, a short staff with a crooked head.
Curchie, a courtesy.
Curler, a player at a game on the ice, practised in Scotland, called curling.
Curling, a well-known game on the ice.
Curpin, the crupper.
Cushat, the dove, or wood-pigeon.
Cutty, short; a spoon broken in the middle.

### D

Daff, to sport.
Daffin, merriment; foolishness.
Daft, merry, giddy; foolish.
Dainty, pleasant; good-humoured; agreeable.
Darklins, darkling.
Daud, to thrash; to abuse.
Daug, overcome.
Daur, to dare.
Daurt, dared.
Daut, caress.
Dawd, a large piece.
Dawtit, or dawtet, fondled, caressed.
Dearies, diminutive of dears.
Deave, to deafen.
Dight, to wipe.
Ding, to crush, depress.
Dink, neat; tidy; trim.
Dinna, do not.
Dirdum, noisy vexation.
Dirk, a highland dagger.
Dirl, a slight tremulous stroke or pain.
Doite, stupified.
Dolt, stupified; crazed.
Donsie, unlucky.
Dool, sorrow; to sing dool, to lament, to mourn.
Doos, doves.
Dorty, saucy; haughty.
Douce, or douse, sober; wise; prudent.
Doughtna, do not.
Doure, stout; durable; sullen; stubborn.
Doosely, soberly; prudently.
Dow, am or are able; can; a dove.
Dowff, or dowf, pithless; wanting force; exhausted; dull.
Dowie, worn with grief; fatigue, &c.; half asleep, tiresome.
Downa, am or are not able; cannot.
Draigle, to soil by trailing; to draggle among wet, &c.
Drap, a drop; to drop.
Drapping, dropping.
Dree, suffer; lose.
Dreep, to ooze; to drop.
Dreigh, tedious; long about it.
Dribble, drizzling.
Drift, a drove.
Drone, part of a bagpipe.
Dronkit, wet.
Drouth, thirst; drought.
Drumly, or drummie, muddy.
Drummock, meal and water mixed in a raw state.
Drury, treasure.
Dub, a small pond.
Duddie, ragged.
Duds, rags; clothes.
Dule, grief.
Dung, worsted; pushed; driven.
Dunted, beaten.
Dwining, pining away.

### E

E'e, the eye.
Een, the eyes.
E'enin, evening.
E'erie, frightened; dreading spirits.

Eild, old age.
Elbuck, the elbow.
Eldritch, ghastly; frightful.
Eneugh, or eneuch, enough.
Ettle, to try; to attempt.

### F

Fa', fall; lot; to fall.
Fa's, does fall; water-falls.
Fae, a foe.
Faem, foam.
Faiket, unknown.
Fain, inclined; desire to embrace, or be embraced.
Fairin, a fairing; a present.
Fand, did find.
Farl, a cake of oaten bread, &c.
Fash, trouble, care; to trouble; to care for.
Fasht, troubled.
Fauld, a fold; to fold.
Fause, false.
Faut, fault.
Faute, want; lack.
Fearfu', frightful.
Fear't, frightened.
Feat, neat; spruce.
Fecht, to fight.
Fechtin', fighting.
Feck, many; plenty.
Feckless, puny; weak; silly.
Feckly, weakly.
Fee, wages.
Feg, a fig.
Fen, successful struggle; fight.
Fend, to live comfortably.
Fere, friend; companion.
Ferlie, or ferley, to wonder; a wonder; a term of contempt.
Fey, fatality.
Fidgin', restless, uneasy.
Fiel, soft; smooth.
Fient, fiend; a petty oath.
Fier, sound, healthy; a brother; a friend.
Fit, a foot.
Fleech, to supplicate in a flattering manner.
Fleech'd, supplicated.
Fleechin, supplicating.
Fleg, a kick; a random blow.
Flether, to decoy by fair words.
Fletherin, flattering.
Fley, to scare; to frighten.
Flittering, fluttering; vibrating.
Flunkie, a servant in livery.
Flyte, to scold.
Foord, a ford.
Forbears, forefathers.
Forbye, besides.
Forfairn, distressed; worn out; jaded.
Forgather, to meet; to encounter.
Forgie, to forgive.
Forpet, a Scottish measure.
Fother, fodder.
Fou, full; drunk.
Foumart, a polecat.
Fouth, plenty; enough, or more than enough.
Fow, a bushel, &c.; also a pitch-fork.
Frae, from; off.
Fraise, cajoling discourse.
Frammit, strange; estranged from; at enmity with.
Freath, froth.
Frien', friend.
Fu', full.
Fyke, trifling cares; to be in a fuss about trifles.
Fyle, to soil; to dirty.
Fyl't, soiled; dirtied.

### G

Gab, the mouth; to speak boldly; to talk nonsense.
Gaberlunzie, a beggar's wallet.
Gaberlunzie-man, a beggar.
Gae, to go; gaed, went; gaen, or gane, gone; gaun, going.
Gaet, or gate, way; manner; road.
Gain, suffice.
Gait, way; manner; road.
Gang, to go; to walk.
Gar, to make; cause.
Gar't, forced to.
Gashin, conversing.
Gaucy, jolly; large.
Gaud, see Jad.

Gawky, half-witted; foolish; romping; ungraceful.
Gear, riches; goods of any kind.
Geck, to toss the head in wantonness or scorn.
Gee, sullen temper, to sulk.
Geordie, a guinea.
Ghaist, a ghost.
Gie, to give; gied, gave; gien, given.
Giftie, diminutive of gift.
Gin, if; against.
Girn, to grin; to twist the features in rage, agony, &c.
Glaikit, inattentive; foolish.
Glaizie, glittering; smooth like glass.
Gleck, sharp; ready.
Gleg, ditto.
Gleib, globe.
Glen, a dale, a deep valley.
Glent, to peep; to shine.
Gley, a squint; to squint; a-gley, off at a side, wrong.
Glint, to peep.
Glinted, peeped.
Glintin, peeping.
Gloamin', the twilight.
Glowr, to stare, to look; a stare, a look.
Glowred, looked, stared.
Gowan, daisy.
Gowd, gold.
Gowff, the game of golf; to strike as the club does the ball at golf.
Gowk, a cuckoo; a term of contempt; a fool.
Gowl, to howl.
Grane, or grain, a groan; to groan.
Grat, wept, shed tears.
Gree, to agree; to bear the gree, to be decidedly victorious.
Greet, to shed tears, to weep.
Greetin, crying, weeping.
Grippet, caught, seized.
Grumphie, a sow.
Grunzie, mouth.
Grup, the bridle or rein.
Grushie, thick; of thriving growth.
Gude, the Supreme Being; good.
Guid, good.
Guid-e'en, good evening.
Guidman and guidwife, the master and mistress of the house; young guidman, a man newly married.
Guid-morning, good-morning.
Guid-willie, liberal; cordial.
Gully, or gullie, a large knife.
Gumlie, muddy.
Gutcher, grandfather.

### H

Ha', hall.
Ha'-Bible, the great bible that lies in the hall.
Hadden, the stocking of a farm or house.
Ha'e, to have.
Haen, had.
Haet, feint haet, a petty oath of negation.
Haggis, a kind of pudding boiled in the stomach of a cow or sheep.
Haight, see Hecht.
Hain, to spare; to save.
Hain'd, spared.
Haith, a petty oath.
Haivers, nonsense; speaking without thought.
Hale, whole; tight; healthy.
Hallan shaker, a beggarly knave.
Haly, holy.
Hallowmas, Hallow-e'en, the 31st of October.
Hame, home.
Hamely, homely; affable.
Han', hand.
Hap, an outer garment, mantle, plaid, &c.; to wrap, to cover; to hop.
Harkit, hearkened.
Hastit, hastened.
Haud, to hold.
Haughs, low-lying, rich lands; valleys.
Havrin, talking foolishly.
Hawkie, a cow, properly one with a white face.
Hawse, to embrace.
Hawse-bane, the neck.

Healsome, healthful, wholesome.
Heapit, heaped.
Hech! oh! strange!
Hecht, promised; to foretell something that is to be got or given; foretold; the thing foretold; offered.
Heigh, high.
Herd, to tend flocks; one who tends flocks.
Herrin', a herring.
Herry, to plunder; most properly to plunder birds' nests.
Het, hot.
Heugh, a crag, a steep place.
Hilty-skilty, thoughtlessly; playful.
Hiney, honey.
Hing, to hang.
Hirple, to walk feebly; to creep.
Hirplin, limping.
Hizzie, a hussy, a young girl.
Hoastin, coughing.
Hool, the outer skin or case, the shell.
Hoolie, slowly; leisurely.
Hoolie, take leisure; stop.
Hornie, one of the many names of tho devil.
Houlet, an owl.
Housie, diminutive of house.
Howe, hollow; a hollow or dell.
Howff, a tippling house; a house of resort.
Howk, to dig.
Howkit, digged.
Howkin, digging.
Howlet, an owl.
Howms, valleys, or riversides.
Hurklin', crouching.
Hussyfskip, household affairs, housewifeship.

### I

I', in.
Ilk, or ilka, each; every.
Ill-willie, ill-natured; malicious; niggardly.
Ingle, or ingle-neuk, fire; fire-place.
Ise, I shall, or will.
Ither, other; one another.

### J

Jad, jade; also a familiar term among country folks for a giddy young girl.
Jag, raw leather.
Jauk, to dally, to trifle.
Jaukin, trifling, dallying.
Jaupit, bespattered.
Jaw, coarse raillery; to pour out; to shut.
Jee, move; change.
Jeel, jelly.
Jimp, to jump; slender in the waist; handsome.
Jink, to dodge, to turn a corner; a sudden turning; a corner.
Jinker, that turns quickly; a gay, sprightly girl; a wag.
Jinkin, dodging; gambolling.
Jo, sweetheart.
Jouk, to stoop, to bow the head.
Jow, peal.

### K

Kae, a daw.
Kail, a kind of broth.
Kame, comb.
Kebbuck, a cheese.
Keckle, to giggle; to titter.
Keek, a peep, to peep.
Keil, paint.
Kelpies, a sort of mischievous spirits, said to haunt fords and ferries at night, especially in storms.
Ken, to know; kent, or kenn'd, knew.
Kent, shepherd's staff.
Kepp, to catch.
Kilt, to truss up the clothes.
Kimmer, a young girl, a gossip, a neighbour (commère, French).
Kin, kindred; kin', kind, obj.
Kirn, the harvest supper; a churn.

Kirsen, to christen, or baptize.
Kirtle, an upper garment.
Kist, a chest ; a shop counter.
Kith, kindred.
Kittle, to tickle ; ticklish ; lively, apt.
Kittlin, a young cat.
Knowe, a small round hillock.
Knurl, a dwarf.
Kurtch, a linen cap.
Kye, cows.
Kyle, a district in Ayrshire.

**L**

Laddie, diminutive of lad.
Laigh, low.
Lairing, wading, sinking in snow, mud, &c.
Laith, loath.
Laithfu', bashful, sheepish.
Lambie, diminutive of lamb.
Lamiter, cripple.
Lan', land ; estate.
Lane, lone ; my lane, thy lane, &c., myself alone, &c.
Lanely, lonely.
Lang, long ; to think lang, to long, to weary.
Lap, did leap.
Lauch, laugh ; privilege.
Lave, the rest, the remainder, the others.
Laverock, the lark.
Lawlan, lowland.
Leal, loyal, true, faithful.
Lea-rig, grassy ridge.
Lear (pronounce lare), learning.
Lee-lang, live-long.
Leesome, pleasant.
Leeze-me, a phrase of strong endearment.
Leugh, did laugh.
Leuk, a look ; to look.
Libbet, gelded.
Lift, the sky, the firmament.
Lightly, sneeringly ; to sneer at.
Lilt, a ballad ; a tune ; to sing.
Limmer, a kept mistress.
Limp't, limped, hobbled.
Link, to trip along.
Linkin, tripping.
Linn, a waterfall ; a precipice.
Lint, flax ; lint i' the bell, flax in flower.
Lintie, a linnet.
Lintwhite, a linnet.
Loof, the palm of the hand.
Loorgeon, a sailing vessel.
Loot, did let.
Looves, plural of loof.
Loun, a fellow, a ragamuffin.
Loup, jump, leap.
Lowe, or low, a flame.
Lowin, flaming.
Lowpin, leaping.
Lowse, to loose.
Lows'd, loosed.
Lug, the ear ; a handle.
Lum, the chimney.
Lunt, a column of smoke ; to smoke.
Luntin, smoking.

**M**

Mae, more.
Mailen, a farm.
Mair, more.
Maist, most, almost.
Maistly, mostly.
Mak', to make.
Makin', making.
Mang, among.
Manse, the parsonage house, where the minister lives.
Marled, variegated ; spotted.
Marmalete, marmalade.
Maud, maud, a plaid worn by shepherds &c.
Maukin, a hare.
Maun, must.
Mavis, the thrush.
Maw, to mow.
Mawin', mowing.
May, maid.
Meikle, meikle, much.
Men', to mend.
Midden, a dunghill.
Midden-hole, a gutter at the bottom of a dunghill.
Mim, prim, affectedly meek.

Min', mind ; resemblance.
Mind't, mind it ; resolved, intending.
Minnie, mother, dam.
Mirk, mirkest, dark, darkest.
Misca'd, abused.
Misca'd, to abuse, to call names.
Mischievous ; unmannerly.
Mither, a mother.
Mony, or monie, many.
Moorlan', of, or belonging to moors.
Morn, the next day, to-morrow.
Mou', the mouth.
Moudiwort, a mole.
Mousie, diminutive of mouse.
Muckit, cleaned.
Muckle, or mickle, great, big, much.
Murlain, a fish basket.
Moslin-kail, broth, composed simply of water, shelled barley, and greens.
Mutch, a linen hood.
Mutchkin, an English pint.
Mysel', myself.

**N**

Na, no, not, nor.
Nae, no, not, any.
Naething, or naitring, nothing.
Naig, a horse.
Nane, none.
Nappy, ale ; to be tipsy.
Negleckit, neglected.
Neuk, a nook.
Niest, next.
Nieve, the first.
Nievefu', handful.
Niffer, an exchange ; to exchange ; to barter.
Niger, a negro.
Nit, a nut.
Norland, of, or belonging to the north.
Notic't, noticed.
Nowte, black cattle.

**O**

O', of.
O'ercome, see Owreword.
O' faith, O faith ! an exclamation.
Ony, or onie, any.
Or, is often used for ere, before.
Ora, or orra, supernumerary, that can be spared.
O't, of it.
Ouk, a week.
Ourie, shivering ; drooping.
Oursel, or oursels, ourselves.
Outlers, cattle not housed.
Ower, over ; too.
Owre-hip, a way of fetching a blow with the hammer over the arm.
Owreword, the strain of a song, the theme.
Owsen, oxen.

**P**

Pack, intimate, familiar ; twelve stone of wool.
Paidelt, waded or walked backwards and forwards.
Paitch, paunch.
Paitrick, a partridge.
Pang, to cram.
Pappit, popped.
Parle, speech.
Parlins, see Pearlins.
Parritch, porridge (a well-known Scotch dish).
Pat, did put ; a pot.
Pattle, or pettle, a plough-staff.
Paughty, proud, haughty.
Pawky, cunning, sly.
Pawky, see Pauky.
Pay't, paid ; beat.
Pearlins, ornaments of lace.
Pech, to fetch the breath short, as in asthma.
Pechan, the crop, the stomach.
Peelin', peeling, the rind of fruit.
Pelf, money, worldly goods.
Pet, a domesticated sheep, &c.

Pettle, to cherish ; a plough-staff.
Phillibegs, the kilt worn by the Highlanders.
Phraise, fair speeches, flattery ; to flatter.
Phraisin, flattery.
Pibroch, a Highland war tune for the bagpipe.
Pickle, a small quantity.
Pine, pain, uneasiness.
Pit, to put.
Placad, a public proclamation.
Plack, an old Scotch coin, the third part of a Scotch penny, twelve of which make an English penny.
Plackless, penniless, without money.
Platie, diminutive of plate.
Pleugh, see Plow.
Plew, or pleugh, a plough.
Pliskie, a trick.
Poind, to seize cattle or goods for rent, as the laws of Scotland allow.
Poortith, poverty.
Pou, to pull.
Pouk, to pluck.
Poussie, a hare, or cat.
Pout, a poult, a chick.
Pou't, did pull.
Pow, the head, the skull.
Pownie, a little horse, a pony.
Powther, or pouther, powder.
Powthery, like powder.
Preen, a pin.
Prent, to print ; print.
Pree, to taste.
Prie'd, tasted.
Prief, proof.
Prig, to cheapen ; to dispute.
Priggin, cheapening.
Primsie, demure ; precise.
Propone, to lay down, to propose.
Provost, Mayor.
Puddock-stool, a mushroom, fungus.
Puirtith, see Poortith.
Pund, pound ; pounds.
Pyle,—a pyle o' caff, a single husk of chaff.

**Q**

Quak, to quake.
Quat, to quit.
Quey, a heifer.

**R**

Raible, to rattle nonsense.
Rair, to roar.
Raize, to madden, to inflame.
Ram-feez'd, fatigued ; over-spread.
Ram-stam, thoughtless, forward.
Rant, talk, recite.
Raploch, a coarse cloth ; coarse.
Rarely, excellently, very well.
Rash, a rush ; rash-buss, a tuft of rushes.
Ratton, a rat.
Raucle, rash ; stout ; fearless.
Raught, reached.
Raw, a row.
Rax, to stretch.
Ream, cream ; to cream.
Reaming, brimful, frothing.
Reave, rove.
Reck, to take heed.
Rede, counsel ; to counsel.
Red-wat-shod, walking in blood over the shoe-tops.
Red-wud, stark mad.
Ree, half drunk, fuddled.
Reek, smoke.
Reekin, smoking.
Reekit, smoked ; smoky.
Remead, remedy.
Requite, requited.
Rest, to stand restive.
Restit, stood restive ; stunted ; withered.
Restricked, restricted.
Rew, to repent ; to compassionate.
Rief-randies, sturdy beggars.
Rig, a ridge.

Rigwiddie, rigwoodie, the rope or chain that crosses the saddle of a horse to support the shafts of a cart ; spare, withered, sapless.
Riu, to run, to melt ; rinnin, running.
Rink, the course of the stones ; a term in curling on ice.
Rip, a handful of unthreshed corn.
Riskit, to make a noise like the tearing of roots.
Rockin, spinning on the rock, or distaff.
Rokelay, a short cloak.
Rood, the fourth part of an acre.
Roon, a shred, a border or selvage.
Roose, to praise, to commend.
Roosty, rusty.
Roun', round, in the circle of neighbourhood.
Roupet, hoarse, as with a cold.
Routh, plenty.
Row, to roll, to wrap.
Row't, rolled, wrapped.
Rowte, to low, to bellow.
Rowth, or routh, plenty.
Rowtin, lowing.
Rozet, rosin.
Rung, a cudgel.
Runkled, wrinkled.
Runt, the stem of colewort or cabbage.
Ruth, sorrow.
Ryke, to reach.

**S**

Sae, so.
Saft, soft.
Sair, to serve ; a sore.
Sairly, or sairlie, sorely.
Sair't, served.
Sark, a shirt ; a shift.
Sarkit, provided in shirts.
Saugh, the willow.
Saul, soul.
Saumont, salmon.
Saunt, a saint.
Saut, salt, adj. salt.
Saw, to sow.
Sawin, sowing.
Sawt, see Saut.
Sax, six.
Scaith, to damage, to injure, injury.
Scar, a cliff.
Scaud, to scald.
Scauld, to scold.
Scaur, apt to be scared.
Scawl, a scold ; a termagant.
Scone, a thin wheaten cake.
Sconner, or scunner, a loathing ; to loathe.
Scraich, to scream as a hen, partridge, &c.
Screed, to tear ; a rent.
Scrieve, to glide swiftly along.
Scrievin, gleesomely ; swiftly.
Scrimp, to stint.
Scrimpet, did scant ; scanty.
See'd, saw.
Seizin, seizing.
Sel, self ; a body's sel, one's self alone.
Sell't, did sell.
Sen', to send.
Sen't, I, &c. sent, or did send it ; send it.
Servan', servant.
Settlin, settling ; to get a settlin, to be frightened into quietness.
Sets, sets off, goes away.
Sey, a home-made woollen stuff.
Shachled, distorted ; shapeless.
Shaird, a shred, a shard.
Shanchle, distort.
Shaver, a humorous wag ; a barber.
Shaw, to show ; a small wood in a hollow.
Sheen, shoes.
Sheen, bright, shining.
Sheep-shank ; to think one's self nae sheepshank, to be conceited.
Sherra-moor, Sheriff-moor,— the famous battle fought in the rebellion, a.d. 1715.
Sheugh, a ditch, a trench, a sluice.
Shiel, a shed.
Shill, shrill.
Shog, a shock ; a push off at one side.

Shool, a shovel.
Shoon, shoes.
Shore, to offer, to threaten.
Shor'd, offered.
Shouther, the shoulder.
Shure, did shear, shore.
Sic, such.
Sicker, sure, steady.
Sidelins, sidelong, slanting.
Siller, silver; money.
Simmer, summer.
Sin, a son.
Sin', since.
Skaith, see Scaith.
Skaithless, unharmed.
Skeigh, proud, saucy.
Skelp, to strike, to slap.
Skiegh, or skeigh, proud, nice, high-mettled.
Skirl, to shriek, to cry shrilly.
Skirling, shrieking, crying.
Skirl't, shrieked.
Skleut, slant; to run aslant, to deviate from truth.
Sklented, ran, or hit, in an oblique direction.
Skouth, freedom to converse without restraint; range, scope.
Skriegh, a scream; to scream.
Skyrin, shining; making a great show.
Slae, a sloe.
Slaps, doors, gates.
Slaver, saliva; to emit saliva.
Slaw, slow.
Slee, sly; sleest, slyest.
Sleekit, sleek; sly.
Sliddery, slippery.
Slypet, fell.
Sma', small.
Smiddy, a smithy.
Smoor, to smother.
Smoor'd, smothered.
Snaw, snow; to snow.
Sneck, snick, the latch of a door.
Sneeshin, snuff.
Snell, sharp, piercing.
Snishin, see Sneeshin.
Snood, a ribbon for binding the hair.
Sousie, or sonsy, sweet, engaging; lucky, jolly.
Soom, to swim.
Sooth, truth; a petty oath.
Sough, a heavy sigh, a sound dying on the ear.
Souk, to drink, to suck.
Souter, a shoemaker.
Southron, southern; an old name for the English nation.
Sowens, a dish made of oatmeal; the seeds of oatmeal soured, &c., flummery.
Sowp, a spoonful, a small quantity of anything liquid.
Soy, material.
Spae, to prophesy, to divine.
Sparena, not hesitate.
Speat, or spate, a sweeping torrent, after rain or thaw.
Speel, to climb.
Spence, the country parlour.
Spier, to ask, to inquire.
Spier't, inquired.
Spring, a quick tune; a Scottish reel.
Spunk, fire, mettle; wit.
Spunkie, mettlesome, fiery; will-o'-the-wisp, or ignis fatuus.
Squad, a crew, a party.
Squeel, a scream, a screech; to scream.
Stane, a stone.
Stark, stout.
Steek, to close.
Steer, stir, commotion.
Steut, tightened.
Stents, tribute; dues of any kind.
Stey, steep; steyest, steepest.
Stirk, a cow or bullock a year old.
Stock, a plant or root of colewort, cabbage, &c.
Stockin, a stocking.
Stooks, stacks of corn, &c.

Stoor, sounding hollow, strong, and hoarse.
Stoun, pang.
Stoup, or stowp, a kind of jug or dish with a handle.
Stoure, dust, more particularly dust in motion.
Stown, stolen.
Strae, straw.
Stralk, did strike.
Straikit, stroked.
Straith, fault.
Strakod, clasped.
Strath, district.
Strappan, tall and handsome.
Streek, stretched, tight; to stretch.
Sturt, trouble; to molest.
Sturtin, frightened.
Styme, a whit, a glance.
Sud, should.
Sugh, the continued rushing noise of wind or water.
Swap, an exchange; to barter.
Swat, did sweat.
Swats, drink, good ale.
Sweaten, sweating.
Sweer, or sweir, lazy, averse; dead-sweer, extremely averse.
Swinge, to beat, to whip.
Swirl, a curve; an eddying blast or pool: a knot in wood.
Swirlie, knaggie, full of knots.
Swith, get away.
Swither, to hesitate in choice; an irresolute wavering in choice.
Swoor, swore, did swear.
Syne, since, ago; then.

**T**

Tackets, a kind of nails for driving into the heels of shoes.
Tae, a toe; three-taed, having three prongs.
Tak, to take; takin, taking.
Tangle, a sea-weed.
Tap, the top.
Tapetless, heedless, foolish.
Tapsalteerie, topsy-turvy.
Tauld, or tald, told.
Teat, a small quantity.
Tedding, spreading after the mower.
Teen, to provoke; provocation.
Tent, heed, caution; to take heed.
Tentie, heedful, cautious.
Tentless, heedless.
Tough, tough.
Thack, thatch.
Thae, these.
Thairms, small guts; fiddle-strings.
Thaukit, thanked.
Theekit, thatched.
Thegither, together.
Themsel, themselves.
Thieveless, a cold demeanour; spiteful, repelling.
Thir, these.
Thirl, to thrill.
Thirled, trilled, vibrated.
Thole, to suffer, to endure.
Thowless, slack, lazy, spiritless.
Thrang, throng; a crowd.
Thrapple, throat, windpipe.
Thraw, to sprain, to twist; to contradict.
Threap, to maintain by dint of assertion.
Threshin, threshing.
Threteen, thirteen.
Thretty, thirty.
Thristle, thistle.
Through, to go on with; to make out.
Thud, to make a loud intermittent noise.
Thumpit, thumped.
Thysel, thyself.
Till't, to it.
Timmer, timber.

Tine, to lose.
Tinkier, a tinker.
Tint, lost.
Tint the gate, lost the way.
Tippence, twopence.
Tirl, to make a slight noise; to uncover.
Tirlin, uncovering.
Tither, the other.
Tittle, to whisper.
Tocher, marriage portion, dowry.
Tod, a fox.
Toddle, to totter, like the walk of a child.
Toddlin, tottering.
Tooly, fight, contend.
Toom, empty, to empty.
Toun, a hamlet; a farm-house.
Tow, a rope.
Towzie, rough, shaggy.
Toy, a very old fashion of female headdress.
Trews, trousers.
Trickie, full of tricks.
Trig, spruce, neat.
Trimly, excellently.
Trow, to believe.
Trowth, truth, a petty oath.
Tryste, an appointment; a fair.
Trysted, appointed; to tryste, to make an appointment.
Tulzie, a quarrel, to quarrel, to fight.
Twa, two.
Twal, twelve.
Twin, to part.
Tyke, a dog.

**U**

Unco, strange, uncouth; very, very great, prodigious.
Uncos, news.
Unkenn'd, unknown.
Unsicker, unsure, unsteady.
Unskaith'd, undamaged, unhurt.
Upo', upon.

**V**

Vera, very.
Virl, a ring round a column, &c.
Vittle, corn of all kind; food.

**W**

Wa', wall; wa's, walls.
Wab, web.
Wabster, a weaver.
Wad, would; to bet; a bet, a pledge.
Wadna, would not.
Wae, wo; sorrowful.
Waefu', woful, sorrowful, wailing.
Waes me! alas! O the pity.
Wal'd, chose, chosen.
Wale, choice; to choose.
Walie, or waly, ample, large, jolly; also an interjection of distress.
Walloch, a dance.
Wallop, dangle, thrash.
Wame, the belly, womb.
Wamefu', a belly-full.
Wark, work.
Warl, or warld, world.
Warlock, a wizard.
Warly, worldly, eager on amassing wealth.
Warran, a warrant; to warrant.
Warst, worst.
Warsti'd, or warsl'd, wrestled.
Wat, wet; I wat, I wot, I know.
Water-brose, soup made of meal and water simply, without the addition of milk, butter, &c.

Wattle, a twig, a wand.
Wauble, to swing, to reel.
Waught, a draught.
Waukit, thickened, as fullers do cloth.
Waukrife, wakeful, sleepless.
Waur, worse; to worst.
Waur't, worsted.
Wean, or weanie, a child.
Wear, to gather in cautiously.
Wearie, or weary; many a weary body, many a different person.
Wee, little · wee things, little ones; wee bit, a small matter.
Weel, well; weelfare, welfare.
Weet, rain, wetness.
Weir, see Wear.
Weird, fate.
We'se, we shall.
Wha, who.
Whare, where; whare'er, wherever.
Whase, whose.
Whatreck, nevertheless.
Whilk, which.
Whinging, crying, complaining, fretting.
Whirligigums, useless ornaments, trifling appendages.
Whisht, silence; to hold one's whisht, to be silent.
Whisk, to sweep, to lash.
Whiskit, lashed.
Whissle, a whistle; to whistle.
Wi', with.
Wicker, willow (the smaller sort).
Wiel, a small whirlpool.
Wifie, a diminutive or endearing term for wife.
Wimple, to meander.
Wimplin, waving, meandering.
Wimpl't, meandered.
Win, to win, to winnow.
Winna, will not.
Winnock, a window.
Winsome, handsome, pleasing, gay.
Wizen'd, hide-bound, dried, shrunk.
Won, dwell.
Woo', wool.
Woo, to court, to make love.
Worset, worsted.
Wow, an exclamation of pleasure or wonder.
Wrack, to teaze, to vex.
Wraith, a spirit, or ghost; an apparition exactly like a living person, whose appearance is said to forebode the person's approaching death.
Wraug, wrong; to wrong.
Wreath, a drifted heap of snow.
Wud, mad, distracted.
Wumble, a wimble.
Wyle, to beguile.
Wylie, cunning, artful.
Wyte, blame; to blame.

**Y**

Yad, an old mare; a worn out horse.
Ye; this pronoun is frequently used for thou.
Yearlings, born in the same year, coevals.
Yeard, earn; an eagle, an osprey; to loup.
Yerk, to lash, to jerk.
Yerkit, jerked, lashed.
Ye'se, you shall.
Yestreen, yesternight.
Yett, a gate, such as is usually at the entrance into a farmyard or field.
Yill, ale.
Yird, earth.
Yont, beyond.
Yoursel, yourself.
Yowe, a ewe.
Yowie, diminutive of yowe.

www.ingramcontent.com/pod-product-compliance
Lightning Source LLC
Chambersburg PA
CBHW031408270326
41929CB00010BA/1379